A CULTURAL HISTORY
OF MEMORY

VOLUME 4

A Cultural History of Memory
General Editors: Stefan Berger and Jeffrey Olick

Volume 1
A Cultural History of Memory in Antiquity
Edited by Beate Dignas

Volume 2
A Cultural History of Memory in the Middle Ages
Edited by Gerald Schwedler

Volume 3
A Cultural History of Memory in the Early Modern Age
Edited by Marek Tamm and Alessandro Ancangeli

Volume 4
A Cultural History of Memory in the Eighteenth Century
Edited by Patrick H. Hutton

Volume 5
A Cultural History of Memory in the Nineteenth Century
Edited by Susan A. Crane

Volume 6
A Cultural History of Memory in the Long Twentieth Century
Edited by Stefan Berger and William Niven

A CULTURAL HISTORY OF MEMORY

IN THE EIGHTEENTH CENTURY

Edited by Patrick H. Hutton

BLOOMSBURY ACADEMIC
LONDON • NEW YORK • OXFORD • NEW DELHI • SYDNEY

BLOOMSBURY ACADEMIC
Bloomsbury Publishing Plc
50 Bedford Square, London, WC1B 3DP, UK
1385 Broadway, New York, NY 10018, USA
29 Earlsfort Terrace, Dublin 2, Ireland

BLOOMSBURY, BLOOMSBURY ACADEMIC and the Diana logo are trademarks of
Bloomsbury Publishing Plc

First published in Great Britain 2022
Paperback edition first published 2024

Copyright © Bloomsbury Publishing, 2022

Patrick H. Hutton has asserted his right under the Copyright, Designs and Patents Act, 1988, to be identified as Editor of this work.

Cover image © Heritage Images/Getty Images

All rights reserved. No part of this publication may be reproduced or transmitted in any form or by any means, electronic or mechanical, including photocopying, recording, or any information storage or retrieval system, without prior permission in writing from the publishers.

Bloomsbury Publishing Plc does not have any control over, or responsibility for, any third-party websites referred to or in this book. All internet addresses given in this book were correct at the time of going to press. The author and publisher regret any inconvenience caused if addresses have changed or sites have ceased to exist, but can accept no responsibility for any such changes.

A catalogue record for this book is available from the British Library.

A catalog record for this book is available from the Library of Congress.

ISBN: HB: 978-1-4742-7348-0
PB: 978-1-3504-0860-9
Set: 978-1-4742-7384-8

Series: The Cultural Histories Series

Typeset by RefineCatch Limited, Bungay, Suffolk
Printed and bound in Great Britain

To find out more about our authors and books visit www.bloomsbury.com and sign up for our newsletters.

CONTENTS

LIST OF ILLUSTRATIONS		vi
GENERAL EDITORS' PREFACE		xiv
	Stefan Berger and Jeffrey Olick	
	Introduction	1
	Patrick H. Hutton	
1	Power and Politics	19
	Kirsten L. Cooper	
2	Time and Space	37
	Gabriel Wick	
3	Media and Technology	57
	Patrick H. Hutton	
4	Knowledge: Science and Education	73
	Tom Simone	
5	Ideas: Philosophy, Religion, and History	93
	Patrick H. Hutton	
6	High Culture and Popular Culture	113
	Fiona McIntosh-Varjabédian	
7	The Social: Rituals, Faith, Practices, and the Everyday	129
	Jennifer Hillman	
8	Remembering and Forgetting	143
	Victoria E. Thompson	
BIBLIOGRAPHY		161
NOTES ON CONTRIBUTORS		179
INDEX		181

ILLUSTRATIONS

INTRODUCTION

0.1	*Writers of the Republic of Letters*, 1772.	4
0.2	Frontispiece of the *Encyclopédie*, 1751–72.	6
0.3	Caspar David Friedrich, *The Abbey in the Oak Wood*, 1809.	10
0.4	Hubert Robert, *The Grand Gallery of the Louvre*, Paris, 1801.	15
0.5	Hubert Robert, *Demolition of the Bastille, July 20, 1789*.	17

CHAPTER 1

1.1	*Völkertafel of Styria*, early eighteenth century.	21
1.2	*Execution of Louis XVI, January 21, 1793*.	28
1.3	*The Caledonians Arrival in Money-Land*, 1762.	30
1.4	*In Commemoration of the Providential Escape of His Most Sacred Majesty King George the Third from the daring Attack of an Assassin when at Drury Lane Theatre, August 2, 1786*.	31
1.5	Friedrich Carl von Moser, *Von dem Deutschen Nationalgeist*, title page, 1765.	32
1.6	Friedrich Carl von Moser, *Von dem Deutschen Nationalgeist*, first page, 1765.	33

CHAPTER 2

2.1	Hubert Robert, *The Finding of the Laocoön, 1773*.	39
2.2	Hubert Robert, *The Ruins of the Palace of Nero, c. 1765*.	41
2.3	Hubert Robert, *The Discoverers of Antiquities*.	42
2.4	*The Tomb of Jean-Jacques Rousseau at Ermenonville*, engraving by Godefroy after a drawing by Gandat.	44
2.5	Giovanni Battista Piranesi, *View of a Mausoleum, called of Nero, on the via Cassia*, from Le Antichità Romane.	45
2.6	Hubert Robert, *View of the Tower of Guy, at La Roche-Guyon*.	47
2.7	Hubert Robert, *View of Méréville from the Lake, 1790*.	50
2.8	Hubert Robert, *View of Château and Temple of Méréville*.	50
2.9	Gabriel Wick, *Illustration*—lateral section, plan, elevation and axonometric view of the Laiterie of Rambouillet, pen and ink, 2017.	53
2.10	Piranesi, *View of the fountain and grotto of Egeria near the Porta Capena, c. 1766*.	54

ILLUSTRATIONS vii

CHAPTER 3

3.1	Jean-Honoré Fragonard, *Young Woman Reading Silently*, c. 1769.	62
3.2	Joshua Reynolds, *Portrait of Samuel Johnson*, 1756.	65
3.3	Anicet Lemonnier, *A Reading of a Work by Voltaire at the Salon of Mme. Geoffron*, 1812.	68
3.4	*London Coffee House*, c. 1710.	68
3.5	*Installation of the Remains of Jean-Jacques Rousseau in the Pantheon, Paris*, 1794.	70

CHAPTER 4

4.1	Nicholas Rowe, *Portrait of Shakespeare*, 1709.	78
4.2	Shakespeare Memorial in Westminster Abbey, engraved for the *London Magazine*, 1751.	83
4.3	William Hogarth and C. Grignion, *David Garrick as Richard III*.	84
4.4	*Garrick Speaking the Jubilee Ode*, engraving by Caroline Watson, after the painting by Robert Edge Pine, 1784.	88
4.5	"The Weird Sisters" *in Macbeth,* Act 1, engraving by John Raphael Smith, after Henry Fuseli, 1785.	89

CHAPTER 5

5.1	*Portrait of Jacques Bénigne Bossuet.*	97
5.2	*Portrait of Nicholas, marquis de Condorcet.*	99
5.3	*Discovery and excavation of the Temple of Isis at Pompeii*, 1776.	102
5.4	*Portrait of Giambattista Vico.*	103
5.5	*Portrait of David Hume*, 1767.	107
5.6	*The Elderly Rousseau, Walking.*	110

CHAPTER 6

6.1	Title page of a poem published by James Macpherson, 1789.	120
6.2	*Portrait of Louis Mandrin in the prison at Valence prior to his execution in 1755.*	122
6.3	*A Party on Lake Urner-See.*	125
6.4	*Portrait of Mary Stuart, Queen of Scots*, engraving by Jacobus Houbraken, 1738, after Hans Holbein.	127

CHAPTER 7

7.1	Pierre Mignard, *Portrait of Madame Marie de Miramion.*	133
7.2	Title page of Marie-Catherine Homassel's *Life* of her aunt Michelle Homassel.	137
7.3	From the *Life of Michelle Homassel* by Marie-Catherine Homassel.	138

CHAPTER 8

8.1	*Translation of Voltaire's Remains to the Panthéon français, Paris, 1794.*	146
8.2	Commemorative print on the Occasion of the Death of Mirabeau, 1791.	148
8.3	*Apotheosis of Louis XVI, 1793*, engraving by Francesco Bartolozzi.	151
8.4	*"Ici l'on danse" (Here we dance): a view of the decorations and lighting constructed on the former site of the Bastille for the Festival of the French Confederation, July 14, 1790.*	154
8.5	*A Temple dedicated to liberty, proposed for the site of the ruins of the Bastille.*	155
8.6	*Government by Robespierre, 1794.*	158

GENERAL EDITORS' PREFACE

STEFAN BERGER AND JEFFREY K. OLICK

Any project titled *A Cultural History of Memory* begs a number of questions from the very beginning. For instance: What does it mean that this project is a *cultural* history, rather than some other kind of history? (What other kind of history might it have been?) In turn, what makes memory a feasible and interesting topic for such a history? (It certainly isn't immediately obvious that it would be.) Finally, why a cultural history rather than *the* cultural history? (After all, with forty-eight chapters spread over six volumes, how many more cultural histories of memory could one imagine?)

CULTURAL HISTORY

A Cultural History of Memory is but one entry in a series of cultural histories already and soon to be published by Bloomsbury, including cultural histories of Animals, the Human Body, Food, Gardens, Women, the Senses, Dress and Fashion, the Theatre, Work, Law, Money, and Hair, among many others. The publisher has taken a light hand in prescribing the orientation of these projects, leaving the definition of cultural history to each project's senior editors. And this is very well, as there are many different ways to inflect the idea of cultural history, and different approaches are likely appropriate to the different subject matters. In turn, we have not imposed any particular definition on the editors of the six volumes in this current project, nor have they on the authors of the forty-eight chapters that comprise the total product. That being said, we have relied on a broadly shared understanding of the purposes and tools of cultural history in framing this particular entry in the series, and it is clear that its many authors have as well, though perhaps with occasional divergences.

Namely, contemporary cultural history, at least as it has been practiced in and on the West (and this is one of the important limitations on the project we will discuss below), has defined itself in contrast to at least three other approaches (on the historiographical developments sketched in the following pages see in greater detail Berger, Feldner, and Passmore (2020)). First, there is a broadly defined "traditional" political historiography, dominant in the nineteenth century, that wrote the story of states, their leaders, and their wars. These "high politics" approaches, of course, fully advanced the claim to "objectivity," particularly since the matters they studied—states, their leaders, and their wars—have been quite well documented. These approaches, nevertheless, not only studied the world of nation-states and their high politics but were often part of defining the claims of those states and glorifying the achievements of their leaders, so their claims to be value-free and scientific were obviously dubious ones.

Following this, though at different times in different parts of the world, and only partly under the influence of Marxist perspectives, there developed a vibrant interest in "economic" and "social" history alongside, and sometimes in contrast to, the traditional political histories: the stories not of the "great men" and the great achievements, but of economic processes and social structures. Like political history, this was often presented in national containers and sometimes served the purpose of highlighting the particular "achievements" of nations in the economic and social spheres. Only later did a nascent Marxist historiography, often relatively weak in the universities before the 1970s, come to understand this study of history to be part of a struggle not merely to interpret or understand history, but to change it, as Marx famously put it in his eleventh thesis on Feuerbach.

A stronger concern for ordinary people in social history, however, only occurred with the turn to "history from below," sometimes also referred to as history of everyday life, micro-history, or historical anthropology. This was largely a development that gathered momentum from the 1970s onwards. "History workshop" movements that often became supporters of this new, more human-agency centered understanding of social history, critiqued older forms of social history for being too focused on structures and processes and thereby for ignoring human agency. Furthermore, these approaches criticized the adherence of much of social and economic history to modernization theories and teleologies of progress that appeared to many practitioners of historical anthropology as outdated. The interest of these historians in the everyday had made them turn to anthropology and, inspired by anthropological methods and theories, they set out to change understandings of the social and cultural. As Robert Darnton has put it, "The anthropological mode of history [. . .] begins from the premise that individual expression takes place within a general idiom" (quoted in Hunt 1989: 12). In other words: history had to start from individual human agency and then locate it within a wider collective field.

More difficult to understand is the next form of "traditional" historical interest that was always a lesser strand when compared to political and economic/social history: namely, intellectual history or the history of ideas. Like "traditional" forms of history that focused on states, wars, and high politics, intellectual history has often focused on a narrow slice of life as well: the thoughts and ideas of other great men than politicians (though sometimes them too), mainly artists, scientists, philosophers, and others whose writings are seen to have captured, defined, and led the "spirit" of an age. To be sure, intellectual historians are quite interested in the contexts and structures that enabled the great thinkers to produce their great works, as well as in how those great works affected the less great thoughts of the cultures and societies that produced them. The recent influence of the so-called "Cambridge school" around Quentin Skinner and J.G.A. Pocock is a good example of such contextualization of great thinkers. Internationally even more influential has been the "history of concepts"—shaped seminally by the German historical theorist Reinhart Koselleck. Conceptual history is now a truly global undertaking and one that takes seriously the belief that we need to thoroughly historicize our key concepts in order to understand how people made sense of the world and how they consequently acted in the world.

Next to political history, economic and social history, historical anthropology, and intellectual history, cultural history now forms one of the great traditions of historical writing, reaching back to the very beginnings of professional historiography. Jacob Burckhardt and Johan Huizinga are just two examples of classical representatives of cultural history that can still be read with great pleasure and benefit by contemporary cohorts of students. However, older cultural history often had a strong emphasis on studying "high culture" and thereby distinguishing what was "true" and "worthwhile" culture from "popular culture" or simply "trash." When a "new cultural history" began to conquer history departments in the 1980s, it democratized older forms of cultural history by redefining culture in broader and more inclusive terms. Furthermore, many of its practitioners were much influenced by the "linguistic turn" and theories associated with poststructuralist approaches (Toews 1987: 879–907). Like historical anthropology the new cultural history was dissatisfied not only with an older political history interested mainly in "high politics" but an older social and economic history reducing the past to structures and processes. Unlike an older intellectual history, it was also not so much interested in "great ideas" but instead in ordinary thoughts and practices. Whilst the initial interest in language led cultural historians to study discourses, many soon realized that discourses had to be related back to practices. Furthermore, practices had much to do with things and objects, in other words, materials that needed to be considered to have an agency of their own in history. The history of material culture could thus build on the linguistic turn and practice theory, but it carved out a niche of its own in a field of cultural history that became increasingly compartmentalized as we enter the new millennium after 2000.

Marxist social historians like E.P. Thompson and Geoff Eley spearheaded new understandings of the history of society that took on board many of the insights of the new cultural history without ever abandoning an appreciation of the Marxist understanding of social developments. Thompson, for example, focused not only on the economic condition that made the English working class, but on "the way [. . .] material experiences are handled . . . in cultural ways" (Merrill 1972: 20 f). This happened, according to Thompson, through "cultural and moral mediations." In turn, however, Gareth Stedman Jones moved the discussion even farther afield from economic reduction when he declared that "We [. . .] cannot decode political language to reach a primal and material expression of interest since it is the discursive structure of political language which conceives and defines interest in the first place" (Stedman Jones 1983: 21-22). For the "new cultural historians" in this tradition, then, what they, in part following Emile Durkheim among others, called "representations" became of primary interest. And, as Roger Chartier put it, "The Representations of the social world themselves are the constituents of social reality" (Chartier 1982: 30). This is because, as Lynn Hunt writes, "All practices, whether economic or cultural, depend on the representations individuals use to make sense of their world" (Hunt 1989: 19). The goal of cultural history is thus, as again Chartier defines it, to show "how, in different times and places, a specific social reality was constructed, how people conceived of it and how they interpreted it to others" (Chartier 1998: 4). In this, Chartier followed Lucien Goldmann, who had defined worldviews—the true subject for intellectual historians who were interested in culture more broadly—as "the whole complex of ideas, aspirations and feelings which links together the members of a social group [. . .] and which opposed them to members of other social groups" (Goldmann 1967: 17). And this is indeed the approach that most of the authors in these six volumes have taken, though in an obviously wide variety of ways in and for a wide variety of contexts.

MEMORY

The turn toward memory, especially understood as a collective or cultural phenomenon, can in fact be seen as—though not only as—another inflection of the new cultural history (Berger and Niven 2014). Its interest in representations and discourses encouraged an interest in memories as constituting those representations and discourses. Whether it was written in pursuit of a nostalgic longing for a great national past, as is evident in some of the contributions to Pierre Nora's seminal seven-volume study on the realms of memory of France (Nora 1981–7), or whether it was conducted in the search for understanding and possibly overcoming the consequences of traumatic events in the past, like genocides or wars, memory history has linked contemporary memories to processes of sense-production in the present that gave rise to very different and always contested understandings of the past.

It should already be obvious, then, that the cultural history of memory undertaken in the forty-eight chapters that follow is not just about recall or other basic cognitive processes. Though the concept of memory employed across these six volumes is sometimes the lay understanding of memory as what and how people can recall in different times and places, the majority of the chapters take memory to be something broader. Memory may seem to take place within individual minds, yet for most of the last century numerous scholars both within and beyond cultural history have understood memory more broadly (Olick, Vinitzky-Seroussi, and Levy 2011). Individual memory always takes place within social contexts, with social materials, from social positions, and in response to social cues. So whatever neurological or mental processes it involves, these are obviously deeply embedded in structures and contexts that extend far beyond the individuals whose minds engage in remembering, traditionally understood. Individuals, moreover, employ many technologies of memory—for instance, chanting or writing—which exist outside of themselves and are not part of their brains, and which vary across social settings and in their impacts on individual mnemonic processes. In this way, it becomes perhaps clearer why memory is such a rich terrain for cultural (and other!) forms of history.

However, many of the chapters that constitute this cultural history of memory take yet another step beyond the mind—that is, beyond what Maurice Halbwachs, one of the key figures in contemporary thinking about memory, called the social frameworks of memory, to see memory as an inherently social activity (Halbwachs 1950). We often—even most often—remember together. Social psychologists understand that there are significant differences between remembering alone and remembering in a group, whether this is a matter of simple recall (e.g. when a group of individuals can reconstruct memorized lists more completely than the sum of individuals alone via cuing and other social processes) or in narrative process (e.g. when a family retells a story of an experience they have shared, and the complete narrative emerges from the many voices involved, which bring different pieces than everyone necessarily would have recalled). However, some scholars argue that groups themselves remember; for instance, they build libraries and fill them with materials, they curate representations of the past in museums and elsewhere in ways that transcend the resources of individuals, and they preserve knowledge that very few individuals recall (Assmann 1992). As such, scholars often refer to social, collective, or cultural memory—the forms and traces of the past that transcend the capacities or even interests of individuals—and many do not believe these forms of memories are merely metaphors (see Erll 2008). The field of memory is thus a vast one, and it is clear that understanding all the different forms of memory—from the neurological to the museological—requires, and is an appropriate subject for, all the resources of cultural history.

Having said that, the development of memory studies since the 1980s has been characterized by the gradual constitution of a new discipline that was self-consciously transdisciplinary. Of all the disciplines that constituted this new field, historians were arguably in a minority. Literary scholars and sociologists were far more numerous, and, as all six volumes in this series demonstrate, a cultural history of memory cannot do without referencing a range of literary, sociological and other disciplinary approaches to memory.

Apart from its characteristic transdisciplinarity, which had a major impact on memory history, however, the latter also remained, for quite some time, tied to the national container that, as we have already discussed, had been so strongly established in the historical sciences in the century roughly between 1850 and 1950. The move of memory history to *transnational* forms of memory has only been a relatively recent development, following a general trend in historical studies to criticize "methodological nationalism" and move to more transnational forms of historical writing, emphasizing interlinkages, adaptations, and transfers. However, as a perusal of any of the hugely successful conferences of the Memory Studies Association will show, most scholars today still focus on national memory.[1] Transnational, let alone global memory is not practiced very widely,[2] which also reflects a major difficulty for a cultural history of memory; there are simply not enough scholars who can truly synthesize vast amounts of work on a particular theme in a global perspective. Here we can only trust that our failure will be an inspiration to future generations of scholars to move to more global perspectives on memory history.

Where our six volumes have hopefully been more successful has been in moving histories of memory away from their fixation with trauma, especially national trauma. The huge body of work on the memory of genocides, in particular the Holocaust, and the equally massive amount of work on the memory of wars, especially the two world wars, but also the Vietnam war and a range of civil wars, is an indicator of to what extent memory scholars have homed in on traumatic events in the past. Undoubtedly, much of this work has been incredibly valuable and inspirational, but the six volumes that we introduce here, whilst not ignoring genocides and war, also intend to highlight a range of other areas in which memory history can be usefully applied.

If *A Cultural History of Memory* tries to escape memory history's bias toward "methodological nationalism" and toward traumatic events in the past, it also deliberately—and structurally—seeks to introduce a longer-term perspective and to show how memory history is a relevant and intriguing exercise for older periods of time. Once again, looking from a bird's eye perspective over the field of memory history, we see a massive concentration of work in the modern period, basically from the late eighteenth century to the present day. But the first four of our six volumes underline to what an extent the history of memory benefits from considering older time periods. As general editors, we particularly hope that modernists (of whom we are culpable examples) may delve into the writings on pre-modern times, as it will reveal not only substantial differences, but also, and certainly more striking to us, amazing similarities when considering the role of memory for cultural sense-production.

A CULTURAL HISTORY

Finally, what of the definite article "A" Cultural History of Memory. In the first place, across a work as extensive as this one (or these ones), it is obvious that there are many different approaches to the subject matters. Though all contributing to this cultural history, the authors come from numerous different disciplines and specialties, have different foci, bring to bear different interests and expertise even within this "one" work. We do so, moreover, from numerous different countries, languages of origin, and periods of study, though the list, however extensive, is still limited in significant ways. In the second place, however, much as the publishers did not lay a heavy hand on the forms of cultural history to be employed, they did determine that all the volumes should have the same structure. Hence, we came up with eight themes that had to be the same across all six volumes. In choosing broad themes—power and politics, media and technology, knowledge: science and education, time and space, ideas: philosophy, religion, and history, high and popular culture, the social: rituals, practices, and the everyday, and remembering and forgetting—we sought to give the volume editors the space to adapt those themes to the particular foci appropriate to different times and geographies. As any reader of the six volumes will realize, the editors made good use of that leeway, but this also leads to the phenomenon that different authors have put the emphasis of their respective chapters differently and usually in line with their own specialisms.

The publisher also dictated the epochal labels we employed, and they determined that the eight topics addressed in each chronologically constituted volume should be nominally the same as the topics in the other volumes. Much as we appreciated the reasons for this—for instance, so that a particular theme could be followed across the epochs, or that someone interested in a particular epoch could recombine the history of memory we have produced for that epoch with the history of something else addressed in other entries in the series—this constraint did raise concerns for us and our colleagues. For instance, no single chronology labeling applies uniformly for different areas of the world (e.g. not every society or culture identifies the same antiquity, or an antiquity at all). And the present chronology is a very Western one indeed. Moreover, the application of these labels can be anachronistic. After all, the people whose forms of memory we are studying in a particular age did not understand themselves as having that particular place in history (e.g. the people in the antiquity we have studied did not think of themselves as inhabiting an ancient world). Finally, had we not understood the imperative of recombination of themes and periods, the editors of each epochally-defined volume might have wanted to label the eight chapters differently from the editors of the other volumes, since the same relevances did not necessarily obtain in the same ways in different periods.

Nevertheless, much as the ground we have collectively covered here is vast indeed, we might still hope—if not for other, at least for additional work in this vibrant field on this fascinating subject. We hope that, despite the additional works that might be possible—and that we hope will be produced—what we have to offer here will be of use to as many as possible. The field of memory studies is a relatively new one. But the sophistication of the chapters (and volume introductions) we have the pleasure of presenting here shows that much as the field has a long way to go, it is well on its way.

Notes

1 https://www.memorystudiesassociation.org/ (accessed February 3, 2020).
2 Agenda-setting in this respect was Cesari and Rigney (2014). For a review, see Erll 2011: 4–18.

Introduction

PATRICK H. HUTTON

HISTORIOGRAPHICAL PRELUDE: IDEAS ABOUT MEMORY IN THE CULTURAL HISTORY OF THE EIGHTEENTH CENTURY

The cultural history of the eighteenth century places in sharp relief the contrast between philosophies that heralded an auspicious future and cultural traditions that cherished a vanishing past. They would shape the contours of collective memory differently. Waxing large during that era was the European Enlightenment, with its projects for reform and optimistic forecasts about the prospect of making a better world. For reformers, little in the "old regime" seemed worth remembering, and so its heritage tended to be disparaged when it was not ignored. Leading critics of the day delivered polemics against the inheritance of a past that blocked innovation by virtue of its reliance on legal privilege, arbitrary justice, tyrannical rule, and most tellingly the dogma of revealed religion. Reserving his most acerbic invectives for the Christian clergy, French essayist and historian Voltaire famously demanded that it was time to *"écraser l'infâme"* (rid ourselves of such infamy). For him, the eighteenth century had ushered in an age that would apply the rational resources of science to solve the problems then faced by humanity. Accordingly, the arbitrary and obscurantist practices of a medieval inheritance were to be consigned to oblivion as a menace to civilization's advance. Among progressive-minded philosophers, alternative memories long neglected were pressed into service to advance the cause of fashioning a more auspicious future. Heritage was to be reframed in a history in which martyrs for the cause of religious liberty and heroes for the promotion of the arts and sciences would be enshrined in a new pantheon, icons marking historical stages along the pathway toward a coming age of Enlightenment in which reason would triumph over superstition to guide the course of human affairs. The idea gave reformers a new sense of collective identity, an imagined community acting in the name of progress.

Insofar as the philosophers harked back to earlier times, it was to the deep past of Greco-Roman antiquity that they turned. As appealing as the idea of the role of the new science was in advancing the human prospect, there remained among philosophers a devotion to the Greco-Roman legacy for learning. As a tradition that had long taught the enduring value of the wisdom of the ancients, it continued to be honored among educated people alongside the new science of nature. Until well into the eighteenth century, Latin remained the *lingua franca* of scholars, and the masterpieces of ancient literature and philosophy continued to hold the preeminent place within the canon of higher education. This classical tradition extolled eternal verities, timeless values of balance and proportion that the Romans had regarded as basic to the ethics of the good life. A running debate between Ancients and Moderns about the comparative value of the humane learning of the classics vis-à-vis new scientific experimentation spanned the seventeenth and eighteenth centuries (Levine 1999: 75–153).

Respect for the learning of Greco-Roman times, moreover, set an eighteenth-century agenda dedicated to fathoming an even deeper realm of wisdom in the preliterate past. Just as some philosophers wished to speculate on the prospects of the future, so some historians sought to find the sources of human understanding in a past that predated Greco-Roman antiquity, one that held the secrets of the obscure beginnings of civil society (Rossi 1984: 123–36). To delve into that primordial realm was to descend from the world of manuscript literacy into that of primary orality, one known mostly for its folk tales and mythologies transmitted in popular culture across that threshold. Scholarly interest in oral tradition added a new dimension to historical inquiry. Its appeal was easy to understand, for vestiges of the cultural mores of those times endured in the living traditions of rural people who clung tenaciously to ways of life cultivated in that distant past. Some eighteenth-century philosophers sang their praises as the deep sources of modern cultural identity among the nations of Europe. Residing near rural folk in Latvia, German pastor Johann Herder idealized the hidden wisdom within popular folklore, and so introduced into high culture a hint of nostalgia for a time and a way of life that was passing. He and other folklorists pointed to a cultural heritage that drew upon the inspiring poetic sources of language, transparency in communication of the emotions of the heart, religious piety as a source of community, particular landscapes underpinning the distinctive cultures of nations, and most significantly the goodness and moral virtue of the common man. Exalting in such values, they portrayed sympathetically a rural way of life based upon the customs of immemorial tradition, in part because they were poignantly aware that these were vulnerable to economic forces shaping a newly emerging urban culture. Common sense distilled from long experience was the watchword of this folk culture, an antidote, in the words of the visionary German poet Novalis, to "the villain reason" that would dispel the wonder of a profound heritage. Such sentiments came to be understood as the cultural foundation of modern German identity by the turn of the nineteenth century (Mosse 1961: 46–7).

Our interest in cultural memory during the eighteenth century, therefore, opens upon the relationship between these opposing ways of remembering the past. It was a time in history noteworthy for the wide divide between attitudes in popular versus those in high culture, and so for what it reveals about changing perspectives on the meaning that collective memory held among different elements of European society. One sees how the juxtaposition of a mnemonics of remembrance with one of expectation exposed the ambiguity of recourse to memory's resources, as the ancient Greeks recognized in the concept of mimesis: memory is at once the source of preservation and imagination. Our study explores both sides of memory's paradoxical nature. From the vantage point of remembrance, memory is the essential mode for carrying forward the common sense of ordinary people filtered through immemorial tradition. But from that of its inspirational "enlightened" mode, memory provides the animating spark to envision a different kind of future. Over the course of the eighteenth century, inheritance and innovation clashed more and more in their encounters *en route* to the political revolutions of century's end in Europe and the Americas.

To account for collective memory's influence in shaping the mental horizons of the eighteenth century, one discerns an ongoing reconfiguration of the relationship between continuity and change. Old ways of thinking may have faded over time, but they did so with the countervailing force of habit, sometimes resistance, and never completely. Transformative change, even in the most radical phase of the French Revolution, never obliterated the past, nor did innovation ever develop as anticipated.

The historians' interest in this interaction of continuity and change played out over the course of the twentieth century, reflecting updates in what historians found memorable about the eighteenth century in their efforts to illuminate the meaning of the past for their own times. Accordingly, the issue of memory is deeply implicated in revisionist scholarship. I note the succession of historiographical reorientations as follows.

Early Twentieth Century: Collective Memory and an Imagined Future

Historians of the early to mid-twentieth century emphasized the philosophers' great expectations for the future. Those who favored this approach to historical scholarship were attuned to efforts by statesmen following each of the twentieth-century's world wars to rebuild European political and social institutions upon foundations of liberalism that they held to be a principal legacy of the Enlightenment. According to historian Carl Becker writing during the interwar years, the eighteenth-century philosophers had been intent upon bringing Augustine's heavenly City of God down to earth in all of its perfection (Becker 1932). Peter Gay, challenging Becker's thesis after the Second World War, argued for the philosophers' more modest hopes, based on practical strategies for improvement and reform in a world rife with difficult problems (Gay 1958: 27–51). But both interpretations directed attention to the philosophers' critique of outworn institutions, antiquated legal systems based upon privilege, and deep-seated attitudes imbued with bias, prejudice, and parochialism that stood as obstacles to their efforts. The Enlightenment of the eighteenth century, they explained, was the portal to modernity and as such a passageway out of a culture blighted by vestiges of a timeworn past. Both stressed its unity as a progressive intellectual movement. To that end, collective memory was refashioned in what sociologist Eviatar Zerubavel has characterized as a "mnemonics of progress" (Zerubavel 2003: 14–15).

This interpretation of the cultural history of the Enlightenment largely concerned its intellectuals, an imagined community bound together by corresponding societies, and accordingly referred to as the "republic of letters." Though few in numbers, they exercised a profound influence upon a society whose literacy rates were rising rapidly (D. Goodman 1994: 34–52). Its leading intellectuals became celebrities, and much sought after to adorn the famous salons and literary academies of an emerging social elite (Lilti 2015: 91–108). They publicized the notion that their age was burdened by a political order that was senescent, arbitrary, and outmoded, and for which no one any longer offered a defense. Their work, considered in its ensemble over the course of the late eighteenth century, encouraged critical thought, undermined commitment to extant public institutions, and prepared the way for the coming of the French Revolution (Chartier 1991: 15–19, 161–8). For this event, the venerable historian Georges Lefebvre argued, popular protest issuing from economic discontent, an unfair and inequitable tax system, together with learned critique of a regime based upon legal privilege, converged in a dramatic moment of "conjuncture" that made possible this vast and unprecedented upheaval (Lefebvre 1947: 177–87). From that time on, the eighteenth century as perceived in living memory was divided between an old and a new regime, with the weight of attention to the latter. To justify their conception of a new politics for a new age, its leaders harked back to Roman antiquity in search of edifying models in which to invest their ideals (Hunt 1986: 20, 28–9, 60).

FIGURE 0.1: *Writers of the Republic of Letters*, 1772. Iconic celebrities epitomized an emerging culture of writers and readers. Courtesy of Getty Images, UK.

Mid- to Late-Twentieth Century: Collective Memory and the Traditions of Ordinary People

Scholarly interest in the Enlightenment perceived from the vantage point of its counter-culture became prominent during the 1970s. British historian Isaiah Berlin signaled the influence of hitherto neglected philosophers, such as Giambattista Vico and Johann Herder, who would contribute to what he characterized as the thought of the "Counter-Enlightenment." Just as some philosophers directed their attention to a transforming future, Berlin explained, these philosophers looked deep into the preliterate past of oral tradition. There they discovered the workings of collective memory within a mentality strikingly at odds with modern ways of thinking but full of wisdom, nonetheless. As they probed these origins of human thought, they encountered the poetical sources of an ancient cultural heritage, a resource for finding meaning hidden in the past that they believed might inspire their present age (Berlin 1976; idem 2013: 1–32). Those drawn to this line of inquiry often looked to the political radicals of the eighteenth century rather than to the liberals, and so were wont to invest great expectations in the future as well. Such, too, were the dreams of social visionaries, such as Henri de Saint-Simon, Charles Fourier, and other utopian socialists, who spun futurist conceptions of planned communities (Manuel 1962; Beecher 1986).

A following approach in mid- to late-twentieth century scholarship looked beyond the intellectuals to the "collective mentalities" of ordinary people, who, for better or worse, made do with existing social and economic practices as strategies for survival. This line of inquiry is associated with French Annales scholarship, which sought to identify the deep economic, social, and environmental structures that must have seemed to most eighteenth-century observers as timeless (Le Roy Ladurie 1981: 1–27). The Annalistes directed attention to the "mental equipment" that shaped thinking in popular culture, psychosocial states of mind elaborated over time out of deep-seated emotions, attitudes and habits (Febvre [1952] 1992: 221–38). Such studies focused on the stabilizing customs of immemorial tradition—the stuff of the inertial power of the past—all elements of memory's workings. Repetition of ancestral ways of life reflected the practical wisdom of the ages. The mores of everyday life in the rural world continued to provide comfort and psychological security for substantial elements of the population. Progressive-minded attitudes succeeded in some quarters, but always against stubborn resistance and the overwhelming odds of the common sense of the ages. Studies of collective mentalities, therefore, tended to deflate the excesses of the philosophers' idealization of popular traditions by evaluating them in light of the often harsh realities of social life in that era. In contrast with the skepticism in the critical thought advanced by the philosophers of high culture, one notes credulity in some remnants of the illiterate population, still susceptible to volatile emotions and given to fabulous beliefs (Ariès 1988: 167–90).

This foray into the attitudes and cultural practices of ordinary people generated much scholarly interest from the 1960s through the 1980s, though its practitioners did not think of their inquiry into psychosocial history as a problem of collective memory, at least as we have come to think of it today. Still, the Annalistes' term for "mental equipment" incorporates that of "habits of mind," and therefore collective memory may be said to have figured in their investigations. Collective memory was treated as an element within the larger field of collective mentalities. It was not until the late 1990s that memory emerged as the dominant historiographical interest, displacing mentalities as an organizing principle for work in cultural history (Confino 2008: 77–84).

Late Twentieth–Early Twenty-First Century: The Institutional Foundations of Cultural Memory

The historiographical turn to memory suggests the cultural historians' reflections on the erosion of Enlightenment ideals over the course of the twentieth century. The horrors of mass warfare and genocide prepared the way for the breakup of a long-standing master narrative about the rise of Western civilization in which the Enlightenment had figured so prominently as its foundational point of departure (Rousso 2016: 62–4). The waning appeal of this once guiding mnemonic timeline led some scholars to revisit the past randomly in search of lost causes worthy of remembrance, a perspective characterized by the Russian literary critic Svetlana Boym as a future-oriented "reflective nostalgia," a past that might have been and might yet again inspire posterity (2002: 49–55, 337–43).

In the late twentieth century, scholarship in cultural history returned to an interest in the high Enlightenment, but redirected attention from ideas to cultural practices (Ferrone 2015: 76, 92–4). The deconstructive tenor of scholarship in academia at large may have been an influence on this "rhetorical turn" among cultural historians, particularly in their appreciation of the originality of the scholarship of French philosopher Michel Foucault, who privileged the text over the author in order to redirect attention from the creation to the implementation of the reformist ideals of the late eighteenth century. Foucault discussed the power of discourse about reform-minded asylums and practices of self-care designed to put Enlightenment theory into practice. In the name of reason, he argued, these institution-building reformers advanced a rationale for the normalization of social mores through efficient disciplinary techniques in the treatment of unruly behavior by the criminal, the sick, and the psychologically disturbed. Foucault argued that the eighteenth-century discourse about asylums—prisons, hospitals, and madhouses—championed the soft technologies of management and control, reining in the impulse to stray from social convention (Foucault 1980: 124–5, 170–1). These institutional practices constituted new, more disciplined forms of ritual remembrance than had the customs of immemorial tradition, and so highlighted the role of political power in shaping collective memory.

Scholars writing in this "post-modern" vein pointed out that the influence of the eighteenth-century philosophers was greatly enhanced by new agencies of communication that publicized their agenda through an appeal to widening readership, thanks to the

FIGURE 0.2: Frontispiece of the *Encyclopédie*, 1751–72. A manifesto of the Enlightenment and a compendium of practical knowledge. Courtesy of Getty Images, UK.

democratization of literacy within the population at large. More people were learning to read and so were able to apply critical thought to the problems of the day. Of particular significance within the world of publishing were compendia of scientific knowledge, notably the French *Encyclopédie* (1751–72), edited by Jean le Rond d'Alembert and Denis Diderot, which inscribed the scientific and technological advances of the century. In this way, the practical accomplishments of the high culture of the eighteenth century were preserved in this readily available archive of knowledge. The acclaim accorded the *Encyclopédie* heralded the coming of a golden age of enlightenment (Darnton 1979).

Students of the rise of print culture emphasized the varieties among its modes of transmission. The success of the celebrated republic of letters, they explained, was greatly enhanced by the institutionalization of its projects in scientific academies, scholarly associations, and fraternal organizations, with a reformist agenda promoted in the name of a science of society (Ferrone 2015: 74–8). The influence of their ideas spread far and wide among educated people in the salons of the well-born and the coffee houses of the middle class (Melton 2001: 205–24, 247–50). In their ensemble, these media permitted the emergence of what German scholar Jürgen Habermas has characterized as the public sphere—a realm for the exchange and cultivation of public opinion outside that of government (Habermas [1962] 1989). The power of these new agencies to communicate the reform-minded agenda of the philosophers contributed to the vision of a different kind of future. From this perspective, the Enlightenment was a more pluralist venture than earlier generations of scholars had believed, revealing a broader spectrum of progressive views. There was, moreover, a gender issue ignored in earlier studies. The literary salons where philosophers gathered were never exclusively conclaves of men. Women of keen intellect presided over many of them, some as writers of distinction themselves (D. Goodman 2009: 1–15; Lilti 2015: 1–11). The Enlightenment, this younger generation of scholars contended, was more than an affair of Parisian intellectuals. There were other places that advanced the new learning in the arts and sciences. By the turn of the twenty-first century, scholars were investigating currents of thought emanating out of centers of learning in other parts of Europe, notably Edinburgh, Amsterdam, Naples, and Vienna, as well as in the seaboard cities of the American colonies aspiring to independence (Withers 2007: 51–4). They also began to discriminate among phases of the Enlightenment over the course of the eighteenth century, each with its particular interests. Mid-century marked the heyday of liberal ideas. By the end of the century, a radical intellectual current distinguished itself from the liberal one, by then well-established. Materialist atheism began to claim adherents apart from the idealist deism of the liberals (Israel 2001: 11, 704–13).

Our study pursues one further line of inquiry into the history of cultural memory. Alongside the wish to remember lies the will to forget, and it introduces another perspective on the workings of collective memory. The repression of trauma is implicated in almost any discussion of its nature. Some forms were subtle, as in the subversive effects of scientific discovery upon immemorial religious belief, inciting anxiety of the sort evinced in Baroque art and architecture well into the eighteenth century in central Europe (Martin 1977: 170–4). Others possessed greater immediacy. As Daniel Defoe's novel about the visitation of the bubonic plague upon London in 1665 reveals, latent fears of its return were never far below the surface of the popular psyche (Defoe [1722] 2003). Moreover, a variety of political events troubled the conscience of the eighteenth century. Wars throughout the century were conducted on a grand scale in the name of colonial conquest, independence, political revolution, and the making of empire, yet haunted by following reflections on the realities of terror, exile, destruction, and death. Memories of the divisive effects of the religious crisis of the Thirty Years' War (1618–48) were revived toward the end of the century, as the movement for German unification became a political cause (Cramer 2007: 1–17, 24–38). Most dramatically, the French Revolution (1789–99) was remembered by those displaced or persecuted in its name not only for its terrifying atrocities, but also for the lost heritage of the old regime (Fritzsche 2004: 127–8; Steinberg 2019: 90–116, 146–52).

Finally, the eighteenth century is the crucial era for understanding the changing relationship between memory and history on the threshold of modernity. Once judged interchangeable, they parted ways during that era. History as the story of exemplary lives yielded place to grandiose schemes of history's temporal patterns considered over the long run (Koselleck 1985: 17, 21–38). Within this transition emerged a genre of philosophical history, given to speculation about human destiny. Its proponents plotted stages along the way on a mnemonic timeline. As its reach extended, cultural history, conceived as the story of manners and mores, began to flourish within the interstices of this new conceptualization of historical time, as exemplified in the writings of Voltaire and Herder. But memory was not to be eclipsed. It would reassert its claims upon the past by retreating into private spheres of introspection, out of which would emerge a new genre of autobiography conceived as soul-searching in the quest for fathoming personal identity (Olney 1980).

UNDERLYING THEMES IN THE USES OF MEMORY IN EIGHTEENTH-CENTURY EUROPEAN CULTURES

Scholarly research permits a broad spectrum of approaches to memory's multi-faceted domain, among them commemorative practices, modes of communication, methods of preservation, issues of identity, the effects of trauma, techniques of introspection, mnemonic framing and remodeling. Among issues concerning memory raised by long-range trends in the cultural history of the eighteenth century, I underscore the importance of the following.

Mnemonic Schemes in the Transition from Theist to Scientific Cosmology

Advances in astronomy challenged long-standing cosmological conceptions identified with Hellenistic religions, leading to their remodeling in a different mnemonic register. The Copernican revolution of the sixteenth century ushered in a new paradigm of scientific understanding that displaced notions about the nature of the universe derived from medieval religious teaching. A Christian version of Claudius Ptolemy's universe (*c.* 150 CE), articulated in wondrous poetical detail by Dante Alighieri in the late Middle Ages, disintegrated in the face of a design that culminated in the model of Isaac Newton in the late seventeenth century (Kuhn 1970: 23–51, 82–91). Thenceforth astronomers would look out upon a largely unknown universe, orderly in its workings yet infinite in its reach. In this way, the scientific revolution precipitated a crisis of identity of cosmic proportions, since it called into question long-standing conceptions of the place of humankind within the universe. To put it more sententiously, the metaphysics of theology gave way to the physics of cosmology. Cultural memory during this era mirrored the contrasting appeals of scientific versus religious understanding. Studies of its places provide insight into what the century judged to be memorable in the context of the transformative changes that were underway. One notes a shift in the objects of commemoration, from venerable saints to intellectual heroes in the making of the new sciences.

During the following eighteenth century, inquiry into new fields of chemistry, biology, and natural history called attention to the dynamic character of scientific ideas as they diversified and expanded their repertoire. To portray the development of the sciences as a mnemonic scheme, d'Alembert and Diderot in their *Encyclopédie* diagrammed the elaboration of this branching tree of knowledge. The new science soon acquired a political edge, as fraternal societies emerged to link its principles to the understanding of society. On the fringes, these spawned cults of sorts. Freemasons, for example, are well-known for the mnemonic props they employed to popularize incipient notions about the constitutional foundations of civil society. Through their lodges, they employed symbols and rituals as a means of initiating members into a movement that for all its secrecy was invested in political and social progress (Jacob 1991: 34–5, 42, 49, 123–4). The natural sciences flourished, and came to be institutionalized in scientific academies, learned societies, and university life. Savants of the eighteenth century such as David Hume explored the epistemological implications of this paradigm shift, deepening skepticism about the teachings of revealed religion.

It is not that religious faith for ordinary people waned in light of this formulation of a new cosmological paradigm. Rather, it came to be conceived differently. Baroque art and architecture of the seventeenth and early-eighteenth century, with its evocation of intense passions in religious experience, revealed the depth of anxiety the new cosmological paradigm introduced. The architectural rebuilding and the artistic decoration of St. Peter's basilica in Rome during the sixteenth and seventeenth centuries, together with the pomp and ceremony attending the funerals of popes during that era, might be construed as the supernova of a kind of religious remembrance intended to reaffirm Christian evangelism by heightening the sense of mystery and awe in religious experience through visceral appeal to the senses. Themes of the Catholic reform for the edification of the laity remained visible in the frescos of the imperial and episcopal palaces of Rhineland prince bishops and the Habsburg empire of Maria Theresa through the eighteenth century. Among intellectuals, the interventionist God of medieval theology gave way to one who was removed, and whose purposes were hidden (Goldmann 1964: 36–7, 303–9). Among ordinary people, piety took precedence over theology and stern moral codes dictated by Christian tradition continued to prevail. Religious practices retained their mnemonic power among the Catholic laity, apart from disputes among the theologians (Delumeau 1971: 274–92). Protestantism, however, shunned the iconographic and ritual trappings of Catholic Baroque culture, with its appeal to elemental emotions, in favor of an ideal of simplicity in the evocation of humankind's relationship to God. Higher education within the universities of Europe and America was still conducted under the auspices of religious authorities, but the framing theological cosmology was gone. Increasingly, the authenticity of religious experience was judged to be an affair of the heart, not of the heavens.

At the same time, a new spirit of religious toleration was in the making. The controversies that had set Catholics and Protestants at war with one another from the sixteenth into the mid-seventeenth century lost their fervor. In that sense, the Peace of Westphalia (1648), which marked the end of the long era of "wars of religion," signifies a turning point in religious sensibilities. People no longer killed one another to alter a religious settlement. Attitudes voiced by religious leaders became more accepting of varied stances on religious faith. Political authorities made toleration official policy, as

FIGURE 0.3: Caspar David Friedrich, *The Abbey in the Oak Wood*, 1809. The romantic mystique of religious ruins lingered in Catholic culture. Courtesy of Getty Images, UK.

exemplified by Joseph II of the Habsburg empire. New religious cults of quietism and of enthusiasm took their place alongside long established churches. Judaism came to be viewed with greater respect and understanding. A humanist agnosticism gained currency within the interstices of this cultural transition (Hecht 2003: 341–67). Jean-Jacques Rousseau's depiction of the religious musings of a Savoyard priest in his treatise on education, *Emile*, epitomized the more open religious sentiments of the late eighteenth century, deepening the connection between introspection and religious understanding. Nature, represented in the Baroque culture of the seventeenth century in spectral images of biological decay, was a century later recast in images of tranquil landscapes that nurture the human soul. There, the God within the human psyche and the God within nature resonated in harmony (Taylor 1989: 355–63).

Memory and the Democratization of Print Culture

The long revolution in the technologies of typographic communication is a centerpiece of the historiography of cultural memory during this era. The eighteenth century witnessed the exponential expansion and diversification of print matter. It would lead to the archiving of knowledge in new ways and on an unprecedented scale. Memory banks were institutionalized in state-sponsored archives, university libraries, scientific academies, museums, encyclopedias and similar compendia of knowledge, all calculated to stabilize cultural memory (Rossi 2001: 192–202). It marked the end of reliance on the well-ordered mind as the primary resource for holding knowledge fast in favor of these external memory banks, which functioned as an extension of the human mind. The ancient art of memory, once the mainstay of erudition in the orator's rhetoric, rapidly lost its once prized significance as an essential skill (Hutton 1993: 30–2).

The print revolution also prepared the way for a divide in the understanding of public versus private memory. In the public sphere, the eighteenth century witnessed the democratization of literacy within the making of print culture. More people were able to read—more than half the population of western Europe by the turn of the nineteenth century—and they were learning to do so in new ways (Melton 2001: 82). With some difficulty, they began to read silently, and there was ever expanding variety in the literature to which they turned. These skills of literacy transformed the way people perceived, learned, and organized knowledge. Over the course of the century, reading and writing became tools of empowerment for more and more people. In the private sphere, these technologies deepened the capacity for critical thought (Ong 1982: 117–23). Public opinion mattered in a way it never had before, and writers were discovering new ways of exercising their influence. Social institutions, such as coffee houses and salons, became forums for discussion among intellectuals, and through these intermediaries the transmission of new ideas to wider audiences open to them. Crucial to the politics of government was public insistence upon written constitutions as the foundation of law to complement and in some measure displace the hazy conception of unwritten constitutional traditions that battened upon the precedents of case law. Printed texts were indispensable for publicizing these documents (Warner 1990).

Individualism and Introspection

The rising respect for individualism has been studied in depth as a political struggle for personal autonomy and legal rights, and the eighteenth century is a key era for enshrining them in constitutional documents. Less researched but equally important is the century's rehabilitation of the open expression of sentiment, which made possible a new conception of memory as a resource for personal awakening and self-discovery. Self-conscious awareness of the nature of emotional life and sympathy for its needs entered public discourse. The effect was to widen the divide between public (collective) and private (personal) memory. The cultivation of introspection was closely linked to the emerging preoccupation with the nature of the self (Taylor 1989: 355–67). This was the age that gave rise to autobiography as a mode of self-exploration, as opposed to a celebration of one's public achievements, the genre's ancient form. Jean-Jacques Rousseau has long been heralded as a pioneer of this kind of soul-searching, and his influence as autobiographer and as novelist was far-reaching. He is the most famous example of the cult of sentiment that developed over the course of the eighteenth century (Grimsley 1969: 85–115; Reddy 2001: 161–72). But ordinary people, too, kept diaries, wrote journals, and copied their reflections on their reading in commonplace books (Darnton, 2009: 149–58). Personal fulfillment became a newly cherished ideal, epitomized in the motto of the "pursuit of happiness." Developmental self-fashioning (as opposed to role-playing) appealed as never before. Education, too, was becoming more formalized, and the idea of stages in the cognitive development of children began to influence teaching (Ariès [1960] 1973: 199–216). The opportunity for higher education expanded in Europe and the Americas.

All of these developments put a decided accent on remembrance of the personality of the individual, as bodied forth in particular character traits. Portrait painting, unadorned by religious or symbolic connotations, came into vogue. Biography emerged as a newly important literary genre, discarding the trope of the edifying life in favor of a more realistic assessment of an individual's complex personality. The rituals attending death and mourning were simplified, judging the individual life in simple humanist terms rather than grandiose spiritual ones. Gravestone epitaphs etching the dates of the individual lives of ordinary people became commonplace in cemeteries across Europe and America. Cemeteries themselves were redesigned as gardens for reflection (Vovelle 1974: 186, 200–7; 1983: 464–70).

Closely related was the reconfiguration of the family as a unit of intimacy. Mutual affection was a route to personal fulfillment, and so was beginning to undercut genealogical status as a basis for marriage. The concept of companionate marriage became the new ideal of marital happiness (Stone 1977: 217–53). A focus on the well-being of children, especially in their development, revised conceptions of parenting (Gélis 1989). It was in this context that the modern novel made its appearance. This genre featured personal relationships. Readers responded to the representation of the emotions of its characters and identified these with their own feelings of love reawakened (Watt [1957] 2001: 198–206). In France, Rousseau was lionized for his *Nouvelle Héloise*, a story of young lovers pouring out their hearts to one another. In Germany, Johann von Goethe's *Sorrows of Young Werther* spoke to those disappointed in unrequited love. All of these cultural practices gave new force of appeal to the cultivation of memory as a private affair. Long a technique for rhetorical display, the art of memory was reconceived as one for soul-searching for the child hidden within the recesses of the adult psyche.

Imagining a Politics of Enlightenment

One long-range trend across the era of the Enlightenment concerns the move from politics that provided security (law and order) to politics that promoted the well-being of the community (the pursuit of happiness). At the highest echelons of political power, one notes the move from dynastic monarchies based upon a heterogeneous network of personal allegiances toward abstract conceptions of the nation as an imagined community of citizens that share belief in its principles and acknowledge common civic obligations in its name (Anderson 2006: 19–22, 37–46). Dynastic monarchy was based on an ancient politics of families and was justified by appeal to a divinely ordained right of genealogical succession. Sovereignty was invested in the body of the king, and the mythology of kingship was commemorated in rituals of coronation and ceremonial pageantry. By the mid-seventeenth century, the principle of absolute personal rule had become inadequate for meeting the complex needs of governmental responsibility. Governments had always been expected to provide security, a notion reaffirmed yet updated in the writings of seventeenth-century political theorist Thomas Hobbes. Hobbes's favor for an abstract conception of sovereignty over a concrete one of personal rule undermined the primordial foundations of the ancient politics of families. Such had been the fate of England in the mid-seventeenth century, when the monarchy was abandoned in favor of a republic. After a decade, the monarchy was restored, but thenceforth would play a ceremonial role as the personification of the nation to which the populace could relate, even though real power was passing to parliament.

With the coming of the eighteenth century, more was asked of government than security; expectations rose about enhancing opportunities for advancement in life as well as for enjoyment of its amenities. In continental Europe, kings held fast to their power, and the rituals of life in royal households persisted much as before. But the idea of royal absolutism, based on a theory of political sovereignty as the divine right of kings over their subjects, ceded place to "enlightened despotism," with its accent on the responsibility of rulers to promote the well-being of their citizens. During the French Revolution, the concept of monarchy itself was abandoned. The execution of the king and queen (1793) symbolically sounded the death knell of sovereignty based upon genealogical inheritance (Hunt 1992: 1–16). A new conception of the republic arose, as the revolution's leaders aspired to re-imagine the nation in the guise of a civic religion, appealing to idealized memories of the Roman republic. In the course of these events, a new kind of political discourse based on popular sovereignty emerged, and it required a new set of mnemonic props of political allegiance (Furet 1981: 46–61). The ceremonies attending kingship gave way to the festivals of the nation (Aulard 1904: 52–6, 307–22). For political festivals to rouse popular emotions effectively, they needed to be made emotionally appealing in the aesthetics of their choreography. In this respect, it is worth noting that Jean-Jacques Rousseau, in his 1772 essay on the government of Poland, had anticipated the importance attributed to ritual remembrance of the historical development of nationhood as a means of localizing abstract conceptions of sovereignty. In Germany, where political sovereignty remained widely dispersed among a variety of kingdoms, principalities, bishoprics, and independent city-states, all loosely confederated under the tenuous authority of the Holy Roman Emperor, philosophers, keen on finding a way to a conception of a unified German identity, turned to cultural conceptions based upon shared language, heritage, landscape, and folklore (Mosse 1975: 21–46, 73–4).

The Nature of Tradition Reconceived

Tradition is a capacious concept and thinking about its nature became more complex over the course of the eighteenth century. This cultural reconfiguration involved a transition from traditions regarded as "immemorial" (habitual practices received from the past) toward what in recent scholarship has been characterized as traditions that were "invented" (commemorative rituals consciously refashioned by public authority to suit the needs of present circumstances) (Hobsbawm and Ranger 1983: 1–14). This shift in scholarly perspective reveals a more self-conscious political interest in cultural practices.

The appeal to immemorial tradition had its apologists. For German philosopher Johann Herder, national identity resided in the continuity of the collective memory of its folk culture, which reached deep into the past. Sympathizers for the old ways argued for tradition's stabilizing power and expressed misgivings about cutting the present age free of its past in precipitous ways. With the advent of the French Revolution, the English statesman Edmund Burke contended that it is better to reform gradually than to jettison the wisdom of the ages. The disruptive effects of the beginnings and rapid onslaught of the industrial revolution in England upon the mores of the rural world gave rise to nostalgia for a folk culture that was beginning to fade from living memory (Fritzsche 2004: 133–42). On the cultural plane, there was an abiding interest in the classical tradition of education. The intellectual debate between "ancients and moderns" over the literary canon remained a running theme through this era (Levine 1999: x–xi, 127; Kelley 1998: 222).

Yet new thinking about the politics of tradition was underway. As reformers of the day developed the confidence that they might shape their own world, the idea of tradition was remodeled to adapt to these conditions. All parties recognized a quickening of the process of change. Some transformative forces were economic. In England especially, agricultural capitalism had been common practice for more than a century. The scope of its development expanded, as small farms and common land were consolidated into large agricultural holdings, while those displaced among the rural population decamped to the cities to swell the ranks of factory labor. The routines of industrial labor exercised baneful social effects upon the working class amid the insalubrious living conditions of the burgeoning cities. The quality of social life deteriorated, as the uprooted cadres of urban workers lost touch with the social traditions of the rural world they had left behind.

To deal with these social conditions, old religious traditions were remodeled, and new political ones appeared. England witnessed a religious revival in the cities, thanks to the rise of Methodism as a movement of Dissenters under the inspiration of John Wesley. Fiery orators, such as John Wilkes, resurrected a radical, democratizing tradition that dated from the Putney debates a century before (Thompson 1963: 26–76). Popular riots over the high cost of living began to appear from mid-century and played into a living tradition of popular protest with visible effects by the turn of the nineteenth century (Rudé 1964: 33–45). In France, urban food riots were a contributing factor in the coming of the French Revolution. The power of the rising of the people as a "revolution from below" was to become the sustaining legend of a revolutionary tradition, and as such a political touchstone for radical reformers throughout the nineteenth century (Hutton 1981: 1–16).

The Aesthetics of Nostalgia for an Emerging Aristocracy

Amidst the dynamic economic and social change of the eighteenth century, the cultural identity of the nobility of birthright was diluted by the rising power of a new aristocracy of wealth and talent. Titles of nobility were still coveted for the prestige and privileges they conferred, but status was for sale with the advance of capitalism within the European economy. The entrepreneur, who acquired and risked capital, gained unprecedented power in the process of becoming fabulously wealthy, and aspired to a place within a newly emerging aristocracy. The legal foundations of social privilege persisted, while nobility as a status of genealogical inheritance survived as a coveted fiction. In these circumstances, rising entrepreneurs came to rival the old nobility of birthright in their wealth and so aspired to acquire their social standing, either through marriage, appointment to high office, or the purchase of titles of nobility (Behrens 1967).

As for cultural memory among this remodeled aristocracy, the pastoral idyll became a guiding aesthetic fantasy of the good life. The newly formed social elite fostered the protocols of "civilized" behavior within these privileged echelons of high society. The notion may be observed in the elaboration of a cult of manners among the European aristocracy, dating from the time of the Renaissance and culminating in the era of the Enlightenment. Herein the idea of the social was reconceived: the old ideal of informal sociability gravitated toward a more formal one of social etiquette. This generated a psychosocial process through which individuals in polite society learned a code of behavior that made them more aware not only of the sensibilities of others but also of their own. Manners were ritual acts of comportment. One remembered how to behave, at first awkwardly, eventually intuitively. To transgress these codes was to generate self-conscious embarrassment. The cult of manners reached its apogee during the mid-eighteenth century (Elias [1939] 1978: 38, 44–50). Here a new kind of collective memory emerged within high society, based upon an ideal of aesthetic refinement. It is made manifest especially in the books of etiquette on "civilized" behavior, the Rococo style of art and architecture, and the formal gardens in the estates of the well-born. Such were the settings for the salons of the eighteenth century, in which women with intellectual interests presided over gatherings that lionized celebrated writers of the republic of letters (Lilti

FIGURE 0.4: Hubert Robert, *The Grand Gallery of the Louvre*, Paris, 1801. The museum's display of historical, legendary, and pastoral themes characteristic of eighteenth-century aesthetic taste. Courtesy of Getty Images, UK.

2015: 8). During the French Revolution, those driven into exile idealized perceived losses of cherished ways of life during the old regime (Fritzsche 2004: 55–91).

Pastoral art lent an aesthetic dimension to eighteenth-century intellectual interests. It drew forth the artists' approach to the domestication of nature, an analogue to the interest of scientists in nature's vitalism. Nature was no longer perceived to be the dangerous place where evil lurked in the dark woods, but rather as a place of reverent tranquility that drew one's thoughts toward the prospect of transcendence beyond rational understanding. Nature as a source of sentimental remembrance also had a sublime side as the archetypal source of collective memory. For the English poet William Wordsworth, the landscape he roamed as a youth was the wellspring of such memory, for it gave life to disinterested contemplation. In philosophy as in art, the pursuit of the sublime approached nature as if it were a force that nurtures the imagination even as it defies description. As an aesthetic concept, the sublime is ineffable, and as such a sentiment infused with awe.

Mapping Far-Away Places

Travel, commerce, and European colonization expanded during the eighteenth century, creating a global network of encounter and exchange of both goods and ideas. Out of their interplay new conceptions of a globalizing collective memory emerged. By then, the Americas were no longer unknown places to be explored but rather well-mapped regions to be settled and colonized by the nations of western Europe. By century's end they had become settings for rebellion by the settlers themselves in the name of independence and the making of nations of their own. The cultures of Asia and Oceania beckoned as exotic new worlds for exploration. Far-away places once only imagined became recognizable ones now visited, deflating fanciful dreams into earthy realities. Whetting the European imagination were stories about the explorers who actually sailed to the far corners of the world, most famously the voyages of Captain James Cook to Australia and Hawaii, the stories about the mutineers of the ill-fated expedition of the British ship *Bounty*, and of Louis Antoine Bougainville's journeys among islands in the far Pacific (Matsuda 2012: 133–43). The German naturalist Alexander von Humboldt journeyed to the headwaters of the Orinoco River in South America, an area of legendary lore hitherto inaccessible to Europeans (Wulf 2015: 61–74). Map making as the framing of geographical space took on more accurate design (Withers 2007: 201–4). For some outliers, the European Enlightenment became a model for reform. Leaders of nations in the Middle East sought to adapt ideas of European philosophers to the cultural world of Islam (Bellaigue 2017).

The leading European philosophers of the eighteenth century were often savvy about the cultural implications of the collective memory of a wider world. They cast the times in which they lived as an age of cosmopolitanism, open to appreciation of the varieties of manners and mores of people around the world (Harvey 2012: 213–20). The ideal of citizenship in the world was sounded by philosophers such as Montesquieu and Voltaire, who opened European perspectives on the varieties among its cultures. For scholars today, reflections on the encounters between European explorers and indigenous populations serve as subject matter for the "new historicism," the study of the circulation of ideas issuing from encounters between cultures that are strange to one another. Each remembered the encounter differently, and so developed a narrative of its own about its meaning. That of the Western explorers, however, defined its representation (Greenblatt 1991: 6, 119–51). Unacknowledged at the time was the shameful legacy of slavery and transportation wrought by colonization, whose repressed memory would return to haunt the conscience of the twenty-first century.

Trauma in an Age of Revolution

The implications of long-range cultural changes were fully revealed in the dramatic political revolutions of the late eighteenth century in the Atlantic world. The collective memory of the century as a whole is therefore weighted heavily toward its later decades. Its centers of action were the American colonies and France, but their influences rippled in waves through Europe and the Americas (Palmer 1960). In the revolutionary era of the late eighteenth and early nineteenth centuries, modernity came into its own, its cultural memories revised and transformed in the process. Its leaders promoted written constitutions as the foundation of a new political order, based upon the ideals of liberalism. A new political discourse circulated in the literary salons, the press, and the representative assemblies. It brought into being the concept of ideology, which taught that theory implies a practice for its implementation. Each one—liberalism, radicalism, utopian socialism, communism—offered a guiding frame of reference for action, a touchstone against which to measure ongoing progress toward an idealized moral goal (Lichtheim 1967: 4–11). New mores, new events and celebrities to commemorate, and new traumas emerged in the midst of revolutions' disruptions. In the minds of contemporaries, these signaled the dawn of an age in which the making of nations would begin anew. Pointedly, French

FIGURE 0.5: Hubert Robert, *Demolition of the Bastille, July 20, 1789*. Iconoclasm in the cause of erasing the memory of the Old Regime. Courtesy of Getty Images, UK.

revolutionaries devised a new calendar, designed a new flag, revamped the system of weights and measures, systematized the agencies of governmental administration, and instituted an array of civic festivals to commemorate the popular uprisings that had ushered in the new regime (Hunt 1986: 36, 62–5, 96–8). Revolutionary leaders rededicated a newly constructed church as a pantheon, a mausoleum of civic identity in which to bury its heroes (J. Goodman 2017). The French Pantheon was but one among many such commemorative burial places erected across Europe, which in keeping with the ideals of the Enlightenment enshrined writers and statesmen rather than kings and their kin (Bouwers 2012).

The desire to consign the Old Regime to oblivion was not without its baneful consequences. Revolutionary statesmen may have proclaimed new egalitarian ideals, but attempts at their implementation created fratricidal havoc in pursuit of what proved to be an elusive goal. In recent decades, scholarly interest has shifted from the ideological imperatives of the Revolution to the atrocities committed in its name (Andress 2006: 1–7, 371–7). During the Reign of Terror of 1793–4, popular tribunes took measures calculated to obliterate the memory of the old order, culminating sensationally in the execution of the king and queen. For historian Lynn Hunt, the execution of the royal family revealed deep-seated psychological fears about the dissolution of the family as a stabilizing force in society (1992: 124–50). But regicide was only the most notorious manifestation of the summary justice and mass killings carried out in the quixotic cause of creating a "republic of virtue." Memory of the Terror led to revulsion in its aftermath, in which leaders of a moderate government sought to take responsibility to right its wrongs by dispensing retribution for the perpetrators, commemoration of the victims, and compensation for their families. But the long-term psychological effect of that experience was to leave a legacy of profound anxiety, insecurity, and psychological repression that would take decades to work through (Steinberg 2019).

The Emerging Divide Between History and Memory

At the outset of this period, history as a scholarly discipline was still practiced naively as a conflation of history and memory. Historians recounted stories of memorable events and persons, many bordering on the mythological. Such stories were meant to convey edifying lessons out of the past, to be appreciated either as exemplary models or cautionary tales for the present (Koselleck 1985: 21–7). Human nature was thought to be immutable, and the human condition to have changed little through the ages. Hence the value ascribed to the idea of eternal verities. During the era of the Enlightenment, however, changing realities stimulated interest among historians in placing such ideas in historical context. Over the course of the eighteenth century, historians redirected attention from memorable events and personalities to the historical process itself so as to reveal its transformative effects over the long run. The idea of history conceived as exemplary lessons lifted as episodes out of a timeless past yielded place to history reconceived as a patterned continuum of dynamic change reaching toward an anticipated destiny. So was born the idea of progress as the inspiration for a new genre of philosophical history that aspired to contextualize the vast intellectual movement that progressive thinkers believed was under way. Antoine Barnave, Nicholas de Condorcet, and Georg Hegel, historians with a speculative bent, invented easily remembered stages with which to plot their forecasts of the direction of moral intention toward which the course of history was tending. In practice, these were mnemonic schemes on a grand scale (Zerubavel 2003: 14–15).

So reconceived, history aspired to an interpretive overview that distanced past from present, and history from memory. Whereas memory emphasized immersion in the past as if it were a presence, history aspired to establish critical distance from the past as a living experience so as to reveal the nature of long-range change in the human condition (Phillips 2013: 81–90). In the name of history reconceived as a new kind of science, the Neapolitan rhetorician Giambattista Vico sought to expose collective memory's hidden meanings and so to assert the primacy of history's rational critique over memory's emotion-laden poetics. Herein the concept of historicism was born, and with it the subordination of collective memory to its protocols. Historicism taught that humankind, having constructed its own human world, could reconstruct it as the story of that accomplishment. Each age along the way was to be appreciated for its "historicity," i.e., its own timeful conditions (Hartog 2015: 105). As the model of historical interpretation for the modern age, this theory of history suggests why historians came to emphasize the need to correct memory's distorting ways of understanding the past. Unacknowledged was a guiding memory that served as the matrix of this master narrative, as exemplified in the high hopes that history would show how the modern nation-state was the instrument of the advance of civilization over time (Nora 1986: 2: 648–9). Accordingly, histories that traced the origins and development of nation-states began to appear and would in time become the dominant framework for organizing historical scholarship. In this respect, a history of the sort pioneered for England by David Hume in the mid-eighteenth century prepared the way.

CHAPTER ONE

Power and Politics

KIRSTEN L. COOPER

Ideas of nation are significant markers of collective identity in the modern age, and as such it is valuable to appreciate their evolution within the context of cultural memory over the course of the early modern era. The nation is an idea constructed upon the myths of a group of people, and is therefore subject to revision, forgetting, rewriting, and selective recall. Scholars of nations and nationalism have long sought to unpack the inventions underlying projections of the nation, and the ways in which those projections have changed in different contexts. Indeed the work of now-classic theorists of nationalism, such as Benedict Anderson, Ernest Gellner, and Eric Hobsbawm, placed nations within a precise historical moment of "invention" or "imagination" (Anderson 2006; Gellner 1997; Hobsbawm 1992; Hutton 2016: 51–4). These scholars did so as a conscious attempt to strip away the myth that nation and its associated political programs have existed, unchanged, since time immemorial. Instead, scholars have shown how much work went into shaping and spreading national myths and national memories.

The new orthodoxy underlying most of these studies maintains that nations are exclusively modern phenomena invented during the late eighteenth and early nineteenth century, and that national ideas had no relevance for the pre-modern age of dynastic politics. There are many exclusively modern variations of national ideas for which this is undeniably true. But this assumption has led to an understanding of Europe's long eighteenth century as a straightforward transition from dynastic to national politics—a transition often epitomized by the shift from Louis XIV's dynastic absolutism to the national republicanism of the French Revolution. According to this narrative, it was only in opposition to dynasty that the nation emerged as a politically significant concept. In the words of Benedict Anderson, nations and nationalism came into being only "against" the "decomposition" of dynasty and other previously dominant cultural systems (2006: 12).

There is, however, a wealth of evidence to contradict this narrative. Numerous recent studies have noted that national ideas were common well before the eighteenth century and that the "triumph" of modern nationalism was far from universal after 1789. Moreover, the concept of "nation" regularly acted in support of dynastic monarchy before, during, and after the eighteenth century. Instead of a simple shift from dynastic to national politics, the eighteenth century witnessed a far messier process in which the way that national ideas were understood and employed changed dramatically. I argue that the idea of nationhood was a useful rhetorical device long before it was employed to "invent" the modern nation-state. For this reason, I distinguish the concept of "nation" held during the early modern era from that of "nationalism" consciously employed during the late eighteenth century to advance the interests of the emerging nation-state.

The concept of nation is a metonym for a particular way of thinking about collective identity. The metonym itself—the national moniker of "France" or "the French nation," for example—may not have changed significantly over time, but the meaning and idea behind the terms shifted radically. At the beginning of the eighteenth century, and for centuries prior, monarchs had been able to marshal understandings of shared cultural, linguistic, hereditary, geographic and political communities—each a constituency of the "French nation"—to bolster their political power and dynastic identity. During the Wars of Louis XIV, for example, a war of words accompanied the royal armies, as pamphleteers cultivated national loyalty and slung national vitriol to justify the actions of monarchs pursuing glory and power for their royal houses. By the end of the century, that same national language signified different understandings. First, the qualities of what constituted the nation itself had changed. In France, they realized that not all members of the imagined French nation truly comprised a homogenous community, and, far more importantly, this fact was suddenly seen as a pressing political problem. Second, the political associations of the national metonym had changed. By the time of the Revolution, the "nation" signified an independent political force to which the monarchy had to submit. National ideas had been imbued with radical new theories of popular sovereignty, meaning that the same language of memory and community now served a different purpose. This transformation was not simply one from dynasty *to* nation, but from dynasty *and* nation to the possibility of dynasty *versus* nation.

A series of mid-century crises of sovereignty sparked this transformation, prompting thinkers to search for a new way to regenerate the political system. These crises coincided with an Enlightenment drive to investigate, categorize, and define previously unexamined and uncritically accepted concepts. Many thinkers seized upon ideas of nation as solutions to the political problems they faced, and in the process subjected those same ideas to a new level of intellectual scrutiny, debating exactly what the nation was. This "constant fusion and friction of ideas," in the words of Harold Mah, "produced identities that were in crucial senses uncertain or unstable," containing within them "multiple and paradoxical projections" of identity and community (2003: 11, 12). Moreover, these projections differed greatly from earlier understandings of the boundaries and uses of national ideas. As Carla Hesse and Thomas Laqueur summarized, "by the middle of the eighteenth century, gaps were appearing everywhere between the signifiers of national identity and the signified" (1994). One particularly potent understanding that emerged from this intellectual fervor was the reinvention of national ideas as effective tools against dynastic monarchy. Just like the memories upon which they are constructed, ideas of nation have been repeatedly altered and rewritten. National ideas, therefore, should be analyzed as intellectual concepts whose meanings are dependent on historical and rhetorical context.

In this chapter, I explore the reinvention of national ideas as they relate to dynastic sovereignty in Britain, France, and Germany over the long eighteenth century. I do not suggest a universal explanation of the history of the nation, but instead focus on the particular context of each case. The fact that some of these usages do not correspond to modern definitions does not mean that they were irrelevant or insignificant. Indeed, contextualization of these ideas reveals a very different picture. Instead of a smooth transition from dynasty to nation, following prototypical invention of the latter idea in one country, (Greenfeld 1992; Hastings 1997; Bell 2001; Plessner 1959; Sheehan 1981), we see a series of roughly contemporaneous crises in England, France, and Germany that sparked remarkably similar debates and anxieties surrounding the meaning and role of the nation. The answers suggested and seized upon, however, differed in each case. The history of dynasty and nation, therefore, is not a linear process of opposition and replacement, but a story of intertwined political categories that at times reinforced and at times pulled against each other, as understandings and necessities shifted. One outcome of these debates was the creation of the modern understanding of nation. But this was just one product in the complicated story of rewriting and forgetting the longer history of national ideas.

NATION IN THE SERVICE OF DYNASTY

The rhetoric of nationhood was both widespread and politically significant in the early modern period. For centuries prior to the eighteenth, ideas about national communities with distinct characters had been common in Europe (Leerssen 2010; Hirschi 2012). During the Renaissance, for example, much humanist scholarship focused on finding national origins and identity, combined with a healthy dose of nationally-framed intellectual competition (Whaley 2012, 1:102; Münkler, Grünberger, and Mayer 1998). Thinkers offered a variety of analyses of national character that focused on everything from geography and climate, to political organization and language, some viewing the above as cause and some as effect of national differences (Montesquieu [1748] 1989; Mah 1994). One need only look at the *Völkertäfel of Styria* to understand how commonplace and well-developed ideas of nation and national differences were by the early eighteenth century. Though not much is known about the origins of this painting,

FIGURE 1.1: *Völkertafel of Styria*, artist unknown, early eighteenth century. Courtesy of the Austrian Museum of Popular Art, Vienna.

its contents are nevertheless fascinating (Stanzel 1999). Depicting ten males dressed in various "national" habits, the painting systematically categorizes the "characteristics" of each "*Volk*," from their manners to their bad habits, political systems, hobbies, land, and virtue in war. This work visually depicts the many layers upon which ideas of nation and national characters were built and differentiated in early modern Europe.

Such stereotypes no doubt functioned, in the words of David Bell, as "a simple and comforting way for people to come to terms with the array of human diversity," but they were also much more than that (2001: 143). National ideas, symbols, and understandings were common as political tools in support of dynastic monarchy. From the late Middle Ages, monarchs legitimized their hold on power with the help of ideas of shared national communities, memories, and histories. Collette Beaune has shown how the "propaganda of nationhood," including projections of France as a chosen religious community, as a community of shared language, and particularly as a national family united by geography and descent, and protected by their national "father"—the king—did more to "shore up the unsteady trusses of the state" in medieval France than any other institution (1991: 9–10). Peter Roberts has demonstrated that in order to promote Welsh loyalty to the crown, Tudor monarchs intentionally mobilized ideas of an overarching British inheritance that simultaneously linked England and Wales while not threatening the distinctive identities of either (1998). By the beginning of the eighteenth century especially, national ideas were common tools of dynastic political rhetoric. Ellen Welch notes how Louis XIV incorporated representations of nations and national character in court ballets and other diplomatic spectacles to assert French dominance over other European powers (2013). Peter Sahlins argues that national ideas were not exclusive to the highest levels of society, and were indeed a tool for rural, border societies to negotiate their own political interests (1989). But one of the most widespread and fascinating examples is the currency that national rhetoric had within pamphlet propaganda. Steven Pincus has analyzed how the projection of national "hatreds" shifted along with the vicissitudes of war in England (1995). The mass of German propaganda directed at Louis XIV's France during the same period was often saturated with competing conceptions of Frenchness and Germanness (Schillinger 1999; Wrede 2004; Cooper 2019, 2020). In these and other examples, national ideas bolstered and aided the consolidation of dynastic rule and helped to further dynastic political interests.

What is fascinating about the flourishing of early modern national ideas, and the political roles they played, is how much they differ from modern examples. That is no reason, however, to deny their importance. Many modern uses of the term "nation" cannot satisfy the strict requirements that theorists have since placed on them. Even more important, many of the characteristics that scholars use to identify and understand modern nations simply did not exist in the early modern period (Gorski 2006; Hesse and Laqueur 1994: 2). First, the "nation" was not considered to be the foundation of sovereignty and political legitimacy, as it would often come to be in the modern era. The nation in the early modern period was regularly represented by "discourses and practices wholly innocent of democracy, [claims to] sovereignty, or anything that could be construed as 'nationalism'" (Hesse and Laqueur 1994: 3). After all, democratic and republican theories of political sovereignty spread significantly only in the second half of the eighteenth century. Second, the concept of explicitly delineated borders was a development of the nineteenth century (Sahlins 1989). Third, the early modern state had neither the capacity nor the interest to intrude deep into the everyday lives of each of its subjects in order to ensure cultural, political or linguistic conformity, as it would come to do in the modern age (Hastings 1997: 29). Fourth, there was no thought that the nation or national identity required exclusive loyalty and commitment, as nationalists would seek to build in the late nineteenth and early twentieth centuries (Zahra 2008: 5). To hold the pre-modern period to the definitional standard of modern national ideas is to impose not only anachronistic understandings of national ideas themselves, but anachronistic expectations for the state, political theory, identity, and the exercise of sovereignty. Instead, by thinking about national ideas as metonyms with shifting meanings, we can better understand how they functioned in their various historical contexts.

In one such context, early modern national ideas were employed as political rhetoric, playing on a sense of collective belonging and interest that could prove beneficial for dynastic purposes. These ideas included cultural understandings based on shared language, mores and customs, historical understandings based on myths of shared heritage (including celebration of descent from past military and religious heroes), political understandings based on loyalty to a certain dynasty or belonging to a certain type of political system, as well as geographic understandings based on ancestral territory, landscape, or climate. In response to the French consolidation of control over Alsace (1679–84) during the Wars of Louis XIV, for example, German pamphleteers argued that these areas belonged by rights to Germany, not just because they had historically been part of the Holy Roman Empire, but also because it was the birthplace of Charlemagne, who was himself of "German blood," and thus his patrimony belonged to the descendants of his nation. Moreover, these pamphleteers argued, the reason the region had fallen to the French was that the inhabitants of the area had been corrupted from their honest, martial, strong and noble German traits by the influence of the feminine, underhanded, perfidious French. The proof, they believed, could be seen in the French fashions, cuisine, and culture so popular among the area's inhabitants, as well as the frequency with which they spoke French instead of their "native" German. Myths of national patrimony founded on politics, heredity, and geography thus formed the basis for claims of restitution. (Ironically, arguments about national corruption based on mores, culture, clothing, and language had also provided a rationale for why the area fell so easily to the French in the first place.) All of these concepts were then mobilized by pamphleteers to support the Habsburg emperor, Leopold I, in his opposition to Louis XIV's growing power (Cooper 2019).

The French responded with their own attempts to marshal national rhetoric to their benefit. The nuances of the well-developed atmosphere of national rhetoric in early modern Europe are illustrated by a series of propaganda pamphlets authored by Jean de la Chapelle and sponsored by the French crown during the War of the Spanish Succession (1701–14). In the midst of this dynastic conflict *par excellence*, La Chapelle's *Lettres d'un Suisse* employed a wide range of national rhetoric. He mobilized ideas of national character in an attempt to detach England and the Netherlands from the Grand Alliance. "The wise and modest Dutch," he argued, were sacrificing their national interests in the war while leaders of both states papered over "ancient" Anglo-Dutch aversions to "force the two nations to march under the same standard" (La Chapelle 1704, 3:15, 54–5). To legitimize and encourage Spanish support of the Bourbon claimant, La Chapelle contended that "the Spanish nation, the most wise . . . sensitive . . . the most courageous and virtuous in the world" would never become "traitors and rebels to their king and to their *patrie*" by rejecting their "rightful" monarch (La Chapelle 1704, 1:23, 4:25). And to encourage continued French loyalty in a long and difficult war, La Chapelle stressed that the French "love for their king and their *patrie*" and "the honor of their nation" would see them through "even the largest of disasters" (La Chapelle 1704, 5:50). The Portuguese, Swiss,

Hungarians, and Germans, too, all had their own national characters, interests, and rhetorical uses, which, of course, La Chapelle mobilised in his efforts to further the interests of his backer, Louis XIV.

Amidst this regular use of national rhetoric, La Chapelle smartly navigated between dynastic and national categories to isolate Louis XIV's Habsburg rivals. La Chapelle had plenty to say about "the Germans," whom he described as a "wise and warlike nation," "proud," "generous," and "free" (La Chapelle 1704, 1:95, 4:239, 261; 5:213). But, La Chapelle warned, these honorable Germans were being led away from their true national interest by the nefarious influence of the House of Austria. "Austria" is itself an example of how metonymic signifiers can be reinvented, with later national connotations emerging only as a result of the vagaries of modern German politics. In the early modern period, "Austria" was a dynastic category, referring to the House of Habsburg. During the Wars of Louis XIV, the Habsburg Holy Roman Emperor, Leopold I, had regularly portrayed himself as the protector of German national interests (Wrede 2004: 450–5). La Chapelle instead described a Germany that existed *despite* a long history of Habsburg "infidelity, fraud, low tricks, secret conspiracies . . . crimes, treasons, murders, assassinations, poisonings, [and] ambition" (La Chapelle 1704, 2:141–2). La Chapelle sought to isolate the Austrians from the German "nation"—and thus from the Habsburgs' allies in the empire—by repeatedly sketching the Habsburgs as "the disruptors of the repose of the [German] *patrie*" (La Chapelle 1704, 2:172–3). This rhetorical manipulation was part of a French effort to isolate their dynastic rivals by disassociating them from the concept of "Germany" while simultaneously using German national rhetoric to unite the rest of the empire in terms of a common national interest (Cooper 2019). In La Chapelle's argument, of course, that interest was a cessation of hostilities against France.

La Chapelle's pamphlets serve as one of many examples of an early modern political sphere well versed in ideas of nation, national communities, and national difference. One uniting factor across this sphere was the regularity with which complex and detailed understandings of nationhood not only coexisted with old regime dynasties, but actively supported them.

MID-CENTURY CRISES

At the beginning of the eighteenth century, La Chapelle used national ideas in royally-sponsored propaganda to promote support of Louis XIV's political and military decisions at home and abroad. By the end of that same century, revolutionaries in France used national ideas to justify the beheading of Louis XVI and the creation of a new, republican, political system. The events of the intervening years destabilized the relationship between dynasty and nation that had existed for centuries. France provides the most dramatic example, but a remarkably similar process occurred in Britain and the Holy Roman Empire. In all three regions, a series of unique yet roughly contemporaneous events undermined traditional political foundations and prompted consideration of radically new political possibilities.

In France, the period from 1750 to 1770 featured a series of controversies between the crown and the *parlements* that led eventually to the 1771 Maupeou Coup, in which Louis XV and his Lord Chancellor, René de Maupeou, suppressed the *parlements* in an attempt to reassert royal authority. As the king sparred with oppositional factions over issues of taxation and the power of the courts, all sides increasingly appealed to a "neutral" public sphere (Baker 1990; Merrick 1990; Chartier 1991; Van Kley 1996). Tensions were further exacerbated by moral critiques of the king and his court, which became the target of slanderous ridicule both inside and outside the halls of Versailles (Kaiser 1996). Never before had a political atmosphere existed in France in which the monarchy's decisions were so intensely debated. In a country in which the monarch had theoretically absolute power, such debate weakened the monarchy's claim of unqualified legitimacy (Melton 2001: 45–75). Instead, the "public" and the "nation" as abstractions were becoming the arbiters of truth and justice, and their representatives were responsible for judging the actions of the monarch.

Britain, even more than France, experienced a significant realignment in how dynastic sovereignty was understood early in the eighteenth century. The Revolution of 1688, and especially the 1701 Act of Settlement, detached the monarchy from hereditary right, "not just once but many times over," in order to justify a Protestant successor. The foundations of sovereignty now rested on a religiously-founded contract between ruler and ruled, with the understanding that the monarch had been "chosen" by "the nation," or "the people," or at least by a parliament claiming that mantle (Colley 2012: 47; Pincus 2009). The 1707 Acts of Union also left Great Britain in the unique situation of having created a new state with a new national identity. As Linda Colley has shown, the Acts of Union prompted the need to officially promote Britishness over and above its counterparts of Englishness, Scottishness, or Welshness, especially as an attempt to better integrate Scotland into the newly founded Great Britain (2012; Lindfield and Margrave 2015). Loyalty to this new nation and its monarchs was sorely tested by the Jacobite uprising (1745–6). Thousands of Scottish Highlanders rejected their "British" monarch as nothing more than an English oppressor. Moreover, the "often disheveled fashion" in which the rebellion had been suppressed prompted fears about the integrity of Great Britain and the loyalty of its people to this new national identity (Colley 2012: 87). The Stuart claimants posed a significant dynastic challenge to Hanoverian legitimacy. Colley argues that the specter of a Stuart restoration made George I and George II reluctant to employ the rhetoric of a new national ideal. Instead of effectively mobilizing ideas of Britishness to support their new position, they retreated from the public eye, generally giving up the battle for popular appeal and public national display (Colley 2012: 206–8).

As in France and Great Britain, the Holy Roman Empire experienced its own crisis of dynastic sovereignty. The empire was a complicated confederation of individual states, each with its own ruler, but falling, at least in theory, under the ultimate authority of the emperor, who had for centuries been a member of the Austrian Habsburg dynasty. Some have argued that the lack of unity in the empire renders inappropriate any discussion of "Germany" prior to the nineteenth century, but in reality the term "Germany" had been used interchangeably with that of the Holy Roman Empire among its inhabitants since the late Middle Ages (Sheehan 1981; Scales 2012). Emperor Leopold I (r. 1658–1705) was able to build on his effective leadership during a series of major crises in order to portray himself as father of all Germans and protector of the empire (Schumann 2011; Wrede 2004). His heirs, though, could not capitalize on his gains and within a generation the dynasty fell to a female heir, Maria Theresa, which sparked a succession crisis that erupted in the War of the Austrian Succession (1740–1748) (Browning 1993). Suddenly the future of the House of Habsburg was in jeopardy, not to mention its continued tenure as Holy Roman Emperors. After a two-year interregnum, the imperial crown went to a non-Habsburg for the first time in 300 years. The reign of this new Wittelsbach emperor, Charles VII (r. 1742–5), was short and unimpressive. He spent the majority of his rule in exile during the war and was depicted as a pawn of foreign powers (Whaley 2012, 2:371, 373–8). After three years of conflict-filled rule, Charles VII died and the imperial crown returned to the Habsburg family with the elevation of Maria Theresa's husband, Francis I. Yet, without significant ancestral territories of his own and often overshadowed by his extremely competent and strong-willed wife, Francis did not do much to re-solidify the position of the emperor. Instead, his reign witnessed a growing divide between imperial and Austrian politics that would only widen under his son, Joseph II (Whaley 2012, 2:380–92). The weakened Habsburg position at mid-century, combined with a generally disastrous imperial experiment under Charles VII and a shift in Austrian priorities, undermined much of the legitimacy built by Leopold I and opened the door for increased rivalry among the imperial states.

Prussia's emergence as a significant rival to Austrian power further destabilized the emperor's position. There had always been pockets of resistance to Habsburg influence in the empire, but never before had one single imperial state possessed the power to so thoroughly challenge the Austrian position. The rivalry between Austria and Prussia resulted in two devastating wars and a major shift in the balance of power in Germany, as well as consumed much of the attention of the Habsburgs which might otherwise have been spent shoring up the imperial crown. In assessing the impact of the Prusso-Austrian rivalry, one must remember that though these were separate states, they both fell within the imperial entity. Though the War of the Austrian Succession (1740–8) and the Seven Years War (1756–63) are considered distinct conflicts in English and French scholarship, German scholars see them as continuations of the same intra-German conflict, as did German contemporaries. Referred to collectively as the "Silesian Wars," contemporaries viewed these conflicts as civil wars (*Bruderkriege*). Neither side could claim to be waging war in the interest of Germany, for, as onlookers regularly pointed out, Austria and Prussia pursued their own particular interests. More and more, it seemed the interests of the German nation fell neither with the Prussian king nor with the Austrian emperors (Whaley 2012, 2:361–2).

By the middle of the eighteenth century, the foundations of traditional dynastic structures were weakened in Britain, France, and Germany. The supportive relationship between dynastic and national ideas also began to break down as onlookers started to question whether the monarch truly acted in the national interest. Into each of these fraught climates, the Seven Years War acted as a catalyst that sparked both an increased turn to national ideas as a political panacea, and a crisis in how to define, cultivate, and even locate the nation. For France, the Seven Years War was an unmitigated disaster. Defeated in Europe and in the colonies, France lost much of its influence around the globe. This defeat sparked a new series of financial difficulties, attempted reforms, and disastrous controversies—the Maupeou Coup among them—as well as intense "collective soul-searching" (Smith 2005: 143). French thinkers desperately tried to explain their nation's poor performance during the war, with many landing on a lack of "national spirit" (Dziembowski 1998). But debates raged as to what exactly this national spirit was, and how it could best be cultivated. The British problem, ironically, was their stunning victory in the Seven Years War. Whereas they previously had to deal only with the problems of Scottish integration, the British now possessed a host of global territories "at once too vast and too alien" (Colley 2012: 102–5). The rapid expansion of the British empire challenged many assumptions about what it meant to be British and contributed to doubts that the "British" monarchy was indeed the best option. In the Holy Roman Empire, the Seven Years War was devastating in its military impact, and profound in its intellectual significance, prompting the emergence of a "wide-ranging debate about reform and renewal" of the empire and the nation (Whaley 2012, 2:365). Imperial onlookers blamed Austria and Prussia for sacrificing the well-being and interests of Germany to their own ambition. If neither the Austrian emperor nor the Prussian king could be said to reliably represent the best interests of the German nation, then who did? In the aftermath of various crises of sovereignty at mid-century and the ramifications of the Seven Years War, questions such as these elicited intense debate.

DEFINITION AND REINVENTION

In France, Britain, and Germany, the Seven Years War raised a veritable cacophony of calls to regenerate respective national spirits. To do so, however, one needed to know what precisely the "nation" was. Until the mid-eighteenth century, few concerned themselves with debating the precise definitions of national ideas. Despite the extent to which national ideas were used in the preceding centuries, questions of the nation's boundaries, foundations, rights, and political role rarely, if ever, arose. Voltaire and Montesquieu, as late as the 1740s and 1750s, wrote extensively about national characters and national spirits, but as ideas that explained other political and cultural variations. In neither did the idea of the nation or the national character itself come under scrutiny (Montesquieu [1748] 1989; Voltaire [1756] 1963). Not until the crises of the mid- and late-eighteenth century did national ideas become the subject of intense, anxious reflection, as intellectuals proposed myriad ways in which they should be understood, defined, and used.

The culture of the Enlightenment contributed significantly to the new intensity with which national ideas were debated. It is no coincidence that the intellectual interrogation of national ideas occurred in the same climate that gave birth to the *Encyclopédie*, an attempt to collect, classify, and define all human knowledge (Hesse and Laqueur 1994; Mah 2003). Moreover, theories of political sovereignty that emerged out of the Enlightenment both exacerbated crises of traditional sovereignty and imbued national ideas with new political resonances. Rousseau's theories, for example, held the people, conceived as the nation itself, as the source of political sovereignty. No longer something to be protected and nurtured by the monarch alone, the idea of the nation could now be invoked in direct opposition to the king. Moreover, if the nation could change the political and legal system at will per the social contract, then law and history—shared tradition— no longer sufficiently described the nation, as they had in previous centuries. What, then, made the nation and how should it be defined? One of the ironies of this moment is that in determining the answer to this question, Enlightenment thinkers invented an entirely new understanding of "nation." What had previously been a relatively unexamined set of symbolic and rhetorical devices, now took on entirely new meanings and roles.

In France, national ideas increasingly became a tool of opposition to the crown while expanding to encompass an ever more democratic understanding of society. David Bell describes how critics of absolute monarchy prior to 1750 generally framed their opposition in terms of the king's duty to God or respect for traditional laws of the kingdom. This changed with the mid-century crises, as critics of the monarchy seized upon national ideas to frame their opposition. This embrace of national ideas as the language of monarchical critique only multiplied after the Maupeou Coup, when a broad-based opposition movement of *philosophes*, jurists, and their supporters wielded national and patriotic rhetoric to express their outrage against "ministerial despotism" (Bell 2001: 56–7). As Jay Smith explains, "parliamentary agitation over despotism, liberty, and the rights of the nation helped to instill a more self-conscious sense of national identity among the politically engaged classes between 1750 and 1770" (2005: 130, 184–5). This sense of national identity was no longer defined by its support of traditional monarchy, but by its opposition to it. During these debates, a new theory advanced by some *philosophes* contended that the *people*, as the embodiment of the nation, were the true source of political sovereignty.

But who were "the people" that made up "the nation"? Smith's study tracks the variety of answers to these questions that were put forward in the last half of the eighteenth century (2005). Far from the unanimous embrace of a newly invented, modern, democratic nation, intellectuals, nobles, merchants, lawyers, and anonymous pamphlet writers grappled with ever more varied questions: is commerce patriotic; are peasants the true embodiment of national spirit; does the nobility protect or detract from the common good of the nation; to what extent does the crown represent or protect the national interest? In particular, Smith charts how the French nobility expended significant intellectual energy to justify their own claims to be the moral wellspring of the nation, only to be overrun by more egalitarian interpretations in the years leading up to the French Revolution. Smith's analysis reveals not a grand, linear, "awakening" of national thought, but rather a widespread reckoning with old concepts, during which different parties desperately fought to redefine national ideas in ways that were relevant and useful to their own interests, standing, or opinions on France's future.

One of the parties in this struggle over national ideas remained the monarchists, who increased their engagement in the public sphere to defend the king's policies against ever-growing criticism. Bell traces this development well, though in my view too narrowly (2001: 56). He contends that the French crown was wading into uncharted territory when it laid claim to national rhetoric based on concepts invented by the monarchy's opponents. Rather, the crown was doing its best to maintain, and later attempt to wrest

FIGURE 1.2: *Execution of Louis XVI, January 21, 1793*, at Paris, France. Courtesy of Getty Images, UK.

back, control of its own rhetorical tools in the face of a multiplicity of radically new understandings and uses. By the time of the Terror, national ideas had been transformed so radically that Louis XVI was beheaded in the name of the same "French nation" that had so well supported the claims of Louis XIV (Figure 1.2).

In contrast with France, the British monarchy had largely won the battle for national legitimacy by the end of the eighteenth century, but only after a period of similar debate and examination. The dual shots of the Jacobite rebellion and victory in the Seven Years War caused an explosion in efforts to rekindle and nurture British national spirit, while pushing ideas of the nation in novel directions. Many looked around with "anxiety that Britain labored under a malaise and must be regenerated from within" (Colley 2012: 88). Colley details how voluntary associations, patriotic clubs, and national societies were "breaking out like measles over the face of Britain," each with its own ideas about what made a patriot and its own path toward rejuvenating the nation (2012: 89). This explosion of societies to revive the national spirit, however, had two unintended consequences. First, by regularly taking on charitable, economic, and social causes, they highlighted just how much the state left undone. Second, these societies and the claims they made for their work encouraged a more expansive understanding of what it meant to be an "active patriot" and who could fulfill this role (Colley 2012: 94). As in France, claims rang out from different sectors of society as to who was, or was not, the foundation of the nation. Colley remarks that the second half of the eighteenth century was "an intensely creative period in terms of patriotic initiatives and discussion of national identities," most crucially about "the boundaries and meanings of citizenship" (2012: 86). One result was that the British aristocracy, like the French, came under attack as never before (Colley 2012: 154–7, 167). The more that national ideas were taken up in different arenas by different segments of society, the greater the "continuing pressure toward equality" (Smith 2005: 181).

Debate also grew in the second half of the eighteenth century about what "Britishness" was, and whether it was preferable to other configurations of nationality. Great Britain, to a greater extent than France or Germany, had much stronger and more established national categories to compete with. The project of constructing the British nation was one of elevating the category of "British" above, though not necessarily as a replacement for, other reference points, such as "English," "Welsh," and "Scottish" (Colley 2012). In the later eighteenth century, however, debates about Britishness collided with critiques of the monarchy. John Wilkes, in particular, launched a campaign for "old English liberties" and "new English rights," based on criticisms of the monarchy. He and others targeted the monarchy's efforts to better integrate Scotland (Colley 2012: 105). Campaigns and prints often depicted Scotsmen flooding into England and taking privileges and positions otherwise meant for "true" Englishmen. An example from 1762 (Figure 1.3) shows a horde of Scots recently disembarked in England, or, to them, "Money-Land," eager to collect pensions and titles from their kinsman. The xenophobic caption reads "While Englishmen are now turn'd out … Then what must we expect to be, While Laird & Laddies go Scot-free." Like most anti-Scottish imagery of this kind, it inaccurately depicts the Scots in tartan kilts, banned in 1745, to emphasize the immutable "differences" between Scottish and English (Colley 2012: 115). Wilkes draped his opposition politics in the mantle of English patriotism, and portrayed the British government, especially under George III, as betraying past English achievements and leading the country astray (Colley 2012: 105–18). For many, defeat in the American Revolution reinforced such anxieties. After the dazzling successes of the Seven Years' War, defeat by a group of upstart colonists was a shock. Across the political spectrum, the American Revolution forced the

FIGURE 1.3: *The Caledonians Arrival in Money-Land*, 1762. Courtesy of the Lewis Walpole Library, Yale University.

British to reconsider their own identity as well as that of these new, independent "Americans" (Colley 2012: 134–46).

By the end of the century, however, both the nobility and the British crown overcame the critiques, doubts, and attacks mounted against them. While the French dismantled their monarchy and their nobility, the British aristocracy asserted their "rightful place as patriots" who served the "nation" in government and on the battlefield. The British crown, moreover, succeeded in transforming itself into "*the* uncontentious point of national union" (Colley 2012: 158, 171–97, 199–241). Where nation and dynasty had become irreconcilable enemies in France, George III, in all his supposed madness, had become a "national totem" (Colley 2012: 233). One example can be seen in a print commemorating George III's escape from an assassination attempt (Figure 1.4). The figure of Britannia, the physical embodiment of the nation, kneels on a shield decorated with the British flag while staring adoringly up at a portrait of the king. Behind her lies the British lion, glaring menacingly at the shadowy figure of the would-be assassin, suggesting that the nation itself is the protector of the monarch. It is a striking contrast with the relationship between crown and nation seen in the execution of Louis XVI.

The relationship between crown and nation in Germany, like most things in the Holy Roman Empire, was slightly more complicated. In the sixteenth and early seventeenth centuries, rhetoric of the German national interest had often been deployed in attempts to curtail Habsburg power (Schmidt 2001). Leopold I, however, successfully reclaimed this rhetoric and mobilized propaganda about himself as defender the German nation and protector of the national interest (Schumann 2011; Wrede 2004). During his reign, the Empire faced a Turkish invasion that reached the gates of Vienna, and repeated incursions from Louis XIV's aggressive expansionism (Stoye 2006; Lynn 1999).

FIGURE 1.4: *In Commemoration of the Providential Escape of His Most Sacred Majesty King George the Third from the daring Attack of an Assassin when at Drury Lane Theatre, August 2, 1786.* Print by Francesco Bartolozzi, 1802. Courtesy of the British Museum, London.

Throughout these conflicts, "Germanness" was repeatedly defined against stereotypes of the French or the Turks (see Figure 1.1 for examples) and military support for the Emperor's defense was called for in terms of protecting the German nation, national character, and therefore the "national" political institution of the empire itself (Cooper 2019). By the end of Leopold I's reign, his propagandists had strongly linked the position of the emperor with the German nation.

Because the position of the emperor was not technically a dynastic one, however, the position of protector of the nation was linked with the imperial title, rather than the Habsburg family. When the Habsburgs lost the imperial crown during the War of the Austrian Succession, therefore, they also lost the ready ability to mobilize national ideas associated with it. The man who did become emperor, Charles VII, was too often seen as a pawn in the hands of the French to make any plausible claims of serving the German nation. Thus, national rhetoric was noticeably absent in the War of the Austrian Succession. During the Seven Years War as well, a combination of diplomatic reshuffling, intra-German divisions, and the blatant rivalry between Prussia and Austria meant that the possibility for either of them to successfully mobilize national rhetoric was severely diminished (Wrede 2004: 494). As Martin Wrede explained, by the Seven Years War the role of the Emperor was politically and publicly depreciated, and the idea of "the Empire as the foundation of the German nation was massively challenged" (2004: 512).

That is not to say, however, that ideas of a German nation died out in this period. Rather, as in Britain and France, national ideas became unmoored from their dynastic anchor, the emperor. Imperial onlookers criticized Austria and Prussia for embroiling Germany in two long, bloody, and expensive wars. For many, neither Austria nor Prussia had legitimately served the national interest (Vazsonyi 1999: 232). Instead a concept of a "third Germany," neither Austrian- nor Prussian-led, emerged with growing force in the final decades of the eighteenth century (Gagliardo 1980: 295–6, 300).

As in Britain and France, this destabilization of the traditional relationship between dynasty and nation caused a flourishing of intense debate around the meaning of national ideas. In the aftermath of a decade and a half of "civil war," Germans, too, looked to reinvigorate national spirit as a way to strengthen the empire. In 1765, Friedrich Carl von Moser published *On the German National Spirit*, in which he emphasized the shared language, political history, constitution, laws, and mores that united all Germans, while lamenting the divisions and internal conflicts that had for years weakened the empire (Figures 1.5 and 1.6). "We are one people, of one name and language, under one shared sovereign," Moser began, but the lack of national spirit in the empire meant that Germans were more concerned with individual interests than with the good of their nation (Moser

FIGURE 1.5: Friedrich Carl von Moser, *Von dem Deutschen Nationalgeist*, 1765, title page. Courtesy of the Bavarian State Library, Munich.

FIGURE 1.6: Friedrich Carl von Moser, *Von dem Deutschen Nationalgeist*, 1765, first page. Courtesy of the Bavarian State Library, Munich.

1765). Moser, like his contemporaries in France, pitted the "memory" of the German nation against the contemporary reality of defeat and disunity (Vazsonyi 1999: 233). In doing so, Moser recycled many arguments for German nationhood, and therefore imperial unity, that had served Leopold I's publicists so well. In fact, the rhetoric of a German nation based on laws, common interest, mores, shared history, and a shared monarch that Moser proposed reads almost exactly like pamphlets calling for German unity in the face of Louis XIV's armies. The response, however, was astounding in its difference. In the late seventeenth century, pamphlet after pamphlet appeared calling for readers to embrace their "German spirit," with no backlash or intellectual opposition (Wrede 2004; Schillinger 1999; Cooper 2019, 2020). Moser's call to reinvigorate German national spirit and thus ensure the unity and the prosperity of the Empire, however, sparked a heated debate which continued until approximately 1770 and gained significant notoriety in the empire (Vazsonyi 1999: 233–4, 236).

As Nicholas Vazsonyi comments, Moser's tract "struck a nerve" that was particularly raw by the middle of the eighteenth century (1999: 234). In particular, Moser's critics spent considerable energy trying to explicitly define the "national spirit" as an intellectual concept, debating whether it applied to the entire population or only the elite, and arguing over whether it was a top-down or bottom-up phenomenon (Vazsonyi 1999: 236–8). All of this intellectual strife over the precise terms, meaning, and foundation of national ideas was tied to the fundamental problem of whether a German national spirit existed. Moser, writing in older terms that linked the nation with the emperor and empire, argued yes. Others, who suggested the nation was the emanation of a popular shared sentiment—who forwarded a more "modern" and democratic understanding of the nation—argued that such a sentiment could not yet be found in Germany and instead needed to be created. This "National Spirit Debate" was conducted mostly by jurists and legal theorists, but the same concerns also caught the attention of some of the best-known Romantic writers. As the political landscape in Germany and the empire changed, writers such as Herder, Goethe, and Fichte suggested their own interpretations of what the nation was, continuing to redefine and resituate it in terms of political, cultural, linguistic, historical, or geographic notions of community, suggesting new definitions from which to base projects of national renewal, defense, or cooperation (Mah 2003). Read within this longer context, the national theories of even such a "father" of nationalist thought as Herder can be seen as symptomatic of a larger shift in the intellectual landscape, "a historic moment of transition in which a new way of thinking emerges in the midst of the old" (Vazsonyi 1999: 236). For the first time in Germany, as in Britain and France, national ideas generated intense debate as thinkers felt compelled to explicitly define the "nation" or the "national interest." Through such processes of defining, thinkers rewrote the meanings and the political associations behind the metonym, and, to much consternation, often realized that the thing they had just so neatly defined, upon further inspection, did not actually exist.

Nowhere else was this discovery more acutely felt than in France during the Revolution. The intense debates over the precise contours of the French nation and national character that had taken place over the previous half century were sharpened by the collapse of the monarchy. Suddenly there was an opportunity for the "nation" to assume all of the power and legitimacy that French thinkers had gradually bestowed upon it. As revolutionaries stared into that "political void," however, they realized that they could not actually find the nation they had so exalted (Bell 2001: 14). In part, this was due to a radical reevaluation of the French "character," such that previously celebrated traits—noble honor, refinement, sociability—were rejected as frivolous and effeminate in comparison to the stoic, republican masculinity of the radical revolutionaries (Bell 2001: 15; Mah 2003: 116–56). But in part this was the logical end point of the process of redefinition that ideas of nation underwent in the eighteenth century. As the national idea was dislocated from its previous dynastic associations, the concept became ever more democratic, embracing the common peasant as the quintessential member of the patriotic nation, characterized by lofty ideals of a unifying French language and culture. The Revolution itself was proclaimed as the political will of this "nation." Yet when the revolutionaries looked more closely, it was impossible to ignore the fact that the inhabitants of France did not speak any unified version of French, and many did not speak French at all (Bell 2001: 16). As Eugen Weber has shown, most of the French peasantry was not really "nationalized" until well into the nineteenth century (1976). Moreover, significant peasant resistance to the Revolution belied the unity of national will that the revolutionaries had claimed (Tilly 1964). The reality of France did not live up to the revolutionaries' ideals of the French nation. For the revolution to succeed, revolutionaries decided they needed to embark on a process of national construction never before seen in Europe (Bell 2001).

Here, then, was the emergence of national*ism* in France, a political program to actively bring a nation(-state) into existence. Here, too, was the first embodiment of the modern idea of "nation" in France, a political system in which the nation was the basis of all political authority and legitimacy. In rejecting the monarchy, revolutionaries severed all ties between nation and dynasty, exalting the former as an independent entity that could and should stand on its own. The "nation" went from an unexamined assumption of shared cultural, linguistic, and historical community supporting the monarch, to a dire political problem whose boundaries and defining features were the subject of intense debate and which needed concerted effort from the state to construct and protect. Even the triumph of this understanding of nation in France, however, did not immediately rewrite alternative understandings of national ideas across Europe. Among counter-revolutionary *émigrés*, writers like Germaine de Staël continued to link Frenchness with aristocratic values (Mah 2003). No doubt in part as a reaction to the radicalism of the French Revolution, the dynasties of Britain and Germany were able to regain some control over the political situation and national ideas. Indeed, as Brian Vick has carefully shown, national ideas at the Congress of Vienna were still tied to and compatible with dynastic patriotism, "whether of smaller states or supranational empires" (2014: 4–5). German delegates to the Congress in particular believed that strong national sentiment was built up from the local and regional all the way up to the dynastic, and any attempt to unduly weaken or strengthen any of those levels out of proportion with the rest would undermine national identity altogether (Vick 2014: 270–74). Furthermore, as Harold Mah has shown, French and German intellectuals continued to reinvent and reimagine the precise definitions and "phantasies" of the nation during and beyond the Revolutionary era (2003). Thus, even by the nineteenth century, no one understanding of nation had definitively triumphed.

CONCLUSION

The idea of nationhood is a concept of cultural memory with deep historical sources that came to dominate political discourse toward the end of the eighteenth century. Over the course of that century, national ideas underwent a radical reinvention, becoming dislodged to varying degrees from the position they had held for several centuries as supports of dynastic monarchy. This dislocation was greatest in France, with national ideas emerging not only in opposition to dynasty, but as a replacement for monarchy altogether. In Great Britain, mid-century crises prompted repeated interrogation of what it meant to be "British," while opponents of the monarchy instead wielded their own national ideas of "English" or "Scottish" to undermine the crown's policies. In contrast with France, however, the British monarchy and aristocracy restored much of their public legitimacy and political control, reestablishing a firm grip on national rhetoric in the process. In Germany, a series of internal wars at mid-century, combined with the rise of Prussia, challenged Habsburg imperial legitimacy and destabilized previous associations of the emperor as head of the German nation. A strenuous debate arose as to the source of the German national spirit and how best to cultivate it. In the aftermath of the sudden end of the empire at the hands of Napoleon, Germans at the Congress of Vienna sought to build a new constitution that would protect the national interest precisely by reaffirming the value of both local and dynastic legitimacy.

By the end of the eighteenth century, national ideas had taken on a variety of new valences. The popularity and ubiquity of their use expanded exponentially. Understandings of their borders of inclusion were pushed ever outwards and downwards as the concepts became increasingly democratic in scope. National ideas attained a new political legitimacy, as theories of popular sovereignty permeated the political landscape of Europe. And, in numerous cases, opponents of monarchy and traditional old-regime structures seized upon national ideas as a rhetoric of opposition. Monarchies never ceased, however, to use national ideas for their own purposes. It is true that the first iterations of one particular understanding of the nation were "invented" in the eighteenth century—that of a sovereign, democratic, culturally homogenous nation—and that later versions of this understanding came to be the ideal of many modern nationalist programs. But the triumph of this one understanding is a story whose own twists and turns need to be understood in the context of the nineteenth and early twentieth centuries. As Hesse and Laqueur argued, the "overvaluation of [modern] nationalism occludes other histories of national identity that are not connected with the nation-state" (1994: 2). The story of political sovereignty in the eighteenth century is not a question of *either* dynastic *or* national understandings, but an appreciation that all of these ideas coexisted, sometimes as overlapping levels of identification and sometimes as competing claims to political legitimacy. The relationship between them was one of constant flux and renegotiation as contemporaries debated, mobilized, and appropriated different ideas for their own purposes. Understanding this dynamic is crucial to understanding eighteenth-century politics and sovereignty, in terms of how they were viewed, how they were exercised, and, ultimately, how drastically they changed.

Like other artifacts of memory, national ideas are not monolithic, unchanging structures. Indeed, to prove this fact was the foundational project of Anderson, Gellner, Hobsbawm, and others. These theorists intended to unpack the baggage of "nation" to show the many ways in which contingency and historical context contributed to its construction. Unfortunately, in doing so they bequeathed a set of rigid, totalizing, and often teleological definitions that, while useful in highlighting the unique characteristics of modern national ideas, have neglected a corresponding understanding of earlier uses of the concept of nation. By stepping out from under these definitions and appreciating the diversity of ways in which national ideas functioned before the modern era, we can continue the project of these theorists in understanding the myriad ways that national ideas are constructed, invented, and *reinvented*. The invention of the modern, democratic, sovereign nation(-state), and the exclusive, all-encompassing, and often violent side effects that this invention would have in the nineteenth and twentieth centuries is just one side of the history of national ideas. By looking at other possibilities and understandings, we can consider what else these concepts were, and what else they might have been.

CHAPTER TWO

Time and Space

GABRIEL WICK

In the second half of the 1770s, the famed painter of ruins, Hubert Robert (1733–1808) developed a secondary reputation as a "composer of landscapes"—a designer of gardens and "*fabriques*" (the eighteenth-century French term for the ornamental ruins, temples and monuments that embellished landscape gardens). One might legitimately wonder what contributions beyond an unbridled imagination, an instinct for picturesque juxtapositions, and a formidable knowledge of classical culture and history, an artist like Robert could bring to the execution of a built work like a landscape garden. Robert was a "painter of architecture," but not an architect; he had only a fairly rudimentary knowledge of plants, and certainly no expertise in topographical engineering. Indeed, in all of his projects, Robert would be dependent on a host of more qualified professionals who would realize his vision. Yet in his own time Robert achieved a real fame for his built works.

What Robert had was a remarkable command of what we might call the visual language of time. He was adept at endowing his drawn, painted, and built scenes with the visual hallmarks of age, decay, and regeneration. This ability to manipulate and recreate these effects earned him the sobriquet of "the poet of time" from his sometime collaborator on landscape projects, the writer Joseph-Antoine-Joachim Cerutti (1738–92) (Cerutti 1792: 44–5). Robert's creative input was also highly valued because he possessed what his contemporaries considered to be a remarkable sensibility with regard to the presentation and contextualization of historical and artistic artifacts. He was in many senses a pioneer in the field of curating at a time when the concept of the public museum was only just developing. In 1777, the Royal Buildings Administration commissioned him to develop a permanent setting in the gardens of Versailles for the sculptural groups known as the Baths of Apollo, one of the foremost masterpieces of the reign of Louis XIV. The next year, in 1778, he was named to the group studying the transformation of the Grand Gallery of the Louvre into a setting for the display of the royal collections (Sahut and Garnier 1979).

Robert's work as a designer of gardens combined these talents, allowing him to work as both a curator and an artist. Robert's garden projects deftly combined imagery drawn from the culture of antiquity and modern archaeological excavations to create highly realistic simulacra of antique ruins that seamlessly incorporated references to contemporary figures and events. In Robert's hands, the garden was transformed into a passage through time that reinvented and distorted the visitor's sense of temporality and history.

This chapter examines three such landscape projects: the tomb of Jean-Jacques Rousseau at Ermenonville; the "ruining" of the donjon of La Roche-Guyon, and an ensemble of *fabriques* in the gardens of Méréville. In these projects Robert drew upon his classical education and memories of his eleven-year sojourn in Italy to invent picturesque scenes and settings. For his elite patrons these evocations of Italy and classical antiquity activated a form of collective cultural memory—sights and scenes that many visitors would have remembered from their own travels, or experienced indirectly through classical literature and the drawings, engravings, and canvases of Robert and his peers. The landscape garden assembled and embodied these personal, collective, and imagined recollections into an immersive and transporting new setting.

A formative influence on Robert's work and popular perceptions of antiquity in this period were the first systematic excavations of the ancient Greco-Roman cities of Herculaneum, Pompeii, Stabiae, and Paestum. With these discoveries, antiquity erupted in an incredibly vivid and almost animate form into the eighteenth-century present like a sort of hierophany. The excavations of the buried cities also favored the development of a whole range of new scientific and artistic approaches: specialized expeditions were mounted to explore, excavate and document these sites (Ceserani 2013: 327–33). Even for those who could not travel to Italy, a new genre of extensively illustrated folios, such as Johann Joachim Winckelmann's (1717–68) surveys of classical sculpture, Giovanni Battista Piranesi's (1720–78) inventive reconstructions of ancient sites, or the abbé Jean-Claude Richard de Saint-Non's (1727–91) collections of engravings (for which Robert himself produced a number of views) allowed readers to feel that they were in some ways first-hand witnesses to the excavations. The effects of these discoveries were profound and far-reaching: as Louis, chevalier de Jaucourt (1704–80) observed in his extensive 1765 description of Herculaneum in the *Encyclopédie*. For the past decade these discoveries had captivated the imaginations of "all those who cultivated the letters, sciences and arts" (Diderot and d'Alembert 1751–72: vol. 8, 150–4).

As Chantal Grell observes, the atmosphere of the early archaeological digs at Herculaneum and Stabiae was well suited to the taste for the sublime and the terrible that emerged in the second half of the eighteenth century (Grell, 1982: 46–7). Those visitors, privileged enough to gain access to excavations (Neapolitan authorities were stinting with such permissions), accessed the ruins through cold and damp tunnels lit only by torches, and excavations were carried out by condemned prisoners guarded by soldiers.

The remarkably complete set of artifacts and environments these excavations yielded transformed historiography and popular conceptions of the past. These developments effectively transformed antiquarianism from a pedantic, interiorized pastime, into an immersive study of environments that simultaneously engaged all the senses (Blix 2009: 9–32). These developments also transformed the very nature of historical evidence: where once texts and inscriptions on isolated artifacts such as coins, medals, and memorials had constituted the principal form of record, now this new and far more visceral and tactile manner of engaging with the past showed how objects and environments could impart a strangely immediate and vivid form of embodied recollection. Contemplating the array of everyday objects emanating from the excavations, mid-eighteenth-century observers were able to project themselves back into the quotidian reality of the past. This experience was extremely intimate—observers could wander with impunity into the most private or restricted parts of the ancient city's houses, temples, and theaters, thus giving them the sense that they might know this place and its people in a far more comprehensive manner than they could ever know a city of their own time. In examining the living environments and possessions of the long-dead, and even in some instances witnessing the setting and manner of their last moments, observers formed an empathetic bond with these unfortunates that was imbued with all the vividness and immediacy of a personal memory. As Pierre-Jacques-Onésyme Bergeret de Grancourt (1715–85) noted, over the course of a visit, the observer is at once delighted to behold such miraculously preserved

FIGURE 2.1: Hubert Robert, *The Finding of the Laocoön*, 1773. Virginia Museum of Fine Arts.

ancient ruins, but also saddened at the spectacle of a city that had been destroyed so precipitously (Grell 1982: 116–20). Witnessing the remains of the excavated cities also inevitably led eighteenth-century observers to reflect upon how their own lives might one day be viewed by posterity and what material traces would communicate something of their existence and experiences in a future where they were not.

A passage describing a fantastic sort of archaeological expedition from Louis Sébastien Mercier's (1740–1814) best-selling novel, *L'An 2440, un rêve s'il en fut jamais*, shows how excavations had captured the popular imagination and assumed a magical and even pseudo-mystical character:

> I have now more than ever a taste for quarries . . . I descended to 900 feet near ****, and was enraged to be unable to go further. I would have wished to leave my footprints upon [earth's] core and question it on the diversity of nations that had passed upon its surface [. . .] and [learn] how many layers of debris of the human race does she enclose from the center of this darkness to the very limit of her diameter? I would have asked her to read for me all of the catastrophes that she has wiped away [. . .] disasters now engraved incontestably upon metals, but of which the memory has been entirely effaced: disasters that will be reborn when she devours into her flanks this current generation, which, in its own time, will be dug up by numberless generations . . .
>
> —Mercier 1772: note a, 240–2

In Mercier's telling, archaeology offers a means of accessing a form of timeless memory, engraved upon the mineral strata. This notion of a natural memorial, inanimate yet strangely evocative, that could now suddenly be activated by subterranean exploration and excavation held the promise of revealing histories that would contradict the official narratives engraved upon medals and other human artifacts.

This notion that a form of universal collective memory could be inscribed within the natural landscape resonated with the influential writings of Jean-Jacques Rousseau (1712–78). In *Émile*, his 1762 educational treatise in the guise of a novel, Rousseau describes how the exploration and observation of the natural landscape could be a means of instilling virtue and empathy in the young. He imagined that in the golden age that preceded the development of societies, laws, and civil authority, natural features of the landscape constituted the collective record, and served as the witness and guarantor of oaths and agreements:

> Before force was established, the face of the earth was the text wherein we inscribed our archives. Rocks, trees, outcroppings, revered and respected by barbarian man, were the pages in this book, that were always open for all to see ... And the faith of man was all the more assured in the promises of these mute witnesses than it is today by the whole body of laws.
>
> —Rousseau 1966: 421

For Rousseau, the *solitary promeneur*, ever suspicious of the morality and legitimacy of collective institutions and authorities, the promenade in the wilderness offered a means of reconnecting the wayward modern with a commonly accessible, but unrecorded heritage, whose memory lay dormant just below the surface of the present.

The idea of a new form of collective universal memory encoded in the material world was transformative because until the very last days of the French monarchy the past continued to play a pivotal role in defining the standing and power of individuals and institutions. For example, the political and ideological debates on the future of absolutism and the powers of the parlements that so marked the last years of the reign of Louis XV focused far more upon the distant historical origins of these institutions, and thus their eventual claims to historical pre-eminence, than on their effectiveness or rationality (see Bell, 2001: 57–60; Mackrell 1973). History and the historical record played a similarly important role in the lives of elites. In this period, the age of a family's lineage governed its members' ability to claim prestigious and highly remunerative positions in government, the church, and the army. Yet there was also a certain room for creativity and invention in the historical narratives that governed so many aspects of late-eighteenth-century life. The most prized and legitimizing forms of historical precedents were those that were held to be immemorial—practices and histories that were universally known and acknowledged, but whose origins were lost in the mists of time. The right to claim *noblesse immémoriale* dispensed the great court dynasties from the obligation of documenting their noble origins because their lineage was held to pre-date the documentary record.

Robert's built projects would deftly and poetically exploit this imagery of the immemorial—a past that was inscribed in the environment and the material world rather than on the page. His gardens often presented a form of ostensibly ancient, tactile material evidence that appeared in many instances to contradict what the viewer knew to be historical "truth." As Susan Taylor observes in her study of the Baths of Apollo, his projects often inverted temporal relationships by framing artifacts of the eighteenth-century present in the language of antiquity, or situating historical fragments or relics in modern settings that appeared to pre-date them (Taylor 1990). Robert's acuity with the very matter of history allowed him to stage scenes and invent settings that re-wrote or re-presented the past and the heritage of his clients.

Timing and good fortune had conspired to make Robert almost uniquely qualified to craft such elaborate and layered simulacra. Initially destined for the priesthood, he had received an excellent education in classical languages and literature at Paris' college de Navarre. His interest in Latin literature and classical mythology would remain with him for the rest of his life, and he brought to his drawings, paintings and built works an erudition that was rare among artists at this time. In 1754, he traveled to Rome in the entourage of his patron Étienne François de Choiseul, comte de Stainville (1719–85) (future duc de Choiseul and chief minister of Louis XV) who installed him at the French Academy. The curriculum of the Academy emphasized open-air drawing in the countryside and overgrown Renaissance gardens that surrounded the city and the study of Roman architecture and monuments. Robert translated this educational approach into a life-long practice that allowed his art to evolve continually. As his works bear witness, Robert, like many of his peers, was fascinated by the archaeological excavations and discoveries taking place around him. His paintings, such as the *Ruins of the Palace of Nero* (see Figure 2.2), and the *Discoverers of Antiquity* (see Figure 2.3) capture this fascination that the subterranean now held as a repository of ancient culture. As his friend the author and translator the Abbé Delille would retroactively record in his poem *L'Imagination*, Robert's passion for exploring Rome's subterranean vestiges supposedly nearly killed him (1825: 255–6).

After eleven years in Rome, Robert returned to Paris in 1765 and was elected the following year by a unanimous vote to the Royal Academy of Painting as a "painter of

FIGURE 2.2: Hubert Robert, *The Ruins of the Palace of Nero, c. 1765.* © Musée des Beaux-Arts, Besançon.

FIGURE 2.3: Hubert Robert, *The Discoverers of Antiquities*. © Musée des Beaux-Arts, Valence.

architecture." The first canvases that Robert presented at the salon of 1767 received plaudits from the critic and *encyclopédiste* Denis Diderot (1713–84), who had been urging artists to explore the ruin genre's potential to serve as a prompt for secular reflections on the nature of existence (Mortier 1974: 90–2). As Roland Mortier observes, in this increasingly secular and philosophically-oriented society, images of ruin and decay filled the vacuum left by sacred themes whose affective power was increasingly blunted, and provided a new focus for reflections on humanity's relationship to time, mortality, the past and the future (1974: 91). Mortier writes that in this period "the language of history replaced that of the gods," and "in a universe deprived of transcendence and the here-after [. . .] the only eternity would be that of time" (1974: 91). Despite this weighty subtext, however, Robert's paintings also contained scenes of levity and humor that spoke to humanity's ability to adapt to new circumstances.

One of the first gardens in France to exploit the evocative and poetic potential of archaeological imagery was that of René-Louis, marquis de Girardin (1735–1808), who remade the surroundings of his château of Ermenonville in the image of the writings and theories of Rousseau. Robert's involvement in the early stages of the development of this garden has been examined by a number of scholars—most especially with the design of the *fabrique* known as the *Brasserie*—but never conclusively proven (see Wiebenson 1978: 81–8; Cayeux 1987: 93–101; Herzog 1989: 75–94). Girardin was proud of his role as the sole author of his garden, and even had Robert participated in its design, the artist would never have risked offending a powerful and influential figure by asserting his own role too forcefully.

Girardin's Ermenonville offers an excellent example of how an artfully composed evocation of the immemorial past could reframe the status and social standing of the garden owner. The marquis could make no claim to an ancient lineage, at least where France was concerned—his family were Florentine bankers who had immigrated to France in the previous century (Martin-Decaen 1912: 4–6). His maternal grandfather had been a tax-farmer and it was with this wealth that Girardin was able to transform Ermenonville. A soldier who had served in the court of ex-King Stanislas of Poland in Lorraine, he had also traveled extensively, especially in Italy, and the gardens constituted something of a souvenir of his cosmopolitan past. Proud of his accomplishments as an artist and a philosopher, Girardin defined his and his family's identity in unconventional terms: unlike most families of their wealth and stature, the Girardins lived almost exclusively in the country where the marquis played an active role in the Rousseauian education of his children, and where the entire family devoted themselves to the practice of the arts (Gazier 1906: 109).

Girardin's gardens inscribed this "modern" manner of living within an artistically innovative setting that was peppered with evocative references to an immemorial past. The circuit of promenades began with the grotto of the Naiads, a dark and subterranean passage recalling the grottoes or catacombs of Italy. This subterranean interlude was something of a visceral cue that defined the garden as a space that was detached both spatially and temporally from the outside world. Within the garden, particularly within the space known as the Arcadian Prairie, visitors encountered a number of structures and scenes that evoked a distant and almost mythical past. Wooden temples, cabins, and primitive shelters, bearing inscriptions from Ovid or representing scenes from Longus, translated classical literature into immersive, tactile settings.

Moving beyond these fairly conventional prompts to Arcadian reverie, the visitor discovered a far more complex and troubling materialization of the past. Upon a promontory overlooking the gardens, a plaque with a Latin inscription informed visitors that a catacomb filled with the remains of an ancient massacre had been discovered there (Girardin 1788: 35–6). Thus, in the midst of this Arcadian realm, in conducting his visitor's imagination below ground, Girardin forced them to envision a massacre that had happened in the very place where they were standing and confronted them with evidence of mankind's propensity for violence. It was imagery that would have momentarily jolted the visitor out of the peaceful reverie of a garden promenade.

This elaborately contrived set piece allowed Girardin to transform what contemporary theorists such as Thomas Whately had derided as "emblematic" experiences—cultural, literary, or historical references in the garden that viewers perceived and understood through the filter of the intellect into what he termed "expressive" experiences—highly visceral and affective scenes that activated and engaged all the of senses (Hunt 1992: 75–102; Bending 2016; Whately 1770).

In the summer of 1778, Girardin had the opportunity to bring to his garden what would soon become the most revered relics of the cult of philosophy: the mortal remains of Rousseau himself. The marquis had persuaded the ailing misanthrope to spend his last months on the estate. When Rousseau drew his last breath, Girardin set in motion an elaborately scripted rite that included the making of a death-mask by Augustin Pajou (1730–1839), a torch-lit conveyance of the corpse to the Island of Poplars, and its internment under a memorial that the marquis had supposedly made with his own hands. With Rousseau's passing, the Girardins were now forever to be remembered not as mere middling nobles or eccentrically artistic parvenus, but rather as "the last friends of Rousseau." Likewise, their gardens were not a contemporary artistic composition to be criticized, but rather a site rendered holy by the memory of the great philosophe and the presence of his mortal relics.

As a Protestant and a proud apostate, Rousseau could not be buried on consecrated ground. For non-Catholics in France, surreptitious burials in gardens or other out-of-the-way sites had historically been tolerated by officials. Turning this necessity into an advantage, however, Girardin decided to mark Rousseau's resting place with an elaborate ancient Roman-style funerary monument. For classically-educated elites, the tomb's presence here in the landscape would have immediately summoned up the antique practice of interring the dead outside cities, and commemorating their memory with elaborate monuments or mausolea that would inspire the passer-by. In his 1788 guide to Ermenonville, the marquis de Girardin's son, Stanislas wrote: "In its form, they have maintained all of the purity of the antique; it is Monsieur Robert who is responsible for the design" (Girardin 1788: 26). The memorial was carved by the young sculptor Jacques-Philippe Le Sueur (1759–1830), probably after an initial sketch provided by Robert (see Figure 2.4). Robert's intimate familiarity with Roman monuments and his classical education made him a natural choice for such a commission. The simple form of the sarcophagus, embellished at its four extremities with acroteria, would have been

FIGURE 2.4: Engraving by Godefroy after a drawing by Gandat, *The Tomb of Jean-Jacques Rousseau at Ermenonville*. Gabriel Wick.

recognizable to many of Robert's peers as a citation of one of the most famous monuments of antiquity, the erroneously-named tomb of Nero, made famous by an engraving of Piranesi in his *Le Antichità Romane* of 1757 (Figure 2.5).

Thus, the tomb presented something of a temporal contradiction; it was an antique monument that housed the relics of a figure who had been very much of the eighteenth-century present. Girardin was drawing upon the language of antiquity to render a suitable homage to his former guest, but in so doing, also framed these relics in an enduring manner in the expectation that they would continue to be revered in some distant future. As Margaret Fields Denton observes, this most famous and pioneering instance of the interment of a celebrated figure in the open landscape (or a garden that represented the open landscape) played an essential role in redefining mourning as a philosophical and secular rite that facilitated and even celebrated expressions of grief in public (2003: 206). Denton observes that the placement of the tomb upon the Island of Poplars reframed death as a serene and peaceful rest, a natural conclusion to life to be accepted rather than feared. For a society that had only recently embraced sensibility and emotionality, and the expression of highly personal rather than ritualized forms of mourning, the antique idiom also served an important role of distancing loss or abstracting the memory of the defunct. In establishing a sort of temporal barrier between the recently departed and the living, the antique tomb allowed mourners to contemplate the defunct as if they were figures from

FIGURE 2.5: Giovanni Battista Piranesi, *View of a Mausoleum, called of Nero, on the via Cassia, from* Le Antichità Romane. Gabriel Wick.

the ancient past—or, alternatively, to imagine that they were figures from the distant future, looking back upon a life that had been lived centuries before. Contemplating ancient ruins and monuments had taught the eighteenth century to empathize with the dead, to imagine their lives, even while knowing little specifics about the circumstances of their lives or passing. But the pastiche antique tomb works in the opposite sense—it transforms the mourner's immediate sense of loss into one that is mediated and blunted by its situation in a broader arc of time and eternal cycles of disappearance and renewal.

ROBERT AT LA ROCHE-GUYON

A contemporaneous project to the tomb of Rousseau was Robert's transformation of the donjon or hilltop keep at the château of La Roche-Guyon (Val d'Oise). Robert's intervention transformed this twelfth-century fortification into a veritable portal to the subterranean, the gateway to a tunnel that conducted visitors down through the strata of time. Here again, Robert's landscape project played a deft game with collective memory—the re-invention of historical artifacts (in this case, an ancient building) and the artful fabrication of an historical narrative that contradicted the viewer's knowledge of history. Robert's patrons for this project were the collector Louis-Antoine-Auguste de Rohan-Chabot (1733–1807), duc de Chabot and his duchesse, Louise-Élisabeth de Rohan-Chabot (née La Rochefoucauld-Enville) (1740–86). Chabot was a member of the illustrious Rohan family, descendants of the sovereign princes of Brittany. While the fortunes of this branch of the Rohan had not prospered, Chabot was destined to accede to the family's principal title, duc de Rohan, when his childless uncle died. For the moment, however, Chabot was dependent upon allocations from his wife's family, the almost equally ancient and far wealthier La Rochefoucauld. In the late 1760s, Chabot sold his townhouse in the interests of economy, and the couple moved into apartments at the La Rochefoucauld's Parisian hôtel and at La Roche-Guyon, their country seat. Thanks to La Rochefoucauld's generosity, the Chabot were able to spend lavishly on the arts and were important collectors of Robert's drawings. The artist also acted as the teacher of a weekly informal drawing "academy" that the couple organized (Catala and Wick 2017).

Since the mid-1760s, the duchesse de Chabot's mother, Louise-Élisabeth de La Rochefoucauld, duchesse d'Enville (1716–97) chatelaine of La Roche-Guyon, had undertaken the creation of a circuit of landscaped promenades in the environs of her home (Wick 2014). The Chabot played an important role in the most remarkable aspect of this landscape project: the integration of the domain's twelfth century walled keep, known as the Tower of Guy, as a picturesque ruin. The 100-foot tall tower sits on a limestone cliff above the main château at an elevation of about 210-feet above the level of the Seine (although the keep survives, it was partially demolished in the 1790s at the orders of the Revolutionary government). The Tower of Guy and the principal residence below are linked by a medieval subterranean passage that passes through the cliff-side and also provides access to the domain's chapel and burial crypt, which are also set within the cliff.

In 1777, Chabot paid for the reopening of this passage (Germa 2002: 208). In this same period, he also commissioned Robert to study the creation of an entrance portal that would join the keep and its underground complex to the promenades. In May 1778, he ordered a set of stairs to be carved into a breach in the first set of walls surrounding the tower that would allow visitors to climb up and over it (Germa 2002: 211). This project can be related to a sanguine drawing by Robert, now at the museum in Besançon (see Figure 2.6).

FIGURE 2.6: Hubert Robert, *View of the Tower of Guy*. Musée des Beaux-Arts, Besançon.

In July 1778, a monumental portal was built to mark the entrance to the tower from the promenades. A drawing by Robert conserved at the Louvre shows an early proposal for this project—with two termes supporting a lintel surmounted by a bust in a circular niche (Paris, musée du Louvre, département des Arts graphiques, RF 11555 recto). A pair of Robert drawings still in the possession of the duc de Chabot's descendants show the project largely as it was realized—with a pair of half-engaged rough-hewn columns in the same Doric-Tuscan mix he had employed at the Baths of Apollo (these drawings are reproduced in Catala and Wick 2017: 10–11). The portal and its entablature were carved to appear as if they had broken down and become misaligned over time. Yet another drawing can be associated with this project, a sanguine showing two Roman centurions relaxing in front of a tomb in the form of a pedimented gateway flanked by engaged Corinthian columns that resembles the portal as it was built. This portal's entablature bears a largely illegible inscription dedicating the scene to Chabot. Thus, in this invented view, Robert projects the "tomb" of his still-living patron back into antiquity.

Robert's use of such primitive classical architectural forms on this medieval tower transformed it into something resembling the circular mausolea on the Appian Way, such as the tomb of Caecilia Metella, or the Tomb of the Plautii. For viewers who were well-versed in the architecture of antiquity, there would have been a certain humor in the fact that in the medieval period these late imperial tombs had been adapted as defensive keeps, whereas here it was a medieval keep that was being Romanized and transformed into a mausoleum. The artist would similarly recreate in the gardens of the marquis de Montesquiou at Mauperthuis one of the most famed and esoteric mausolea of the late imperial period, the pyramid of Caius Cestius (see Wick 2017: 12). Robert and the Chabots' intervention also represented an inversion of the architectural phenomenon of *spoila*, common in the Italian peninsula, whereby early Christians integrated antique decorative elements as features in their churches. Here of course, the tower itself was the authentically ancient element, and the antique ornaments were deftly crafted simulacra.

The revelation of the confected or recomposed nature of this ruin formed an essential aspect of its reception and appreciation. As Susan Taylor observes in relation to the Baths of Apollo, Robert, much in the tradition of Piranesi and other *vedutistes*, delighted in including idiosyncratic or paradoxical touches in otherwise highly realistic depictions of antique monuments. To paraphrase Taylor's argument, these were touches that allowed the artist to signal their presence and the contrived nature of the composition to the viewer. They showed that what appeared to be a natural accidental work of time and nature had in fact been confected by the artist, who had selected, remade, and recombined elements drawn from reality in order to create a new and more effecting whole (Taylor 1990: 222–34). It was not enough that the viewer should admire the artistry of the result, but they should also be made aware of how the illusion of reality was formed and created (Taylor 1990: 236).

The intention behind the addition of the portal seems to have been to mark the beginning of what might have been an initiatory sequence that led down to the subterranean chapel and crypt—creating a complex with a strong funerary and perhaps also a Masonic resonance. It should be noted that both Chabot and Robert were Masons and members of the Société Olympique, a Masonic association of amateur musicians and music lovers. Much as in the account of Mercier's time-traveler, the subterranean passage allowed visitors to pass from the garden into a far more menacing and sublimely transporting setting. The crypt also had a far more significant meaning for Chabot. It was where he would inter his wife at her death in 1786, and where he would be interred in 1807 (their bodies would remain here until 1828 when the château passed from the hands of the duc's descendants back to the La Rochefoucauld family (La Rochefoucauld 2001: 246). Thus we can see how with the addition of Robert's portal the tower was transformed into what Monique Mosser has termed "a frontispiece grotto"—the forbidding marker of the entryway to subterranean and magical realms (see Mosser 1983).

At La Roche-Guyon we can read in Robert's deft evocation and reinvention of the buried past an attempt to shape and manipulate the viewer's perception of the present. In 1772, the duchesse d'Enville's son Louis-Alexandre, duc de La Rochefoucauld (1743–92) lost his first wife to a riding accident before the couple had produced an heir. In 1780, the duc de La Rochefoucauld married his own niece, the daughter of the duc and duchesse de Chabot. This alliance was probably intended to ensure that the château would not be inherited by a cadet branch of the family at his death. And in fact, this is precisely what happened: when the duc died, La Roche-Guyon passed to his wife and then in turn to her brother and nephew, the Chabots' son, the future seventh duc de Rohan. As the Chabot did not have a château in the Paris region, they would have anticipated that La Roche-Guyon would soon become their principal seat. Thus, Robert's project for the renovation of the Tower of Guy served to literally inscribe the Chabot into an imagined historical narrative of the château and domain that would shortly become their own. Its vague and fanciful evocations of the antique alluded to a wholly imaginary immemorial history that preceded and thus took precedence over the documented history of the château.

ROBERT AT MÉRÉVILLE

In the summer of 1786, Robert was called upon to advise one of the richest men of the kingdom, the retired court banker Jean-Joseph de Laborde (1724–94) on the design of the landscape garden at his newly acquired estate of Méréville (Essonne). Remarkably for this period, Laborde's fortune was entirely of his own making. His financial acumen and the patronage of the duc de Choiseul yielded him a vast fortune, as did his investments in vast plantations in Santo Domingo and the trafficking and labor of enslaved people. As Jill Casid has observed, Laborde, like many of his contemporaries whose fortunes derived from colonial holdings, endeavored to create a remarkable country seat that would serve as an oasis of "seclusion and forgetting," allowing him to re-contextualize the recent mercantile sources of his wealth (Casid 2005: 75–93).

Laborde's project for Méréville was indelibly shaped by the loss of his former country house, the château of Ferté-Vidame (Eure-et-Loir). Since the 1760s, Laborde had been transforming Ferté-Vidame into a country seat that was commensurate with his wealth and standing. In 1783, however, Louis XVI obliged Laborde to sell the estate to the duc de Penthièvre. The king had obliged his cousin Penthièvre to sell him the domain of Rambouillet, and the acquisition of Ferté-Vidame was intended to console the duc for his loss. As the *parvenu* Laborde could stake no claim of an ancestral tie to Ferté-Vidame, it was all the more easy for Louis XVI to dispossess him of it—albeit at an exorbitant purchase price. When Laborde purchased the relatively modest château and estate of Méréville to replace Ferté-Vidame, he made much of the fact that as an old man, his ambitions stopped at creating a peaceful setting for his retirement. He claimed that his only desire was to make the medieval château into a comfortable, habitable residence, and transform its marshy grounds into a healthy environment with a few promenades laid out for the enjoyment of his wife and daughters. For the house he commissioned a project from the fashionable architect Jean-Benoît-Vincent Barré (1735–1824). For the new landscape garden, his choice of designer belied his stated wish for simplicity and economy: he hired François-Joseph Belanger (1744–1818), architect to the brother of the king, the comte d'Artois, who had recently completed Bagatelle and was soon to contribute to the bankruptcy of a treasurer of the Navy with his extravagant designs for the gardens of the Folie Saint-James. As the historian Nicole Gouiric observes, although Belanger was dismissed after only eighteen months for what Laborde felt was his casual attitude toward accounting, during this time he established the general parameters that the project was to follow (Gouiric 2017). With Belanger gone, Laborde expressed his desire to oversee the project himself, and commissioned Hubert Robert to assist him in developing his ideas and overseeing their realization.

After his contentious experience with Belanger, Laborde quite naturally turned to Robert, a man famed for his easy manners, charm and wit. As we have seen, Robert had already proven himself to be adept at discreetly accompanying aristocratic amateurs in their artistic endeavors. The banker and the artist would have already known each other well, as both were closely linked with the duc de Choiseul. After Choiseul's disgrace in 1770, Robert and the Labordes would have crossed paths quite frequently at the duc's domain in exile, Chanteloup. Their visits there served to publicly underline their continued fidelity to the once powerful politician.

In 1786, Laborde had also commissioned Robert to paint six large-scale canvases for the interior of Méréville—just as the artist had done at Bagatelle for Artois. As Paula Rea Radisich observes, Robert's principal decor for the interior of the château, four caprices

FIGURE 2.7: Hubert Robert, *View of Méréville from the Lake, 1790*. Musee d'Île de France.

FIGURE 2.8: Hubert Robert, *View of Château and Temple of Méréville*. François Doury.

of Roman ruins (now at the Chicago Art Institute) were installed in the Petit Salon, a comparatively intimate reception room that opened onto the gardens and which was intended as the setting for informal family meals (Radisich 1995: 401–15). This decor constituted something of a prelude to the experience of the gardens, but its association with this familial space rather than the grander reception rooms nearby, seems to have been intended to emphasize the garden's personal and sentimental character. Two other large format paintings of the garden were executed in 1790 for the château's billiard room—one of these was certainly the *View of the Great Cascade* (private collection) (illustrated in Gouric, 2017: 95). Like the Petit Salon, the billiard room was also a space dedicated to informal gatherings rather than public representation. The two other large format paintings, representing two principal views of the garden—*The Château Seen from the Lake* (Musée d'Île de France at Sceaux) and the *Temple Viewed from the Riverbank* (private collection)—were also executed by Robert for the Laborde's townhouse. (In total, some fourteen canvases by Robert were seized from Laborde's hôtel in 1793) (Boyer 1961) (see Figures 2.7 and 2.8).

In the foreground of all of these views, like Robert's invented Italian and antique scenes, are washerwomen, shepherds and other rustics, who may have been either denizens of the present or the distant past. As Nicole Gouiric notes, the presence of cows and sheep in pasture create a certain ambiguity as to whether we are in the garden or in the Italian *campagna* (Gouiric 2017: 91). Only the distant view of recognizable (but distorted and re-composed) elements of the Méréville landscape such as the château, the temple, and the rostral column, ground these views in the present. With Robert's involvement in the decoration of the social spaces of the Laborde townhouse, the château and its gardens, a consistent visual language that associated the family with antiquity emerged. Guests of the Labordes would have had the pleasing sensation of identifying monuments and motifs from these paintings that they would have recollected seeing at either of the family's residences writ large in the garden.

What sets Méréville apart from other contemporary landscape gardens of its scale and expense is the relative sobriety and solemnity of its settings and ornamental structures. There were no picturesque cottages or farm buildings, flowering bridges or exotic pavilions at Méréville, such as one would have found at the duc de Chartres' Monceau or Monsieur de Monville's Désert. What visitors discovered in their place was a succession of pristine classical style temples and monuments set within a beautiful rolling landscape. With the sole exception of the Cenotaph of Cook, dedicated to the memory of the great navigator, whom Laborde, as a merchant greatly admired, each of these monuments evoked the lives and exploits of members of the marquis' family (Maskill 2006). There was the Rostral Column, celebrating the bravery of the marquis' two young sons who had joined the ill-fated La Perouse expedition. (This monument is depicted in the lower left-hand corner of Figure 2.7.) The Laiterie (see below), which translated into architecture the innocence and purity of his daughters, who would both marry ducs and thus cement the family's entry into the highest echelons of the nobility. The Column of Trajan called initially the "Obélisque antique" was a monument to the marquis himself (Lassus 1976: 285). And finally, the Temple, which initially seemed intended to evoke the mutual devotion of Laborde and his wife and their role as founders of this family.

What saved the gardens of Méréville from a certain sense of monotony and repetition were the counterpoints provided by a perfectly crafted sequence of simulacra of natural geological and hydrological features. Visitors encountered rock bridges and arches, an immense roiling waterfall that seemed to erupt from inside the earth itself, vast grottoes, and a veritable archipelago of small islands set within the river. The promenade itself orchestrated experiences of wonder and terror, leading one unexpectedly to precipices, or across bridges that appeared half ruined. The immediate and visceral character of these episodes framed the "emblematic" experience of the monuments with an "expressive" transporting affect.

Here as at Ermenonville, Robert used his fluent command of the visual and architectural codes of Roman antiquity to reinvent contemporary artifacts and events in a language of the immemorial. At the heart of the composition, the white marble Temple was a nearly exact reproduction, in a restored form and a reduced scale, of the first-century BCE round peripteral temple of Tivoli. The acropolis of Tivoli, one of Robert's favored motifs, is situated dramatically over the falls of the Aniene and a sheer precipice.

In Bélanger's initial plan for Méréville, a similar round temple was to be built on an island in the garden's principal lake. The dampness of this site was unsuitable for such a heavy structure, and this first temple collapsed during construction. Thus, one of the first tasks facing Robert and his collaborator, the architect Barré, in laying out the gardens was to locate a new site for the temple: they chose a rocky promontory at the heart of the gardens that dominated the surrounding landscape. The temple was faithful to its prototype at Tivoli in all but one substantive detail—its lack of windows. As Olivier Choppin de Janvry hypothesizes, this was a modification intended to heighten the building's sublime character (Choppin de Janvry 1969: 83). In this respect, Méréville's Temple had something of a funereal character, as if in building it the elderly Laborde was already anticipating his own disappearance. As David Coffin notes, since the early eighteenth-century British aristocrats had taken the temple of Tivoli as a particularly appropriate form for mausolea—most notably with the mausoleum of Castle Howard, the Pelham Mausoleum at Brocklesby in Lincolnshire of 1786–7, and the Mussenden Temple in Ireland of 1785 (Coffin 1994: 131–45). The Temple was initially intended to house a full-figure sculpture by Pajou of the marquis' wife Rosalie de Nettine de Laborde (1737–1820), holding a shield bearing his portrait in profile (Draper and Scherf 1998: 271–4). These plans had to be modified in 1790 when the marquise insisted that she was too old to be a fitting subject for such a work. Instead the couple's youngest daughter Natalie de Laborde (1774–1835) was sculpted in her place.

Visitors would have accessed the Temple via the ruined bridge, a masonry and Roman-brick structure, built to appear as if it had once forded the valley with a graceful segmental arch that had subsequently collapsed and been repaired in a makeshift manner with rough posts and planks. The apparently precarious condition of the bridge would have added an element of fear and trepidation to the approach to the temple that imparted an "expressive" immediacy to the building's otherwise "emblematic" character. Yet there is another layer to this device, because the bridge erected at Méréville bears a striking resemblance to one depicted in a painting titled *A* (now in the Philadelphia Museum of Art) Robert had exhibited two decades previously in his first salon of 1767. This celebrated canvas had belonged to Laborde's recently deceased brother-in-law, Ange-Laurent de La Live de Jully (1725–79). Thus, the gardens at Méréville materialized the imagined world of Robert's painting, but also the memory of artworks directly associated with Laborde's extended family.

On the opposite shore of the lake from the site originally intended for the temple, was the Laiterie, a structure dedicated to the fabrication and consumption of different dairy products (see Martin 2011). Erected between 1790 and 1792 to a design by Barré and Robert, it was intended to celebrate the marriage in the summer of 1790 of Natalie de Laborde with Charles, comte de Noailles (future duc de Mouchy) (1771–1834). Robert had recently collaborated with the architect-entrepreneur Jacques-Jean Thévenin (1732–1813) on design of the Laiterie at Rambouillet for Marie-Antoinette. For the Queen, Robert re-imagined the traditionally fairly understated typology of the laiterie—a white marble-clad room lit by large windows—into a fantastic classical temple that terminated in a fountain in the form of a grotto. As Monique Mosser notes, the queen's laiterie at Rambouillet translated Cicero's description of his Almatheum at Arpinum into a garden *fabrique* (Mosser and Brunon 2014: 36–8). At Rambouillet, Robert is also credited as having designed the Laiterie's furnishings and tableware in the Etruscan manner, creating for the first time not just a building that evoked antique models, but an immersive and holistic antique environment, that was markedly different from contemporary styles in all its details (Maës 2016: 336–45).

Natalie de Laborde's Laiterie was to be both larger and more complex than its royal predecessor. (See Figure 2.9).

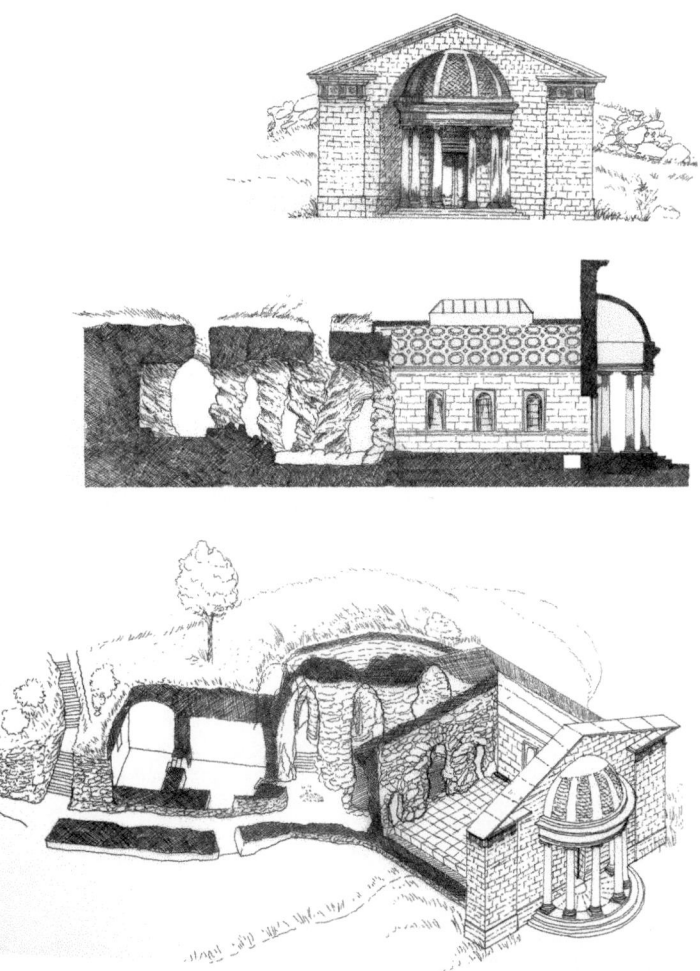

FIGURE 2.9: Gabriel Wick, *Illustration*—lateral section, plan, elevation and axonometric view of the Laiterie of Rambouillet, pen and ink, 2017.

As at Rambouillet, the Méréville Laiterie began with a simple and understated temple front, which gave no indication of the elaborate interiors within. However, whereas the Laiterie of Rambouillet was conceived as a free-standing structure, that of Méréville was set into a small hill and thus further blurred the division between architecture and nature, temple and grotto. Passing through the front door the visitor would have entered directly into a marble-clad rectangular chamber evoking the central chamber or *cella* of a classical temple. The two lateral walls were both inset with three cylindrical niches probably intended for statues, incense-burners or candelabras. The wall opposite the entrance was composed of vast boulders. Three openings in this wall revealed that it masked a grotto beyond, which contained a large pool, fed by a number of small waterfalls that cascaded over a series of roughly formed basins. The water from the pool then flowed around the edge of the *cella* in channels lining the three remaining walls. The visitor could pass through two lateral passages into and around the grotto and then into a series of chambers beyond. Where the *cella* was crisply classical, these subterranean chambers set into the mount were composed of vaults formed of vast boulders, and their floors were inset with large rounded river pebbles. A number of irregular openings set into the rock formation provided indirect sources of daylight. As the research of Nicole Gouiric has revealed, these irregular rock surfaces were tinted in delicate shades of red, yellow and green, thus causing subtle variations in the tone of light within the space (Gouiric 2017: 91).

The form of the rectangular *cella* with its three niches terminating in a fountain set into a hillside would have been recognizable to many of Robert's peers as an evocation of an antique ruin celebrated in the eighteenth century, the so-called *nymphaea* of the deity Egeria on the outskirts of Rome, memorably depicted in an etching by Piranesi (see Figure 2.10).

It was the beautiful nymph Egeria who was said to have revealed to her husband Numa Pompilius, the mythical second king of Rome, the divine laws and rituals that would govern the kingdom. According to Ovid, when Numa died Egeria melted in her tears and

FIGURE 2.10: Piranesi, *View of the fountain and grotto of Egeria near the Porta Capena, c. 1766*, New York, Metropolitan Museum, The Elisha Whittelsey Collection.

was transformed by the gods into a spring that was sacred to the vestal virgins—guardians of the city of Rome's sacred hearth flame. Plutarch identifies the spring near Rome's Porta Capena, whose waters were reserved for the vestal virgins, as that of Egeria.

The architecture of the Laiterie itself, its juxtaposition of a highly refined temple with brute grotto is especially interesting because it implies something of an invented historical narrative woven around the development of what was in fact an entirely modern structure: as we penetrate into the temple and discover the grotto with its pools and cascades behind, we are led to imagine how the primitive well-spring of sacred beliefs, nature and natural phenomenon, was built over, and in a sense de-natured by later additions. This sense that the erection of temples in fact defiles the natural sites that they were intended to embellish was one articulated by Juvenal in his *Satires* (3.17–20) specifically in reference to the Egerian grotto:

> Th' Egerian grots—ah, how unlike the true!
> Nymph of the Spring, more honoured hadst thou been
> If, free from art, an edge of living green
> Thy bubbling fount had circumscribed alone,
> And marble ne'er profaned the native stone.
>
> —Gifford 1802: 70

Thus, as one enters the temple one moves back into time as well as space. From the grotto, the visitor passes through a vast corridor of rough-hewn rock to a winding set of stairs that leads up and out into the Arcadian setting of the garden. The passage from the refined Laiterie to its primitive grotto and then out into the landscape takes the visitor on a voyage into the past from which they emerge in a sense purified of the corrupting influences of civilization and restored to a purer original state.

Taken as an ensemble, we can see how the monuments at Méréville seem to have been intended not just to embellish the landscape, but also to immortalize the marquis and his progeny and represent them to some distant imagined future in the guise of quasi-mythical figures who were to be revered for their roles in the founding of a great new house and lineage. An intriguing but unfortunately now lost painting executed by Robert at Méréville in 1786 seems to reinforce the pseudo-sacred character of this landscape composition: it shows Natalie and her sister Pauline Louise Josèph (1767–92), duchesse des Cars, laying wreaths on an altar dedicated to the *Deis Manibus* (the spirits of ancestors who watch over the household) at the entrance to a grotto (Cayeux 1968).

The re-conceptualization of the garden *fabrique* as the focus of new forms of ritual devotion was a significant development of the 1780s that reflects the increasing knowledge of antique religious practices yielded by the archaeological excavations around the Bay of Naples. This desire to recreate not only the sacred architecture of antiquity but also the rituals that went along with antique monuments and temples was almost certainly driven by a remarkable new publication of this period—the Abbé Saint-Non's five volume illustrated survey of Naples, the *Voyage pittoresque ou description des royaumes de Naples et de Sicile*, published between 1781 and 1786. This survey featured measured archaeological plans and elevations of temples and precise depictions of the ritual instruments discovered there, alongside reconstituted views of sacrifices conducted by figures in antique dress drawn by the architect Louis Jean Desprez (1743–1804) (Pinto 2012: 175–98). Following Girardin's success in making Ermenonville and Rousseau's tomb the object of a new set of secular mourning practices, the landscape garden was invested with a whole new significance as a setting for acts of veneration and memorialization. Ermenonville inspired a host of other garden patrons such as the princesse de Monaco at Betz or the marquis de Montesquiou at Mauperthuis, who also attempted to attract the public to their gardens by installing tombs of notable historical figures or creating pastiche monuments. It is interesting to note that both Monaco and Montesquiou consulted with Robert on the form of their garden *fabriques*. Monaco seems to have been particularly concerned with imparting an air of antiquarian rigor to her garden: when she built her elaborate Temple of Friendship at Betz (designed by the architect Barré, Robert's collaborator at Méréville), she consulted the savant Abbé Barthélemy on the manner in which such structures were furnished in ancient times.

A consistent thread that unites all of Robert's landscape projects is this desire on the part of his patrons to root or inscribe themselves for posterity into the archaeological substrate of their domains. Few of them could have ever even suspected that the social and political order would collapse so dramatically in the years or even months after the completion of these gardens, or that these compositions would so quickly take on a new poignancy as memorials to their creators and their lost world. The marquis de Laborde's son, Alexandre de Laborde (1773–1842), inveterate traveler, archaeologist, writer, and connoisseur of the picturesque, was to eulogize his father's garden and those of many of his contemporaries, in his richly illustrated *Description des nouveaux jardins de la France et de ses anciens châteaux* (Delance: 1808). Writing of the mausoleum that the marquis de Montesquiou had built at Mauperthuis to house the remains of the Admiral de Coligny (1519–72), Alexandre de Laborde mocked the men of his father's generation for having included tombs in their gardens:

> Dramas were wanted on the stage, tombs in gardens. Real misfortunes have but too much brought back our sensibility to the true. We are no longer tempted to sport with grief, and we shall not place at present on the skirts of a road exposed to the risibility of the passengers the tomb of one whose remains were deprived of burial by his fellow citizens. Such misfortunes are become too sacred to be atoned for by such improper reparations.
>
> —1808: 157–8

Given that the remains of Alexandre de Laborde's father, the marquis, had been relegated to a common pit following his execution in April 1794, we can understand how the grandeur and extravagance of these contrived memorials would now be so deeply unpalatable. In the light of the actual historic events that had just overtaken them, the attempts made by men of his father's generation to shape how they would be remembered by the distant future must have seemed all the more tragic and absurd.

CHAPTER THREE

Media and Technology

PATRICK H. HUTTON

THE LONG REVOLUTION IN THE MAKING OF PRINT CULTURE

The cultural history of memory in the modern era is intimately intertwined with the long revolution in the democratization of print culture. The eighteenth century witnessed its acceleration in western Europe and the Americas, a process that had begun some 300 years before with Johannes Gutenberg's invention of the printing press on the eve of the Reformation. Communications theorist Marshall McLuhan characterized entry into this culture as a "Gutenberg galaxy" in which print media permitted the flourishing of a more open and inquisitive mindset (McLuhan [1962] 2011: 79–81). Typographic technology not only greatly enhanced the possibilities of human communication. It also acted as an extension of mind by providing print matter as mirrors for critical reflection (Clark 2008; Foer 2011: 155–61). Thanks to the transforming effects of the interaction between mind and its mnemonic satellites in books, newspapers, and other printed documents, a new style of intellectual life based upon the dynamics of high literacy emerged within the interstices of a manuscript culture resistant to innovation.

The mid-eighteenth century marked the tipping point between that manuscript culture, still framed by the protocols of the spoken word, and a typographic one in which print media asserted its ever more pervasive presence as the dominant mode of cultural communication. Its volume grew exponentially, to become the primary archive of cultural memory during that era and thenceforth into the mid-twentieth century. In manuscript culture, the written text had served the needs of orality; in print culture, the relationship was reversed. The new culture was fashioned around communities that encouraged refined practices of reading and writing as a means for pressing outward the horizons of knowledge. Within this context, oral communication, far from being marginalized, continued to exercise its influence as a vital resource as its uses were redirected toward rumination on the meaning of ideas found in the books, newspapers, and periodicals that now commanded the educated public's attention. A variety of new social institutions—salons, coffee houses, masonic societies, and reading groups—emerged as places for conversation about the writings of a host of innovative philosophers, essayists, literary critics, and novelists (Eisenstein 2005: 102–20). Whereas the rhetoricians of manuscript culture had prided themselves on their intellectual autonomy, employing mnemonic skills in impressive displays of their erudition without recourse to written props, the philosophers of print culture professed their ideas through print media, which served as archives of cultural memory open for the shared appreciation of a diverse and far-flung audience of increasingly sophisticated readers. As conveniently portable tools for learning, books became the guiding force in the circulation of ideas. Some of these writings had a serious side, dealing in issues about advances in the arts and sciences as well as projects for political and social reform. Others provided lighter fare to satisfy a growing interest in the mores and manners of everyday life as experience with which readers could identify. As the century wore on, writers found readers ever farther afield, exercising influence far beyond their numbers in promoting new kinds of cultural discourse. Their reach extended throughout the Western world, and sometimes beyond (Withers 2007: 50–7, 62–83).

In the course of this entry into the galaxy of print culture, the uses of memory were remodeled. The rising production and distribution of books, pamphlets, newspapers, and broadsheets in the second half of the eighteenth century reconfigured the organization and accessibility of knowledge, as well as reshaping methods of learning and practices of communication. As the heritage of human knowledge passed from the collective memory of oral tradition into the cultural memory housed in the vast archives of typographic media, ideas about the uses of memory were elevated to a new plane, where they were sorted into public and private realms. Public memory, as embedded in printed texts, gave rise to the power of public opinion, efficacious but at the same time volatile and easily manipulated. Personal memory, by contrast, came to be appreciated apart as a facile, creative faculty of mind, turning its inquiries inward to explore the deep sources of the self. This kind of memory, too, was empowering, as it inspired the writing of autobiography, the memoir, the personal letter, and the novel. As memory scholar Aleida Assmann characterized this transition in its ensemble, memory as *ars* came to be rivaled by memory as *vis* (A. Assmann 2011: 17–22).

In this chapter, I consider the changing uses of memory along that stretch in the timeline of the eighteenth century during which the narrow pathways of manuscript culture widened into the king's highways of print communication. As a setting for the critical study of memory, the move marks a transformative episode in the long-term passage from religious to secular literature, from intensive to extensive reading, and from subservience to collective judgment issued from on high by public authorities toward the independence of mind of individual writers and readers. Writers once beholden to kings and their courtiers for patronage gained a measure of autonomy, and scholarship, once subjected to censorship by clerical authority, thrived in the intellectually liberating domain of what came to be characterized as a "republic of letters." These topics illuminate the role of cultural memory in the eighteenth century in a variety of ways—in media as a mnemonic resource for publicity, in changing habits of reading, in the search for the self as reflected in the mirrors of literature, and in newly emergent communities of intellectual exchange built around books as a shared resource. Ideas about the law, too, would be reconceived, as immemorial tradition of particular judicial precedents in case law yielded place to written constitutions that laid claim to universal principles, and so introduced new ways of remembering the law.

THE WANING AUTHORITY OF ORAL TRADITIONS

Print literacy marked a dramatic advance in a long-term textualization of culture that harked back to Greco-Roman antiquity. The advent of manuscript literacy dates from the era 700 to 200 BCE, and served as a first step in the process (Havelock 1963: 13–15). Through the Middle Ages and into the early modern era, open access to manuscripts was rare, and of limited influence upon oral communication. Writing continued to serve speaking, and the characteristics of orality determined much as before the way knowledge was classified, presented, and communicated. Manuscripts nonetheless incited a desire for accuracy of recall within the dynamic flow of oral communication, and so functioned as stabilizing places of memory. Such were the circumstances for the formulation of the concept of the canon as a touchstone against which to measure change (J. Assmann 2011: 87–96). In manuscript culture, knowledge was organized mnemonically according to topics, as it had been in cultures of primary orality.

The classical art of memory was modeled on such foundations as a technique of remembering, based on localizing unfamiliar information systematically in familiar places and images (Yates 1966: 1–26). Effective use of the art was coeval with the heyday of manuscript culture, and rose and fell with its fortunes. The art had been an early invention of manuscript culture in antiquity; it would remain a vital practice so long as that culture exercised influence, and so well into the seventeenth century (Rossi 2000b: 1–28). With the advent of print technology, the art of memory, long prized as a technique for preserving the heritage of the past, was marginalized as a skill among scholars. It continued to influence practice in fields such as rhetoric and law, and the effective use of mnemonic props retained a measure of prestige as aphorisms and epigrams to be recited at opportune, impromptu moments. Rhetoric favored rote learning, and the capacity to mobilize knowledge without notes was valued as an impressive resource for speakers delivering sermons in churches, lectures in university halls, and speeches in the diverse bodies of government. Memorization of significant passages of poetry and prose remained a common pedagogical practice until well into the twentieth century. The professor's lecture from handwritten notes served as a staple of university courses until the turn of the twenty-first century.

Manuscript culture, moreover, had its characteristic archival memory banks. These were fixed repositories of learning, closely allied with the political institutions that sponsored them, and some were of long standing. They housed official documents and cultural artifacts. Through the early modern era, state archives expanded; scientific academies and museums were founded; libraries thrived, thanks to the sponsorship of reform-minded monarchs and the largesse of wealthy patrons of learning and the arts (Rossi 2000a: 192–202). But well into the eighteenth century, all of these institutions were identified with the political culture of the absolutist state, which they served as sequestered fortresses of knowledge. Only savants who enjoyed the patronage of kings, princes, or wealthy aristocrats had privileged access to them. The royal archives in France, for example, were organized to serve agencies of state, not scholars. While some scholars were permitted to search their records, the public at large had no access to them (Pomian 1992: 193–200). These archives would play a minimal role in the making of the new public sphere of print communication. The first published scientific journals date only from the late seventeenth century.

During the eighteenth century, moreover, oral communication continued to shape attitudes and opinions within the popular culture of what was still a predominately rural world. Edmund Burke, for example, estimated that the reading public in England during the 1790s may have numbered no more than 80,000 out of a population of six million (Watt [1957] 2001: 36) Oral communication was dynamic, the primary vehicle for everyday communication about domestic life and local issues, as well as rumors conveyed as news from afar, and gossip about scandals closer to home. At the same time, collective mentalities cultivated within cultures of primary orality tended to reaffirm the value of ritual repetition of custom, which battened upon deep-seated habits of mind derived from the common sense of personal experience and traditions believed to issue from the depths of time. Custom advised caution and was suspicious of innovation. Thinking in that milieu was often rife with credulity and susceptible to rumors and the telling of fantastic tales. Faced with the print revolution, some within this culture resisted the deepening textualization of ideas prevalent among educated people. Some clergymen disapproved of ready access to print matter, worrying that readers might stray from ecclesiastical doctrine, or be tempted to engage in immoral behavior. Among the poor, some identified reading with the rich and powerful, and so an instrument of social domination. Others feared the written word as a kind of black magic (Chartier 1989: 122–4). Even learned scholars, such as the rhetorician Giambattista Vico, worried that the printing press was debasing learning. It was becoming easier to print books inexpensively, and he believed that many texts unworthy of the scholars' attention were circulating in the public domain. Print culture, he allowed, opened the floodgates to mediocrity (Vico [1709] 1990: 72).

Yet during the eighteenth century, the democratization of print culture was a trend that would not be stayed. Inexorably, it exercised cumulative effects upon the making of modern ways of thinking. By mid-century, observers noted the diminishing authority of collective memory—conceived as the living memory of oral tradition—as a source of knowledge. There were fewer references to the authority of immemorial tradition in public discourse, and of the value of folklore as a source of wisdom. By the end of the eighteenth century, oral traditions of storytelling were being historicized in printed collections, a sure sign of their waning influence. These folktales, which hitherto had been passed from parents to children, generation upon generation, were now gathered and inventoried in compendia for circulation among interested readers sometimes unfamiliar with the traditions from which they came. Those collated by Charles Perrault in France, Wilhelm and Jacob Grimm in Germany, James Macpherson in Scotland, Thomas Percy in England, and Hans Christian Andersen in Denmark, exemplify this Europe-wide trend. The critical perspective of such folklorists on their heritage betrays a certain nostalgia not only for the passing of a rural way of life but also for the mystique of a vanishing practice of oral communication that had sustained popular culture as living memory (Fritzsche 2004: 143, 148–59).

THE EVOLUTION OF THE ART OF READING

Statistical data on trends in literacy in eighteenth century Europe and America reveal dramatically rising rates, though their interpretation presents complexities. There was considerable variation in the acquisition of the skills of reading and writing from country to country and from place to place. But as historian James Melton has pointed out, a few broad generalizations are possible, and one can discern long-range trends. Overall rates of literacy in western Europe doubled over the course of the century. Literacy was significantly higher in the cities than in the countryside. More men than women could read. There were more readers in western Europe and in the American colonies than in eastern or southern Europe (Chartier 1989: 111–19; Melton 2001: 81–6).

Reading had never been an easy skill to acquire. Written codes of a language differ from its oral codes. Learning to read entails functional adaptations in the neural pathways of the brain, and so requires considerable practice in converting letters into sounds (Ong 1982: 106; Dehaene 2010: 218–19, 228). Neither oral communication, nor for that matter elementary reading skill, was easily subordinated to communication through the printed word. Historian Roger Chartier has researched the history of the uneven development of reading and writing practices during the early modern era in France.

Through that period and in some places well into the eighteenth century, people who read did so differently from the way we do today. Readers lingered over the word, and pronounced it aloud, even when alone. Oral recitation of written texts, therefore, might be characterized as a stage along the way in the transition from manuscript to print literacy. During the early modern era, nearly all readers voiced their readings in small groups such as the family. They returned to the same passages over and over, particularly those in the Bible and works of religious devotion as a ritual reaffirmation of given teachings. Books were expensive and acquisition of them was typically limited to the wealthy. Even in the early eighteenth century, most households possessed only a few. Reading and writing, moreover, were cognitive skills apart from one another, each one drawing on a different region of the brain. Learning to write was a separate act from learning to read, and presented another set of challenges. Not everyone who could read could write, and some people who had rudimentary writing skills (such as signing their names) could not read (Chartier 1989: 112). Even during the eighteenth century, those who could write intelligibly tended to mimic their habits of reading. Consider the popularity of the commonplace book. These were notebooks in which readers cut up and literally copied passages out of the text of the author in order to personalize the thoughts they stimulated, and to make them their own (Darnton 2009: 149–50). Paraphrasing was an act of abstraction that for many readers would only come through practice over long periods of time.

The key to entry into print culture, however, was the capacity to read rapidly and extensively. Silent reading signified a crucial step in advancing that practice. Its effects upon human understanding were profound. Silent reading was well-established among highly literate people as early as the sixteenth century. With the democratization of print literacy during the eighteenth century, it became a common pastime for those who had the opportunity to enjoy it. Well-to-do women especially developed silent reading skills to a high level of attainment (Goodman 1994: 53–4, 73–89). Chartier alludes to the interesting fact that the iconography of the era focuses almost exclusively on women readers (1989: 124–43). In wealthy households, rooms were set aside as libraries for reading alone. The ability to read silently hastened the move from slow reading of a few texts toward canvassing a wide range of reading material with increasing speed. Silent reading accentuated the shift from the ear to the eye as the dominant mode of perception. Those who had once heeded ideas presented in the spoken word now looked for them in texts. The techniques of silent reading permitted personalization of ever wider and more diverse fields of learning, and so paradoxically made possible the privatization of cultural memory. Personal interpretation fostered a capacity for skepticism and introduced a need for independence of mind. It encouraged introspection, and inspired self-criticism (Ong 1982: 117–23). It marked a step toward the autonomy of individual identity and established preconditions for the rise of autobiography as an inquiry into the hidden secrets of the self. In this way, the ancient art of memory was reborn as a modern technique for introspection in which textual representations of the things of the world came to be regarded as mirrors for the soul. The capacity for critical understanding implicit in silent reading also encouraged readers to engage and reflect upon different points of view, and to distinguish among them, signaling the beginnings of an interest in literary criticism as a genre. Readers were thus able to recognize and accept the complexities of personality. Modern biography made manifest this rising sympathy for the subjective mindset of others, in light of such feelings for oneself. James Boswell's biography of the many facets of the personality of the literary critic Samuel Johnson exemplifies this move toward

FIGURE 3.1: Jean-Honoré Fragonard, *Young Woman Reading Silently*, c. 1769 Courtesy of Getty Images, UK.

more realistic and nuanced assessments of the lives of the celebrities of the era (Zaretsky 2015: 49, 56–7, 74–8, 89, 102; Lilti 2017: 74–6).

PRINT LITERACY AND THE DIVERSIFICATION OF READING MATTER

By mid-century, books in print provided a decentralized archive of knowledge that was hastening the democratization of literacy. Printed books served as moveable places of memory, which could travel with the reader. The significance of this easy access to print as the medium of cultural exchange did more than provide incentives for more people to learn to read and write. Print media erected a platform for a kind of literacy oriented toward curiosity about new fields of learning, and manners and mores apart from one's own. Even among an older, religiously oriented understanding of the world, reading encouraged a deeper understanding of one's own faith and a growing tolerance of the religious viewpoints of others. The renewal of Christian piety within what scholars refer to as the "second Reformation" during the seventeenth century had placed a new accent on the importance of learning to read in both Protestant and Catholic communities. Over the course of the eighteenth century, though, publication of reading matter gradually shifted from religious to secular topics to accommodate the changing interests of expanding cadres of readers. More importantly, print culture promoted new habits of reading. Readers in the dawning age of Enlightenment aspired to canvass a wide and diverse range of material. The incentive to read more widely, in turn, prompted them to read faster. The expanding realm of books in print provided an opening for access to innovative ideas as well as to the learning of the ages. The eighteenth century witnessed the acceleration of the transition in reading matter from Scripture and devotional religious literature toward a wide range of humanistic and scientific topics, each elaborated in its own sphere. Religious literature remained popular throughout the eighteenth century, and sales increased. Yet secular literature was expanding at a more rapid rate, in the shift in readers' tastes from intensive to extensive reading. The prior distinction between sacred and profane literature, was superseded by one that contrasted serious and light reading. The categories of genre for reading came to be divided among the morally edifying, the entertaining, and the salacious (Melton 2001: 86–104).

Among these realms of knowledge issuing from the diversification of scholarly inquiry made possible by print technology, one notes first those that played out in the public sphere: philosophy, history, natural history, political theory, applied science, manners and mores, travel, child rearing and pedagogy. Such widespread topics nurtured intellectual curiosity, and generally had a stimulating effect upon extensive reading. Such was the profusion of print matter and the zeal of a public eager to consume it that censorship, whether by church or state, had become impossible. By the late eighteenth century, the government in France acknowledged the economic value of these publications and lessened its oversight. During the French Revolution, regulation of the book trade disappeared completely, and the publication of print matter grew hyperbolically (Melton 2001: 142). At the same time, the surfeit of reading matter led to a concern about distinguishing refined from mediocre literature. Here emerged an interest in the concept of taste as a principle for differentiating reading preferences (Gadamer [1960] 1992: 35–41). Efforts were made to identify the best of the new literature. One notes Samuel Johnson's *Lives of the Poets* (1781), which sought to identify a modern tradition of *belles lettres*. In this way, the ancient concept of the canon as a common standard of measurement was reconceived as a modern designation for books of enduring merit. (Grabes: 2008: 311–18)

Noteworthy in the midst of this network of reading material was the appearance of the encyclopedia, not only as a comprehensive compendium of practical knowledge but also as a critical assessment of the current state of learning and research. The encyclopedia as a scholarly genre developed over the course of the eighteenth century. The prototype was Ephraim Chambers' *Cyclopedia*, published in London in two volumes in 1728. The project culminated in the French *Encyclopédie* of 1751–72, first published in seventeen volumes under the editorial supervision of philosophers Jean le Rond d'Alembert and Denis Diderot. It was heralded by contemporaries as one of the greatest achievements of the European Enlightenment. As historian Robert Darnton has explained, it was at once a work of reference and a manifesto of the Enlightenment, an attempt to present the corpus of the sciences and the humanities as a unified project that ordered knowledge according to rational principles. It was accessed through the innovation of alphabetic indexing as a more abstract code for the organization of knowledge (Darnton 1984: 191–213). In its widespread distribution, the *Encyclopédie* played a key role in the cultural revolution ushered in by print culture. Despite its size and initially large (quarto) format, it was over the long run of its publishing history a best seller, especially after its second and following editions were published in simpler (octavo) page format that ordinary readers could afford (Darnton 1979: 33–7, 136–8).

The democratization of print culture also contributed to inquiry into life's private sphere, which fostered the idea of memory as a technique of introspection (Watt [1957] 2001: 196–200). Memory as soul-searching cultivated reflection on one's own feelings and on the psychology of well-being that it permitted. In his poetical ruminations about human harmony with nature, the English poet William Wordsworth, introduced the idea of levels of memory, an intuitive overture into the field of depth psychology. Screen memories, which he characterized as innocuous "spots of time," provided an aesthetic gloss to cover over disturbing hidden memories of traumatic experience. The former served as place markers for the latter (Hutton 1993: 52–9).

Letters, too, became a popular genre of writing from the mid-seventeenth century, especially among women. Historian Dena Goodman explains how letter-writing gave them a freedom to expand their intellectual horizons beyond their everyday experience, and so to assert an identity of their own in the topics they chose to explore. Women directed attention to personal well-being and the pursuit of happiness and turned the examination of conscience toward shared reflections on feelings (Goodman 2009: 1–4, 329–37). Letters served as a precondition for the appearance of the epistolary novel, with its sentimental appeal to emotions. The cultivation of sentiment led to a remarkable upsurge of interest in novels of manners and mores, fictional accounts of the lives of others with which one could identify intellectually and emotionally (Watt [1957] 2001: 189–96). Interpersonal relations within the dynamics of family life were a typical theme of many of these works, as exemplified in the novels of Jean-Jacques Rousseau, Samuel Richardson, and Johann von Goethe. Darnton portrays Rousseau as the writer who taught his generation how to read novels in a way that deepened their understanding of the dilemmas of their everyday lives (Darnton 1984: 231–49). Interest in this new genre developed rapidly over the course of the second half of the eighteenth century, to such a degree that the purchase of novels surpassed that of religious literature by the end of the century. The novel of mores introduced a gender issue into eighteenth-century literature as well. In her study of the novels of mores in late eighteenth century France, historian Lynn Hunt analyzes their portrayal of dysfunction in family life, noting perceived problems with absent fathers and wayward mothers on the eve of, and during the French Revolution. Such writings, she argues, gave expression to a more pervasive anxiety about the stability of the family, as revealed in the pornographic sexual anarchism portrayed in the writings of the marquis de Sade (Hunt 1992: 17–51, 124–50).

Popular novels, moreover, permitted perspective on the personal experience of falling in love. Entering into the private thoughts and emotions of their characters made readers aware that the inner lives, psychological needs, and erotic fantasies of others were not unlike their own, and so states of mind with which they could vicariously identify (Watt [1957] 2001: 199–200). The novel's depiction of this intimate realm of private life led surreptitiously into a prurient interest in illicit love. Aspects of forbidden love, hitherto cloaked in secrecy, were now made explicit in a literature of erotica that circulated clandestinely. Much of it de-sacralized the private lives of the royal family and its entourage through speculative stories about their scandalous love affairs (Darnton: 1982; 31–5; 1995: 72, 78–9, 241). Pornography as a secret literature of the *ars erotica* was hardly new, and most of these works were of fleeting interest and quickly passed into oblivion. But scholars have recently remarked upon their significance within the genre of the eighteenth-century novel, less for the presentation of secret lives, more for the

FIGURE 3.2: Joshua Reynolds, *Portrait of Samuel Johnson*, celebrated letter writer, 1756. Courtesy of Getty Images, UK.

reinvention of discourse about sexuality as a way of seeking truth about the human condition (Foucault 1978: 20–2; Hunt 1993: 10–35).

PRINT CULTURE AND THE EMERGENCE OF THE "PUBLIC SPHERE"

The power of publicity in the new galaxy of print culture is evinced in the emergence of what philosopher Jürgen Habermas has characterized as a new kind of public sphere, apart from court society, commercial networks, or religious congregations. Based upon emerging methods of critical rational analysis, he argues, its activities were devoted to the propagation of the practical sciences, but from the beginning had a political edge (Habermas [1962] 1989: 69). The idea of a public sphere so conceived was first identified with the politics of oppositional parties that challenged royal authority during the early eighteenth century. Their power resided in their effective use of the press. This newly conceived realm of public life emerged in cities in England and later France, then intruded into those of central Europe as well (Melton 2001: 31, 52, 61). During the late eighteenth century, the public sphere came to be identified more specifically with organizations that gave it a pronounced cultural identity, as increasingly dense networks of readers and writers conjured up an imagined community that they labeled the "Republic of Letters." Its leading figures were known by their celebrity as writers rather than their wealth, martial prowess, or birthright. Citizens of the Republic prided themselves on their cosmopolitan outlook, tolerant attitude toward others, open-mindedness about new ideas, and freedom to roam in the wider world that books and newspapers opened to their imaginations (D. Goodman 1994: 34–52).

This imagined community established a new framework for cultural memory that defined the practices of intellectual life associated with the Enlightenment. The Republic thrived on the power of the publicity that it generated, and so exercised influence upon eighteenth-century culture well beyond its participants in the urban centers of Europe. The power of literate people to define their own cultural domain inserted a wedge of forward-looking attitudes and values between the popular culture of ordinary people, whose collective mentalities were rooted in custom and long-held conventions, and the highly mannered culture of the royal courts and their aristocratic satellites, whose values and rituals of political authority were rooted in the collective memory of an ancient genealogical heritage. The new culture of the Republic of Letters carved out a sphere of influence between them and rapidly surpassed them in its popular prestige. The power of the Republic was in high literacy; print was its medium of publicity. Centered upon social gathering places in the cities, its numbers were comparatively few. But it made manifest its authority in shaping public discourse within the society at large in its intellectual agendas and its circulation of new ideas (Furet 1981: 35–9). In the largest sense, the Republic was committed to civic humanism. Through the synergy generated by this openness toward the human and the natural sciences in all of their possibilities, a progressive-minded agenda was in the making, as the emerging culture fashioned by writers and voraciously consumed by their readers turned a critical eye upon the human predicament with a view to its improvement. Corresponding societies from within its ranks bridged the physical distance that separated its communities and were devoted to exchanging ideas about practical projects for political, legal, and social reform.

As a network of writers and their readers, citizens of the Republic of Letters invented their own unique institutions, rituals, manners and mores. Put more specifically in terms of memory issues, readers and writers cultivated new habits of intellectual inquiry and exchange. They devoted time to reading during the day, and they identified places in which to do so. Even when they lived at great distances from one another and were unknown to one another personally, they developed through their reading a sense that they were vicariously participating in a fellowship based on shared interests, sympathies, and commitments. These included not only the sociability that the vigorous exchange of ideas promoted, but also a need for more intimate forms of communication—with some through informal socializing, with others through letters, and with themselves through introspection. Readers felt a kinship with the authors they appreciated, and sometimes wrote to them to affirm the ideas and emotions they shared (Darnton 1984: 246–9).

Given the expansion of the reading public, writing became a profession to fulfill their need for new books and newspapers, and writers acquired an identity and a social prestige they had never held before. They lived by their ingenuity in building a clientele willing to buy their writings. In the process, the most celebrated among them acquired iconic identities, idolized by readers drawn magnetically to their public persona. The spectrum of writers, however, was broad. There were the famous writers, the *philosophes*, widely known and much lionized within the Republic of Letters. Writers of such distinction still needed a wider milieu within which to publicize their work and build their reputations, and most looked for the financial support of wealthy sponsors, notably those identified with the salons of the aristocracy (Lilti 2015: 109–32). But a much greater number of writers were obscure and lived on the margins of society in what was figuratively called "Grub Street." They eked out a living by writing for fly-by-night commercial ventures, newspapers, or the salacious literature of gossip and scandal (Darnton 1982: 17–40). Publishers and printers were professions that came into being to make communication of the works of these authors possible. Publishing became a significant commercial activity; the writings they published a commodity, and as such a form of intellectual property. Authors asserted their power by laying claim to owning ideas, launching the field of copyright law (Foucault: 1977: 124–5). Once censored for their own content, books were now inspected for plagiarizing that of others.

In the public realm so reconceived, new places of memory emerged to localize the identity of this emerging print culture of high literacy. Salons and coffee houses were their meeting places, books, and newspapers the objects of their conversations. These new institutions facilitated the interchange between writers and readers, a way of social life in which lively discussion extended the reach of literacy. As gathering places for social dialogue, they would animate the development of cultural memory during this era. The salon was the most famous among them. Educated women came to preside over these gatherings, inviting participants and setting the agenda for discussion. These agencies of the emerging public sphere permitted the entry of women into public life, denied them in other social and political settings. Their role marked a tentative first step in the acceptance of the principle that the feminine had a role in that arena (Melton 2001; 14–15, 205–11). The salons featured polite discussion of important writings among invited guests, nearly all of whom were well-born aristocrats or celebrated writers. They were well-known at the time and remembered since as settings for stimulating intellectual discussion, the performance of music, and the cultivation of the fine arts. According to historian Antoine Lilti, however, the salons were given to the cult of appearances based upon rituals of comportment and should not be regarded as completely aligned with the values of the Republic of Letters. They were satellite institutions of court society, still dominated by the well-born in the manners they prescribed. They were primarily places of worldliness and sociability, as much as venues for learned appreciation of literature and the arts (Lilti 2015: 27–9). The notion of the civilizing process as the elaboration of a refined code of manners found its fulfillment within these gatherings (Elias [1939] 1978: 3–7, 38–40, 46–50).

Coffee houses provided an alternative venue for the public sphere that appealed to the lesser ranks of society. They were originally derivative of social life in taverns and public houses, places notorious for boisterous revelry, and drunkenness conducive to forgetting. Coffee houses were instituted to satisfy the needs of a more sober clientele, and robust commerce in coffee prepared the way for this new site for reading and discussion. In contrast with alcohol, coffee acted as a mental stimulant, quickening thought and sparking lively conversation. One could read newspapers there, often aloud in the presence of agreeable companions. Conversation was often serious and less volatile than in the taverns. Emotions were kept under wraps. In principle open to anyone, they were in practice places for socializing among the educated middle class. Coffee houses spread rapidly in London and Paris from the mid-eighteenth century, and played a key role in expanding and democratizing the Republic of Letters (Melton 2001: 229–50).

The Masonic lodges also figured prominently in the cultivation of the Republic of Letters. They were egalitarian in principle, yet distinctive for their symbolic ties to an earlier age in their rituals and secrecy. Though they harked back to a laborite heritage in

FIGURE 3.3: Anicet Lemonnier, *A Reading of a Work by Voltaire at the Salon of Mme. Geoffron*, 1812. A place to be seen as well as heard. Courtesy of Getty Images, UK.

FIGURE 3.4: *London Coffee House, c. 1710*. A place for reading and lively conversation. Courtesy of Getty Images, UK.

the stonemasons of Scotland, there were no stonemasons and few workers among the membership. The lodges were meeting places for the middle rather than the working class. While not overtly political, they fostered discussion of progressive reform in the name of a civic humanism (Jacob 2006: 11–25; Chartier 1991: 161–8). Reading clubs and lending libraries also emerged, sponsored by commercial publishers, not yet municipal governments. One subscribed to them (Melton 2001: 106–8). Learned corresponding societies were credited with some importance on the eve of the French Revolution for building a sense of a common cause (Lefebvre [1939] 1946: 45–6).

It was out of such social settings that the force of public opinion became visible and began to exercise its influence in both social and political realms. Among its most important effects, public opinion gave birth to the idea of the celebrity as a social type. According to Lilti, the idea of celebrity transformed the notion of the memorable personality. Public recognition of celebrities as cultural icons turned attention from older notions of posthumous glory and undying fame toward figures of the moment who had become objects of public adulation. Celebrity was a kind of favor that was usually fleeting, dependent as it was upon fickle public opinion. Voltaire was likely the greatest celebrity of the century, Lilti remarks, and he took pains to promote it. Rousseau rivaled him in the attention accorded him by the reading public and complained about too much public attention. Admirers wanted to see such personalities in the flesh, and even to meet them personally. Statesmen also became celebrities within this milieu, as exemplified in such American notables as George Washington and Benjamin Franklin. Such were the circumstances in which celebrity brought into being the "fan" as a complementary social type (Lilti 2017: 43–9, 62–4, 87–102, 193–206).

By the 1780s, the Republic of Letters had developed a political style in the power of the publicity with which reform-minded writers proclaimed their viewpoints, a prelude to the revolution launched in France that would soon reshape the political institutions of Europe. The persistent and wide-ranging critique of the timeworn institutions of the old regime as obsolete, arbitrary, or tyrannical, waxed large in their writings, and exercised far-reaching influence upon the reading public. The court societies of kings and their retinues had no such agencies for publicizing their viewpoints or replying to their critics. As historian Daniel Mornet pointed out long ago, the old regime in France tottered and became vulnerable to revolt because no one any longer valued its institutions or believed in its role. The new public sphere was ready to discard its ways, and to consign them to oblivion. As an institutional apparatus about which no one any longer cared, that regime seemed unworthy of remembrance, and suggests why it crumbled so precipitously in France in 1789, and elsewhere in Europe following the campaigns of Napoleon at the turn of the nineteenth century (Mornet 1933: 469–77).

By the end of the eighteenth century, the public sphere was sufficiently developed in urban centers across western and central Europe to institute the commemoration of its writers and statesmen, in some measure displacing that of royalty and traditional festival days. The shift is closely associated with the commemorative rituals of the French Revolution. From its early days, its leaders invented festivals to honor its insurgencies (notably the storming of the Bastille) and to celebrate its civic values (such as the festival of Reason) (Aulard 1904: 52–6; Hunt 1984: 35–7, 62–5). Publicly-sponsored pantheons appeared in the late eighteenth century to house the mortal remains of the heroes of the Republic of Letters. In Paris, the church St. Geneviève was converted into a public mausoleum to honor the writers and statesmen of the Republic of Letters. Count Mirabeau, an orator in the early days of the Revolution, was the first to be interred there

FIGURE 3.5: *Installation of the Remains of Jean-Jacques Rousseau in the Pantheon, Paris, 1794*. The French Republic commemorates one of its most celebrated writers. Courtesy of Getty Images, UK.

(briefly); Voltaire shortly thereafter (J. Goodman: 2017). The erection of pantheons in other European centers soon followed (Bouwers 2012).

FROM COLLECTIVE TO CULTURAL MEMORY IN THE INTERPRETATION OF THE LAW

During the eighteenth century, interpreting the law moved from recourse to specific case precedents embedded in immemorial tradition (conceived as a historically developing unwritten constitution) to written constitutions that universalized its principles in an ahistorical way. The idea of a written constitution developed piecemeal over several centuries. Law, enshrined in memory conceived as a cultural depth, conceded some place to law reconceived in the covering wording of documents that guaranteed the rights of specific groups and so supplemented an unwritten constitutional heritage. England provides the most frequently cited example. Constitutional law was conceived as the "common sense" of a historical tradition whose principles for interpreting case law were disclosed in their reiteration over time (Pocock 1972: 237–8). The coming of print culture spurred the case for universalizing the law in foundational principles applicable in all times and places. The late eighteenth century was an age keen about setting them forth explicitly in comprehensive constitutional documents. Case precedent remained a resource for judicial interpretation, but jurists looked to the written constitution as their ultimate reference, its originating place of memory. For this reason, written constitutions became for posterity commemorative documents drafted by statesmen revered as "founding fathers" (Lepore 2010: 16–17, 120–5; Hutton 1988).

The demand for constitution-making across Europe in the late eighteenth century correlates roughly with the move from a manuscript into a print culture. In American jurisprudence, scholars have noted the short timespan that separates the writing of the Declaration of Independence as a manuscript from the American Constitution as a printed document, and helps us to understand what was at issue in the transition (Derrida 1984: 13–32). The Declaration of Independence, signed individually by delegates to the Continental Congress, dramatized personal affirmation in the making of a new sovereign nation. The Constitution, by contrast, was an anonymous presentation of principles that defined the processes through which government was authorized to proceed. Its amendment with a Bill of Rights enshrined those judged universal and inalienable (Warner 1990: 103–6). The problem was in disseminating the document as printed matter, and the printer played a key role in making its publication widely available, one analogous to the webmaster of our own times. Bringing a printer to Vermont in the mid-1770s, for example, was a major concern for framers of the Vermont Constitution of 1775 in establishing its identity as a sovereign republic (Hutton 1992: 279–80, 283).

Consider the making of the French Revolution. It was first and foremost a juridical revolution in the idea of law, through which rational principles came to claim primacy over historical precedent. The French Constitution of 1791 put a formal end to a body of law based on privilege that had been elaborated out of time immemorial. The principle of legal privilege was repudiated and condemned in the French National Assembly as early as August 1789 and the Declaration of the Rights of Man and Citizen published in December of that year set forth the moral principle of the equality of all citizens before the law (Lefebvre [1939] 1946: 145–56). Thus the constitution established a new touchstone against which legal precedents were thenceforth measured in case law, superseding the notion of the common law as the aggregation of historical experience. The American Constitution proved to be unusually stable, amended only marginally over time. Among conservatives, this conception of the durability of the constitution inspired reverence. The French Constitution, by contrast, was a casualty of the French revolutionary tradition, in which the constitution was rewritten several times as one regime replaced another over the course of the nineteenth and twentieth centuries (Kammen 1986: 35–9, 64–7).

CONCLUSION: SUMMING UP MEMORY ISSUES IN THE DEMOCRATIZATION OF PRINT CULTURE

From the vantage point of the cultural history of memory, the eighteenth century in Europe and the Americas marked a transition between a recessional of collective memory, conceived as living memory within a manuscript culture still organized around the practices of orality, and a processional of cultural memory, conceived as the encoding of memory in the mediated resources of the printed word. In the manuscript culture of the early modern era, printed texts might be likened to islands within a sea of collective memory. The text was an artifact that served as a mnemonic aid to collective memory, a prop to support accurate recall of well-established knowledge as a resource for oral presentation. Memory was understood to be a habit that reinforced retrieval of well-established teachings. The democratization of literacy through print culture, therefore, signaled a shift from memory as a means of preserving knowledge to memory as an instrument of intellectual inquiry into new fields of knowledge. The trend was tied to rapidly rising rates of literacy and consumption of reading matter. Literacy transformed the way humans remember, vastly expanding the resources that they could consult at will. Printed texts provided a ubiquitous and reliable network of knowledge on which readers and writers could rely. Books were places of cultural memory that readers and writers shared in common as participants in an imagined "Republic of Letters." The cultural memory contained in print constituted a new galaxy of communication that transformed human understanding of the world.

The coming of print culture with its new technologies of communication might be said to have complicated the ways of remembering. Significantly, it opened a divide between public and personal memory. To trace its history is to recognize the externalization of public memory in print media that promoted social and cultural exchange, and the internalization of personal memory as the living activity of soul-searching for the authentic sources of the self. Habits of reading, once dedicated to reinforcing habits of mind, became habits of inquiry, techniques for exploring worlds of knowledge that transformed the uses of cultural memory. The printed text, in its widening availability to expanding communities of writers and readers, not only permitted them to deepen their knowledge of the world at large but also to use texts as mirrors in which to discover the secrets of their own experience, or as vehicles with which to enter vicariously into the interior lives of others. It inspired the varieties of literary genre devoted to the experience of private life—autobiography, memoir, letters, and the novel.

This transition in the technologies of communication has deepened our awareness today of the way in which the uses of memory have a history, for these have evolved significantly over time. In this dynamic process, the eighteenth century marked a revolution in the uses of memory in the transformation of Western culture through print technologies. It is one about which we have become more aware as we seek to understand the cultural implications of the revolution in electronic communication in our own times.

CHAPTER FOUR

Knowledge: Science and Education

TOM SIMONE

The fortunes of Shakespeare's reputation went through dramatic shifts during the eighteenth century. The question of his reputation involves a great range of cultural complexity from popular performances and printed texts to economic enterprise and commemoration that all helped raise the image and memory of Shakespeare to unique heights. While plays and play texts were generally considered popular ephemera in his era, the vitality of theatrical performance continued after the ban on public drama beginning with the Civil Wars of the 1640s and lasting through the era of the Commonwealth until 1660. Shakespeare was one among a group of notable playwrights from the past whose memory was celebrated in the late eighteenth century. However, the plays of the collaborative playwrights Francis Beaumont and John Fletcher as well as those of Ben Jonson were more frequently performed than his works. But by 1800, Shakespeare had come to be seen as the great national writer, the major author in the English language, and the public icon of cultural genius. The complex process of the development of Shakespeare's reputation shows the growth of his status and serves as a unique example of cultural memory as process rather than fixed concept. What is popularly assumed as the undeniable cultural centrality of Shakespeare was not the case in 1700. The eighteenth century was the period where Shakespeare was elevated to incomparable renown in the major areas of public memory.

Four major elements out of many contributed most directly to the transformation of Shakespeare's reputation in the eighteenth century: rise in popular performances of various kinds attributed to Shakespeare, the promotion of new editions with both popular and scholarly treatment, public monuments and celebrations of Shakespeare, and the expansion of Shakespeare's influence abroad, especially in France and Germany. Using the long eighteenth century, we can consider these four major aspects of Shakespeare's reputation as they evolved and made him a dominant national icon by the time of the rise of Romanticism in the early nineteenth century.

PERFORMANCE AS ENTERTAINMENT AND PROFIT

After the period of closed theaters (1642–60) under Oliver Cromwell, new theatrical styles and spaces emerged in Restoration theater along with the rise of Augustan taste in morality, manners, and aesthetics influenced by French neo-classicism. While Shakespeare was known and often performed, his plays were famously subject to major revisions, adapting them to the artistic conventions and expectations of the late 1600s and early 1700s. According to one couplet in Dryden's 1667 version of *The Rival Ladies*:

> That which the World called Wit in Shakespeare's age,
> Is laught at as improper for our stage.
>
> —Dryden, 1668

John Dryden, the poet laureate of Britain, praised Shakespeare's range and natural talent while criticizing his linguistic and plot elements that seemed outdated to Restoration taste. He also noted that during the years near the end of the seventeenth century two plays of Beaumont and Fletcher were performed for every one of Shakespeare's. Yet, Dryden claimed a richness of imagination and natural talent in Shakespeare that overcame the rougher parts of language and action in the plays.

The closing of the theaters in Cromwell's era was overturned with the Restoration of Charles II in 1660, and new concepts of decorum and taste emerged largely influenced by standards of current French classical style and the appeal of new elaborate scenic spectacle. Shakespeare was an older author among many from the Elizabethan and Jacobean period. Shakespeare's godson (and possibly his illegitimate son) William Davenant (1606–68) championed the plays in revised form, often in his own versions, like *The Tempest, or the Enchanted Isle* (1667) adapted with Dryden. This version was a much-embellished play with multiple additional characters, love plots, and new musical numbers, and this iteration held the stage for almost 200 years. Davenant was instrumental in theatrical activity before and during the Restoration, tutoring Thomas Betterton, the most famous English actor of the late seventeenth century, and reputedly starting the practice of including actresses in dramatic performance. In his public theatrical presentations after the Restoration, Davenant also instituted the new proscenium stage and painted back drops with often spectacular visual effects. Davenant may have influenced his collaborator Dryden, who praised the place of "Nature" in Shakespeare's work.

> To begin then with *Shakespeare*; he was the man who of all Modern, and perhaps Ancient Poets, had the largest and most comprehensive soul. All the Images of Nature were still present to him, and he drew them not laboriously, but luckily: when he describes any thing, you more than see it, you feel it too.
>
> —Dryden 1668: 87

This period is notable for the freedom and extent of dramatic adaptation of earlier plays and especially the plays of Shakespeare. The most famous and infamous adaptation was Nahum Tate's radical rewriting of *King Lear* (1681), eliminating the Fool, arranging Lear's survival, and creating a romantic conclusion with the marriage of Cordelia and Edgar. While the date falls before the eighteenth century, Tate's version held the stage throughout the eighteenth century. There were debates over Tate's treatment from the disdain of Joseph Addison to the approval of Samuel Johnson, who objected to the harshness of Shakespeare's original. However, the reshaping and rewording of Shakespeare's plays was extensive, both on stage and in print in almost all cases. There were a great many adaptations of the plays throughout the eighteenth century and far into the nineteenth, while musical adaptations, influenced by the rise of opera in France, were popular. Purcell's *The Fairy Queen* (1692), derived from *A Midsummer Night's Dream*, was not only popular in its day but has survived as a significant Shakespeare adaptation into the twenty-first century.

The appeal of Shakespeare as a dramatist of "nature" was praised by Dryden and others, even though the language and many aspects of the plots conflicted with a Restoration aspiration to refinement and homage to the French dramatic unities. The criticism of Shakespeare's language and plots was most strongly presented by Thomas Rymer in his *Short View of Tragedy* of 1693. A devotee of French neo-classicism, Rymer devotes a detailed chapter on his rejection of the language and action of *Othello*. His criticism of Shakespeare and *Othello* represents a notable rejection: "the tragical part is, plainly none other, than a Bloody Farce, without salt or savour" (1696: 146).

A survey of performances of Shakespeare's plays in the early eighteenth century shows moderate popularity in the early years and a great preponderance of adaptation and rewriting for the public taste of the day, which favored both spectacle and decorum. Shakespeare maintained importance in the early eighteenth century, but his language and poetry and the boldness of his plots and their variety met with a great deal of resistance. However, the rise of Shakespeare's reputation was in many ways the product of some of the most popular actors of the day, especially David Garrick. While performing Nahum Tate's version of *King Lear* and other altered plays including *Hamlet* without the gravedigger scene, Garrick and others became champions of the icon of Shakespeare in performance and celebration. With popular appeal and the advocacy of various groups, such as the Shakespeare Ladies Club during the 1730s, the number of performances grew significantly by mid-century. At times the two major London theaters, Covent Garden and Drury Lane, put on productions of the same play simultaneously. By 1750 Shakespeare's popularity had risen dramatically in performance.

TEXT AND HISTORY

The collective memory of Shakespeare developed through two major traditions over the course of the eighteenth century, one based on printed texts of his dramas, the other upon their theatrical performance. The treatment of the texts, as exemplified in a succession of critical editions, sought to reconstruct as accurately as possible the original dramatic documents of Shakespeare's plays. The effect was to historicize the author and his plays in an effort to establish the collective memory of both. Editors of his work in this tradition sought to establish critical distance between past and present and made of the bard and his dramas cultural artifacts of their time in history. The process of dramatic performance, by contrast, was dynamic in the effort of actors to adapt theatrical performance of Shakespeare's plays to the sensibility of the ever-moving present age. The actor David Garrick, who merged the persona of Shakespeare with his own, intensified the plays and the author in the popular culture of the eighteenth century. The effect was to celebrate Shakespeare as a living tradition that lifted past into present. This was a tradition that was continually evolving

The history of Shakespeare's text in the eighteenth century traces the growth of Shakespeare's reputation and status through publication and the development of textual scholarship and commentary from naïve adaptation to systematic study. While popular performance produced an expanding appreciation and elevation of Shakespeare, the major editions were monuments of the ever-expanding configuration of Shakespeare in cultural memory. The effect of much of the emphasis of this editorial tradition was to elevate the text and classical status over popular performance. The concept of Shakespeare is deeply embedded in the history and practice of published texts. While performance traditions brought popular immediacy, the steady growth of serious attention to text and specific historical and linguistic meaning provided a scholarly and cultural elevation of Shakespeare as author and literary icon. The scattered publication of individual plays and the Fourth Folio in the latter seventeenth century left a chaotic and unreliable presentation of Shakespeare's texts. Out of more than fifty individual published play texts from 1660 to 1700, all but ten were substantial adaptations, and only thirteen even had Shakespeare's name on them (Dugas: 85–6). The Fourth Folio of 1685, with its seven extra plays, was the last of the supposedly correct collected play texts of early eighteenth-century literary tradition, but it was part of a tradition of ad hoc editing and "improving" of earlier editions. The tradition of improving the texts in terms of Restoration conceptions of taste, language, decorum, and meaning continued throughout the period.

Shakespeare's early status was shown as particularly important seven years after his death with the publication of the First Folio (1623) in which his plays were given the status of "literature" by the very size and format of the folio arrangement. The large folio was organized by his fellow actors John Heminges and Henry Condell. In addition to the literary status of the folio, the actors, together with the publisher Isaac Jaggard, were able to publish eighteen plays that had never before appeared in print. Works like *Macbeth*, *The Tempest*, *Antony and Cleopatra*, and *Twelfth Night* would probably never have been known without the monumental achievement of the folio. This collection followed Ben Jonson's 1616 folio, with poems and masques, as well as eight plays. Both folios were deluxe editions, even when their production was uneven, and claimed a status as literature and not just records of popular play texts. In 1602, the new Bodleian Library in Oxford explicitly excluded these plays as inappropriate for its collection, although an exception was made later for the 1623 First Folio. Three later Shakespeare folios appeared in 1632, 1663, and 1685, the last two supplemented with seven extra plays supposedly by Shakespeare. Various inexpensive single play quartos also appeared over the years. In the late seventeenth and early eighteenth century, publishers considered later but more corrupt editions as more authoritative than the earliest ones, both for libraries and for further editions in the eighteenth century.

The publisher John Tonson bought the rights to the Fourth Folio (1685), and he was among those seeking clearer copyright law, as well as production, sale, and profit from new editions. Thus, both the questions of the contemporary views on language and thought and the expanding business of the book trade were determining factors in the idea of Shakespeare (Dugas 2006: 121). The publication of new editions reflected growing interest in Shakespeare as well as the beginnings of concepts of textual editing and scholarship. In both the performance and evolution of serious published texts, Shakespeare's importance continued to grow in significant ways.

The notable increase in literacy and readership in the eighteenth century provided a critical arena for the growth of Shakespeare's reputation and evolution into a national icon. The critical treatment of Shakespeare's texts was integral to eighteenth-century intellectual and cultural development, and these endeavors were central to initiating what Marcus Walsh characterizes as "the beginnings of interpretive scholarship" (Walsh 1997: 201). An important precedent for the new attention to textual and interpretive commentary on Shakespeare was the beginning of annotation of English literary texts, probably first used for Milton's *Paradise Lost* by Patrick Hume in 1695. Because of Milton's quasi-scriptural topic and narration, the poem was given a theoretical and theological importance that merited interpretive commentary. According to Walsh, Hume's annotations are considered "the first systematic and scholarly commentaries on the text of a modern vernacular author" (1997: 3). He cites René Wellek and John Shawcross as modern critics expressing that view. Of course, this is in the English tradition. Extensive commentaries on Dante, by contrast, began in Italy the year after his death in 1322.

Hume's annotations appeared in the sixth edition of *Paradise Lost* published by John Tonson in 1695. John Tonson and his nephew Jacob Tonson, Jr. were instrumental in the increase of editions and commentary on English language literature. The Tonsons initiated a major change in the nature of Shakespeare's texts when they pursued a series of new multi-volume editions of the plays starting in 1709 and continuing until 1787, when the firm closed. At the outset, they employed the playwright Nicholas Rowe to prepare a new text of the plays. Published in 1709 in six volumes in octavo format, it is considered to be the first modern edition. Much smaller than the folio format, each octavo volume contained four or five plays, most prefaced with an engraved image of a scene from the play. The octavo format was far more portable and convenient than the cumbersome earlier folios. The increase in an educated public in England interested in reading Shakespeare made such a new edition both a popular and a commercial success. Rowe also introduced the first volume with a particularly influential preface: "Some Account of the Life of Mr. William Shakespear." The combination of an interest in the life and work of Shakespeare grew in significant ways throughout the eighteenth century.

In the development of concepts about the importance of Shakespeare's work, most new collected editions reprinted the introductions of earlier notable editions. Consequently, Rowe's narrative and evaluative version of Shakespeare the man was reprinted throughout the century in most of the collected editions that followed. Rowe's biographical sketch, for all its anecdotal material and inaccuracies, remained the best known version of Shakespeare's life until the appearance of the much more factual version by Edmond Malone, published posthumously in 1821. However, Rowe's was the first attempt to give a sketch of Shakespeare's life along with an appreciation and evaluation of his plays (Schoenbaum 1993: 89). The preface included a stylized image of Shakespeare, modernizing but extending the iconic representation of Shakespeare that was initiated by the Droeshout portrait on the title page of the First Folio. This anecdotal biography helped to present the image and narrative of Shakespeare as a dramatic and historical figure himself. Informed by rumors from Stratford-upon-Avon garnered by the actor Thomas Betterton, Rowe first promoted the anecdote that a young William Shakespeare was caught poaching deer at Charlecote estate and was charged before the first Sir Thomas Lucy, the local magistrate. No historical basis for this story has been found, but the poaching episode became a permanent part of the Shakespeare legend. Rowe refers to Ben Jonson's somewhat critical comments on Shakespeare as well as Thomas Rymer's strongly negative views from 1696. But he adds appreciation from Dryden as well as his own favorable views of many of the plays. However, as Edward Capell noted in 1768, Rowe drew exclusively on the compromised Fourth Folio of 1685 for his text.

Nicholas Rowe is considered the first editor of Shakespeare in his modernizing of spelling and punctuation. He used his practical theatrical experience to introduce relatively consistent division of the plays into acts and scenes with marked character entrances and exits and added a list of characters to each play. In the biographical sketch, illustrations, dramatic articulation, and book format, the Rowe/Tonson version brought a new appeal and context for Shakespeare, his biography, and the plays. The Rowe edition of 1709 began a series of eleven major multi-volume editions of Shakespeare in England in the eighteenth century with an influential and expanding audience of sophisticated readers and the evolution of the apparatus of commentary and then textual scholarship (de Grazia 1991: xii). The prestige and profit that Tonson sought apparently met with success as a second Rowe edition followed in 1714 with further versions appearing in the next few years. Readership and Shakespeare's notable achievement began to expand in importance throughout the rest of the century. The growth in editions and the emergence

FIGURE 4.1: Nicholas Rowe, *Portrait of Shakespeare*, 1709. Courtesy of the Folger Library.

of critical commentary paralleled and contributed to the increase in performances in the 1730s and consequently to Shakespeare's fame.

The new eighteenth century multi-volume editions included introductions mixing appreciation and critical responses to the whole range of the plays. And critical as well as interpretive comment grew rapidly. Editions by Alexander Pope in 1725 and Samuel Johnson in 1765 brought two of the major writers of the century into extensive engagement with Shakespeare. Pope introduced many personally drafted revisions to the plays, singled out notable passages, and deleted lines he judged were by other hands. Johnson brought an imposing literary and linguistic awareness to bear on Shakespeare and the plays. As the author of the famous *Dictionary of the English Language* of 1755, Johnson held pre-eminence in matters of language and correctness. In the influential Preface to his 1765 edition, Samuel Johnson confirmed Shakespeare's now elevated status in elegant and measured terms:

> The Poet, of whose works I have undertaken the revision, may now begin to assume the dignity of an ancient, and claim the privilege of established fame and prescriptive veneration. He has long outlived his century, the term commonly fixed as the test of literary merit.
>
> —Johnson 1765. 1.5

Johnson's estimation that Shakespeare had now attained "the dignity of an ancient" marks the culmination of the critical process of elevating his plays to the status of classic literature. Johnson, who stood as the most imposing literary figure in England in the middle of the eighteenth century, added gravity and esteem to Shakespeare that has maintained a solidity from his era to ours. Johnson's critical appreciation particularly appealed to the growing sophisticated readership of the eighteenth century. His Preface is still considered a major contribution to the history of literary criticism in English. Even with his reservations about the paucity of a desired clear morality and the problem of linguistic challenges, Johnson's verdict is both a testimonial and a confirmation of Shakespeare's new place in cultural memory.

Yet Johnson's literary judgment still rested on the suspect text of the Fourth Folio. His articulation of the enduring appeal of Shakespeare is irreproachable, but there were other currents stirring that were to go beyond his eminence. In terms of scholarship and textual exploration the work of Edward Capell in his edition of 1767–8 and then Edmond Malone in his influential edition of 1790 moved the study of Shakespeare into a new understanding of history, language, and culture. Other editions of note include versions edited by Lewis Theobald (1733) and George Steevens (1773). All but one of these versions of Shakespeare's collected plays were published by the Tonson firm until it closed in 1787. Tonson ran a highly regarded publishing house that promoted significant editions of major authors in England's high literary tradition. His early purchasing of the rights to Milton's *Paradise Lost* in 1688 led to popular success and esteem as well as raising awareness of Milton's poem and status through Hume's annotated edition.

Shakespeare was not the only figure of English literature undergoing a rise in status through increasingly scholarly treatment and publication. Chaucer editions by Urry (1722) and Tyrwhitt (1776, 1778), Spenser versions by Upton (1758), Hughes (1715, 1758), and Church (1758), and new editions of Milton by Bentley (1732) are a sample of the scholarly treatment of earlier authors now being viewed as classics (de Gratzia 1991: 195). While the attention to Shakespeare took on unusual breadth with performance and the many forms of publication reinforcing each other, the Tonson publishing firm was influential with its emphasis on scholarly treatment of earlier writers as part of both increased literacy and the development of an historical attitude toward English literary past. The nearly exclusive world of classical learning in the universities was challenged by a broader world of English literature in the publication world of editors and public readers. English literary scholarship emerged in the eighteenth century from outside the strict bounds of the universities and was directed to the increasing reading public.

The evolution of textual editing of Shakespeare in the eighteenth century involves many complexities as well as contested approaches. The interest in providing convincing versions of Shakespeare's plays in the 1720s and 1730s resulted in both sanitizing complex texts through adaptation and the application of modern style, as in Alexander Pope's edition of 1725, and in collections of famous, exemplary passages from the plays. Four editions can serve to outline the shifts and complexities in this creation of scholarly and interpretive editing. Since the universities maintained adherence to classical languages and methods, the major editors were writers and independent scholars who came in large part from legal and literary backgrounds and had the economic means to support their detailed work. And these editions succeeded in economic terms through their popularity with the literate and relatively prosperous reading public. And it is worth noting that Shakespeare's appeal to women gave rise to women's advocacy groups and to a number of influential women who published criticism and interpretation of Shakespeare.

Rowe's 1709 edition was important for its new, more portable format of octavo volumes, the biographical preface, and the regularization, attention to dramatic cues, and a popular imaging of the plays in the engravings prefacing the plays. All of these elements appealed to the reading public. In textual matters, Rowe, a popular playwright himself, offered a straightforward text with no comment or documentation of how he arrived at this text. In general, he drew on the Fourth Folio of 1685 and shaped texts to make general sense and simple presentation. This six-volume edition mediated between the large earlier folios and the popular single play issues. The publishing format was significantly influential, for all the later serious, if expensive, editions of the century appeared in multi-volume versions.

As the textual treatment of Shakespeare became more serious, editors began the process of annotating the plays, questions arose about what the text said in specific difficult passages and how the quality of the work was being evaluated. While Pope's edition of 1725 was a fine poet's retouching with important corrections to many garbled prose and poetry passages in the folios, his general use of the text was based on late, questionable texts. Lewis Theobald published a critique of Pope's edition in 1727 and a collected works edition in 1733 correcting many of Pope's textual errors and adding many annotations for interpretation and clarification of difficult passages. However, his critique of Pope's edition placed him under the satirical pen of the poet, who portrayed Theobald as the mocked hero "Tibbald," the king of dunces, in the early version of *The Dunciad*. While he substituted Colley Cibber for Theobald in the final version of the poem, Pope continued to satirize Theobald's critical apparatus and approach. Pope's antagonism undermined his reputation and influenced a number of later editors, including Johnson, to discount Theobald's better knowledge of the literal text (Deelman 1964: 27–8).

The emergence of a modern approach to textual editing and commentary began with the detailed work of Edward Capell published in 1767–8 and attained it fullest early expression in the edition of Edmond Malone in 1790. The editions of Theobald and Johnson extended the process of annotating and commenting on the text, a sign of the new classic status of Shakespeare in England. But the question of how to approach the text and what were the strongest documents for the foundation of text and meaning took on new detailed and historical attention with Capell. Malone followed later with even more extensive discovery and use of documentary material. A significant evolution in the approach to Shakespeare was the development of these textual and documentary studies and the establishing of an historical awareness of the differences of language, dramatic procedures, and cultural circumstances between Shakespeare's lifetime and the eighteenth century. Where Rowe and Pope tried to accommodate Shakespeare's text to early eighteenth-century values of the cultural and linguistic excellence of their time, Capell and Malone saw a clear and marked difference between the era of Shakespeare's career and their own. This sense of historical difference and specificity affected the study of textual editing and initiated inquiry into the documentary evidence of Shakespeare's historical time.

Capell began work on a Shakespeare edition in 1749 but also worked in parallel on *Prolusions* (1760), a volume of Elizabethan texts in which he presented his assertion that only the earliest editions could be primary textual sources. He also prepared in manuscript a critical text of *Paradise Lost*, which was not published, based on close textual study of the earliest editions of the poem (Walsh 1997: 177). With this background in earlier texts Capell worked for nearly seventeen years on his edition of Shakespeare that appeared in 1767–8. This edition was a radical rethinking of the nature of Shakespeare's text based on the earliest printings of the plays.

Capell published his ten-volume edition with Tonson in 1767–8. He prefaced the edition with a lengthy discussion of the nature, characteristics, and limitations of the earlier eighteenth century versions that preceded his work, but in his arrangement of the plays he presented a straight text with only the briefest of notes to clarify individual words. The text itself was based on close adherence to the evidence of the First Folio and the earliest quarto printings at his disposal, drawn from his extensive library, although the choice among variants was still based upon his editorial decisions. Capell's version was the most careful and accurate to appear by that time. However, the strength of his research and textual editing was withheld until the publication of his *Notes and Various Readings to Shakespeare* in three volumes over a decade later in 1779. As Marcus Walsh concludes:

> In terms of the evolution of Shakespearean editing in the eighteenth century, Capell's textual openness and thoroughness, his return to the first printed texts, and his consistently critical method, amounted to a revolution.
>
> —Walsh 1997: 182

However, both his critique of earlier editions and the delay of the presentation of the evidence for his text left Capell open to personal criticism and relative neglect. Nonetheless, his work was in significant ways the beginning of modern textual scholarship.

In terms of overt influence and recognition, Edmond Malone extended Capell's "revolution" in textual scholarship and established even more strictly the concept of documentary and factual evidence. In many ways, the earlier editors of Shakespeare relied on taste and personal discrimination in their establishment of text and context. Even Johnson, for all his literary and linguistic status, saw no differences among the four folios and paid little attention to the quartos. Thus, accretions of error and editorial change were accepted as part of the textual tradition. Malone, who had been in the law before his editorial career, had the intention of stripping away the personal judgments and changes within the tradition by editors and printers. As Margareta de Grazia describes Malone's work:

> We can see here how the emphasis on authenticity exempted Shakespeare's text from the warring judgements of earlier editors and positioned it in a new realm in which information pre-empted evaluation, factual scholarship phased out literary judgment.
>
> —de Grazia 1991: 70

In his ten-volume 1790 edition, Malone presented the edited text, commentary, theatrical history, and documentary evidence. One key element was his thorough critique of Rowe's widely reprinted version of Shakespeare's life, refuting virtually every so-called event that had become popular lore. He continued to work on a second edition, including a new documentary life of Shakespeare as well as an extension of his history of English theater. Malone died before completion of the second edition, but his work was completed by his collaborator, James Boswell, Jr. The second edition of 1821 can be considered an extension of the first edition, and it added the printing of as many original documents related to Shakespeare as Malone could amass.

MONUMENTS, ICONS, AND PUBLIC CELEBRATION OF SHAKESPEARE

Through its prominence the large Droeshout engraving on the title page of the First Folio presented an icon of Shakespeare that began the extensive process of imaging Shakespeare as author and authority. Both the second and third folios also used the worn plate of the Droeshout portrait on their title pages, and the image has been copied and imitated innumerable times. A stodgy funerary monument to Shakespeare had previously been installed over his grave in Trinity Church in Stratford, which Leonard Digges notes as subject to the ravages of time in his brief poetic tribute in front matter of the First Folio. Both images have elements that present ambiguous versions of what Shakespeare might have looked like. Neither is a portrait from life, and each one betrays a lack of originality. The folio portrait is best known, but while it has an iconic pervasiveness, the image has been questioned for its quality and source. However, many have interpreted Ben Jonson's short poem facing the title page of the folio as confirming resemblance to Shakespeare, writing that the artist has "hit his face." Droeshout might have been using an earlier portrait that has disappeared, but there is no certain evidence of that. The Stratford funeral monument seems to portray a rather prosperous merchant. The history of Shakespeare's appearance largely can be seen as adapting the Droeshout image to both popular and artistic expectation.

The inclusion of engraved portraits of Shakespeare became common in most eighteenth-century editions, as can be seen in the image from the Rowe edition above. Margareta de Grazia includes ten different versions of Shakespeare's portrait for different editions in her work on the development of textual editing in the period (de Grazia 1991: 116–17). The popularizing of Shakespeare's image is linked in this way to the growth of publication of books, newspapers, and magazines, and the expanding use of engraved or etched images in printing throughout the eighteenth century. The spread of print images of Shakespeare is paralleled and extended by plate images representing scenes from the plays in Rowe's 1709 edition.

The image of Shakespeare was to some degree shaped by politics. In the eighteenth century, various political struggles over the monarchy and the role of parliament stirred debates over English national identity, in the aftermath of the Civil War and even the "Glorious Revolution" of 1688. While Robert Walpole as a Whig held the greatest political position in the 1720s, a number of forces agitated for greater emphasis on traditional national representatives. A loose group of cultural and political organizations, sometimes called the Patriots, stood in opposition to Walpole's influence and turned to the past achievements of England as symbols (Dobson 1992: 138).

The elaborate gardens and buildings at Stowe, Buckinghamshire, under the ownership and political opposition to Walpole of Richard Temple, Viscount Cobham, became an arena for commemorating the English past. In a building on the Stowe estate called the Temple of Worthies, completed in 1735, sixteen busts of notable figures of the English past were kept on display. The building honored both figures of action and of culture. Busts, sculpted by Dutch artists, portrayed political figures including Elizabeth I, Raleigh, Drake, and others. Among the cultural figures enshrined in the Temple were Milton, Shakespeare, Inigo Jones, and the contemporary Alexander Pope (Dobson 1992: 135–6).

Shakespeare as national icon, however, was receiving growing public attention. The Temple of Worthies, while localized, concentrated public energies that led to a Shakespeare monument in the uniquely public and historical arena of Westminster Abbey. One of the main challengers to Walpole, Richard Boyle, Earl of Burlington, commissioned the Dutch sculptor Peter Scheemakers, one of the artists of the Temple of Worthies, to create a statue of Shakespeare for Poet's Corner in Westminster Abbey. His effort was supported by a group of major political and literary figures, including Pope. The statue and its setting were planned by the garden designer William Kent and sculpted by Scheemakers (Dobson

1992: 138). A major element in the project was the Shakespeare Ladies Club, which campaigned vigorously for more performances of the plays in the late 1730s. They persuaded John Rich, the manager of Covent Garden theater, to put on a benefit performance of *Julius Caesar* on April 28, 1738. According to the *London Daily Post*, the performance and donations raised £200 for the project. The sculpture was executed and installed in the Abbey on January 29, 1741 (Deelman 1964: 33). While Poets' Corner had many figures at the time, the memorial to Shakespeare became the largest, most recognized, and, arguably, the most influential cultural image in the Abbey and eventually in the country. The figure of Shakespeare stands five feet, six inches high, leaning in a pensive mood on a pedestal with books. The statue rests on a five-foot platform and is framed by recessed pillars and an imposing cornice above with images of Elizabeth I, Henry V, and Richard III carved below.

The Shakespeare memorial in Westminster Abbey was widely reproduced in published printed images and in physical facsimiles and imitations that were used in a variety of later dramatic presentations. Its location and imposing size were notable in its day, and the memorial continues to preside over all others for visitors to the Abbey from around the

FIGURE 4.2: Shakespeare Memorial in Westminster Abbey, engraved for the *London Magazine*, 1751. Courtesy of the Folger Library.

world. There were few visitors to Stratford-upon-Avon in the early eighteenth century, and the expansive gardens and temples at Stowe would have drawn mainly privileged viewers, but the memorial in Westminster Abbey could not have been in a more significant place, where monarchs are crowned and buried. The tradition of commemorative statues of Shakespeare has its origin in the Abbey memorial.

All of these efforts to enshrine Shakespeare in stable commemorative imagery complemented the dynamics of the theatrical performance of his plays. The influence of these images parallels the growth of theatrical popularity of the plays and the rise of the star actor, most notably David Garrick. While Thomas Betterton set the mode at the turn of the century, Charles Macklin, Spranger Barry, and David Garrick gained fame for their acting in the middle of the century. The two most central theaters were Covent Garden and Drury Lane, still in contemporary form and times just blocks from each other in central London. And there are numerous accounts of the presentation of the same Shakespeare plays at the same time in both theaters. David Garrick was the most famous and central actor of his time. He is described as preforming in a detailed and newly natural style. He set his mobility of voice and gesture against the more stately and rhetorical style of earlier times, and he was praised for his convincing performances of both tragic and comic roles. He was renowned for his portrayals of Benedick in *Much Ado about Nothing*, Richard III, Hamlet, and King Lear. While his repertory was notably broad, he came to be identified with his portrayals and championing of Shakespeare and

FIGURE 4.3: *David Garrick as Richard III*, engraving by William Hogarth and C. Grignion, from the painting by Hogarth, 1746. Courtesy of the Metropolitan Museum of Art, New York.

his plays. Samuel Johnson, with all his measured comments, characterized Garrick as a uniquely convincing actor:

> He was then only actor I ever saw whom I would call a master both in tragedy and comedy; though I liked him best in comedy. A true conception of character, and natural expression of it, were his distinguishing excellences.
>
> —Deelman 1964: 91

Garrick developed a strong personal identification with Shakespeare in his acting and in his public persona. In addition to the great popularity of his performances, he had a temple to Shakespeare erected at his home Hampton. He collected a statue, paintings, and artifacts associated with Shakespeare, and he often entertained guests in this sanctuary. The extension of Garrick's identification with Shakespeare and Shakespearean roles led to perhaps the grandest and most contradictory elevation of Shakespeare in the eighteenth century, Garrick's "Shakespeare's Jubilee" in Stratford-upon-Avon in early September 1769.

Stratford, the birthplace of Shakespeare, was a small market town in Warwickshire about 100 miles northwest of London. While it retained a distinctly provincial appearance, the growing interest in Shakespeare brought occasional visitors, who increased in numbers in the eighteenth century. One telling, if puzzling, anecdote concerns the cantankerous Reverend Gastrel, who had bought the remodeled house New Place, Shakespeare's impressive final home in Stratford. Shakespeare supposedly planted a mulberry tree in the yard that became an object of pilgrimage and veneration. Gastrel became ever more irritated by numerous visitors calling at his house asking to see the mulberry tree. In a fit of pique, Gastrel had the tree cut down in 1753, which caused much public protest. In 1759, the tradesman Thomas Sharp bought the wood from the tree and began making Shakespearean mementos out of it. Later, while living outside Stratford, Gastrel was angered by the town window tax on New Place, and out of even greater resentment he had the building destroyed (Deelman 1964: 46–8).

When the town decided to build a new town hall, the council proposed granting the famous Garrick the "freedom of Stratford" and suggested it would welcome as gifts images of him and Shakespeare. The connection of Stratford to Garrick and the growing fame of Shakespeare led through innumerable complexities to the three-day Shakespeare Jubilee of 1769. Garrick entered into serious planning for it in the spring of that year. He was part owner and major actor of Drury Lane Theatre, and his performances and personal identification with Shakespeare were unequalled. However, even with his adoration of Shakespeare, in theatrical reality Garrick played mainly in heavily adapted versions of the plays. He played more of the folio text of *Macbeth* than had been the tradition, but he cut nearly 300 lines and added his own final speech for the dying character. He was famous for his King Lear and the character's pathos in the storm, but he retained Tate's adaptation and saved Lear in the end. And yet his championing of Shakespeare as master playwright continued throughout his career, and many ascribed the increased reputation of Shakespeare to Garrick's sustained success and effort (Deelman 1964: 91–2). To represent his identification with Shakespeare, Garrick negotiated with Gainsborough for a portrait that juxtaposed his own image with that of Shakespeare.

Although planning was just beginning in spring of 1769, Garrick sent announcements of the Jubilee to London papers on May 9. The publicity campaign started early and continued unabated through the spring and summer months. While the jubilee in theory was to celebrate the 200th anniversary of Shakespeare's birth in 1564, the event only took shape five years later. Garrick's fame and the expanding national status of Shakespeare combined to create a media event of unprecedented proportion and energy. The density of commentary and published letters in the press leading up to the Jubilee both for and against Garrick's celebration shows the complexities of a cultural process of commemoration that was unique at the time and seldom equaled since. Newspaper articles, together with much correspondence and a great range of personal letters and documents, show the intense involvement of public attention and national definition focused on the Jubilee.

The Jubilee was planned as an extensive celebration of Shakespeare in Stratford that drew on Garrick's fame and the expanded role of Shakespeare in British culture beyond being an author of plays. The event was to be three days long with an elaborate plan of activities. A large wood rotunda called the Amphitheatre, with a capacity of 1,000 people, was erected near the Avon for many central events from meals to the major delivery of Garrick's *Ode to Shakespeare*, as well as dancing, concerts, and an elaborate masquerade. While the outside of the building was plain, wooden columns and extensive painting in the building gave an impression of elegance (Stochholm 1964: 23–4).

With all the publicity and novelty of the Jubilee, travel to Stratford and logistics of lodging and food presented great challenges. The overall cost was also steep, so that members of the upper middle class and an impressive range of the aristocracy made up most of the attendees. Estimates place the number of visitors at nearly 2,000, almost the equal of the population of Stratford. While the townspeople had the chance for notable financial gain, the contrast between prosperous visitors and ordinary residents caused conflicts on both sides. The influx of so many people and the events put great pressure on Stratford and the surrounding towns to accommodate them.

The first day opened on Wednesday, September 6 at 6 a.m. with the firing of seventeen cannons plus mortars, followed by breakfast and the mid-day presentation of Thomas Arne's oratorio *Judith* in the church. After dinner, a musical concert was followed by a ball. The second day brought both the height of the Jubilee in Garrick's *Ode* and the ominous onset of rain that continued through the third day, which caused both inconvenience and major disruption of elaborately planned spectacles. The projected fireworks at the end of the second and third days were cancelled because of the rain. Perhaps the biggest disappointment was the cancellation of the widely publicized procession through Stratford of Shakespearean characters grouped by play. The costumes provided by the Drury Lane Theatre would have been ruined by the rain, and Garrick would have had to reimburse large sums to the theater for the damage (Deelman 1964: 239). The idea of the procession, though, was resurrected theatrically in London after the Jubilee.

The central and most successful event of the Jubilee was Garrick's *Ode*. At noon on Thursday, September 7, an audience of more than 1,000 gathered in the Amphitheatre for Garrick's central event. Many had expected him to appear in Elizabethan costume, but he wore his formal steward's velvet suit with gilt waistcoat, carrying a staff and wearing his special mulberry Shakespeare medallion on a ribbon around his neck. Similar commemorative finery was worn by most of the crowd, but Garrick's had extra size and touches. Surrounded by the musicians and singers, Garrick stood in front of the iconic statue of Shakespeare patterned on the Westminster memorial (Deelman 1964: 232–3).

The *Ode*, like most of the speeches, had been printed before the Jubilee and was the product of Garrick's major efforts for the great presentation. He had written a number of plays and many prologues and epilogues for performance, but he was not a poet of unusual talent. He was, however, a master of dramatic presentation and knew how to stir a crowd. One particular novelty of the *Ode* was the combination of music and Garrick's declamation. The music was written and arranged by Thomas Arne, a famous composer of oratorios and theatrical music on an expansive scale. Arne was also the composer of both *Rule, Britannia* and *God Save the King*, thus adding a national musical aura to the performance. The *Ode* included choral versions of parts of the text and recitative spoken passages with orchestral accompaniment.

After the overture, Garrick rose to begin his declamation:

> To what blest genius of the isle
> Shall gratitude her tribute pay . . .?

Accompanied by a soft orchestral background he called forth the spirit of the Jubilee:

> Now swell at once the choral song,
> Roll the full tide of harmony along;
> Let Rapture sweep the trembling strings,
> And Fame expanding all her wings,
> With all her trumpet-tongues proclaim,
> The lov'd, rever'd, immortal name!
> SHAKESPEARE! SHAKESPEARE! SHAKESPEARE!
>
> —Garrick, 1769: 2

And the music swelled with the chorus singing forth: the effect was unexpected and impressive. Many considered this the greatest performance of Garrick's life. One attendee wrote: "There never was exhibited in England a Performance more pleasing, more grand, or more worthy of the Memory of Shakespeare, and the Genius and Talents of Garrick" (Deelman 1964: 216–7).

The *Ode* was reprinted in many newspapers and magazines after the Jubilee, though stripped of the dramatic and musical elements that were so impressive in the Amphitheatre. As straight text, the purpose of Garrick's work was recognized, but there were strong debates about whether the words did proper honor to Shakespeare. Writers both for and against the Ode as well as the Jubilee carried on debates about the festival at great length.

After the *Ode* ceremony, one of the communal meals took place, but the continuing rain cancelled the grand fireworks display. The grand masquerade, however, did take place. James Boswell, one who enjoyed the Jubilee greatly, proudly appeared as a Corsican chief to the amusement of many. But the rain continued with the nearby Avon River overflowing its banks and threatening the Jubilee building. A muddy horserace was held on the third day, but most other events were dampened or cancelled as the crowds scrambled to find conveyances out of Stratford. Garrick was unhappy with the disruptions, many of which he ascribed to the reluctant townspeople of Stratford. On his return to London, he considered much of the Jubilee a failure.

There were many letters of complaint to the newspapers about cost and weather and the effect of the Jubilee, but sufficient attendees found the occasion novel and appealing and offered many positive reports. Boswell, generally known as a cheerful character, published a major review of the event in *The Pubic Advertiser* on September 16, which painted a congenial appraisal:

> I will always be of the Opinion that Shakespeare's Jubilee at Stratford upon Avon is an institution which does Honor not only to our immortal Bard, but to all who have contributed towards it, and I hope that every seven Years it shall be celebrated with equal Ardour of Enthusiasm as has been in 1769.
>
> —Stochholm 1964: 111

The London newspapers were full of reports and debates about the Jubilee, and this age given to satire witnessed many sallies against the proceedings in print and in dramatic commentary. But after the struggles of the Jubilee, Garrick recovered, and while his rival George Coleman at the Covent Garden Theatre turned out a fairly weak parody on October 7, he made his own case. On October 14, he staged the first performance of his theatrical *Jubilee*, which ended with an elaborate pageant of a great number of actors representing characters from the plays and carrying banners with the titles of the works they were evoking. Thus, the rained-out pageant in Stratford came to life on the Drury Lane stage (Stochholm 1964: 153). Garrick's theatrical transformation of the Jubilee went on to be the most successful play of its day, running to ninety performances over the next year.

FIGURE 4.4: *Garrick Speaking the Jubilee Ode*, engraved by Caroline Watson, after Robert Edge Pine, 1784. Around Garrick declaiming, and the statue of Shakespeare, are images of Shakespeare characters, including Falstaff, Lear and Cordelia, and the ghost of Hamlet's father. Courtesy of the Metropolitan Museum of Art, New York City.

Garrick's Jubilee not only put emphasis on Stratford for its connection to Shakespeare, but also confirmed the English sense of the preeminence of the figure of Shakespeare as an emblem of national identity and of his central role in the cultural memory of the late eighteenth century. The tradition of continuing Shakespeare festivals did not take hold as Boswell wished until the next century, as was the case with monumental statues. But the flourishing commemoration of Shakespeare was born in the energies of the eighteenth century.

The memorializing of Shakespeare continued through the end of the century in the expanded use of printed images, many copied from paintings from artists as well-known as Hogarth, Gainsborough, Reynolds, and the imaginative Swiss artist Henry Fuseli. The publisher John Boydell drew on enthusiasm for Shakespeare in his plans for a deluxe folio edition illustrated by an ambitious range of artists (West 2012: 246–8). He created a Shakespeare Gallery with a portrait statue of the author over the entrance that opened in 1789 to exhibit the original paintings, and he commissioned both the original art work and the engraving of the images in prints. To the satisfaction of the artists his payments for their work were notably generous.

The grand project ultimately grew to over 150 canvasses in mixed style, ranging from classically restrained to exuberantly romantic. The gallery and project were popular as part of the great interest in Shakespeare, but the extended delay of creating prints of

FIGURE 4.5: "The Weird Sisters" in *Macbeth*, Act 1, engraved by John Raphael Smith, after Henry Fuseli, 1785. Courtesy of the Metropolitan Museum of Art, New York City.

varying quality and publishing the folio edition drew a good deal of criticism, and Boydell was forced to sell the gallery and art works shortly before his death in 1805. Yet Boydell encouraged English artists in substantial ways and provided impressive portable memorials to Shakespeare. The prints were reproduced throughout the nineteenth century and in certain ways stimulated the visual appetite that anticipates the media world of contemporary treatment of Shakespeare. While Garrick was the more dramatic, Boydell enriched the visual presentation of Shakespeare's work with enduring effect.

SHAKESPEARE BEYOND ENGLAND

While Shakespeare had become the great English writer by the time of Garrick's Jubilee, he was also becoming a presence of note in Germany and France, though with mixed reception. The struggle between French neo-classicism and Shakespeare's vivid drama, which was often called barbaric, slowed his appearance in France. Voltaire's critiques of Shakespeare were sharp and influential. Voltaire, a vigorous and provocative proponent of Enlightenment artistic and political values, claimed to have introduced Shakespeare to France through commentary on English drama with passages on *Hamlet* that, while written in 1719, appeared in print only in 1728.

After two imprisonments in the Bastille, Voltaire went into exile to London from May 1726 to February 1729, where he attended to improving his English and encountering English drama and Shakespeare in particular. To understand the live performances at Drury Lane better, he followed the text in copies supplied to him by the prompter. Voltaire's passion for French classical drama made him quickly antagonistic to the dramatic and vivid scenes he observed, such as the murder of Desdemona and the gravedigger scene in *Hamlet*. He wrote in English to Lord Lytton: "The taste of your politest countrymen in point of tragedy differs not much from the taste of the mobs at the Beargarden" (Pemble 2005: 3).

Voltaire could not abide the contrast between the decorum of the classical tragedy of Corneille and the variety of action and tone of the Shakespeare plays he saw. And these were the adapted versions that were standard on the London stage of the day. However, while acknowledging certain passages of note, Voltaire began a long battle against the unclassical and, for him, offensive aspects of the Shakespeare plays he knew. He wrote satirically about *Hamlet,* presenting detailed summaries that paraphrased and distorted the play as he knew it. He found the ghost an affront, and he even picked at individual passages and plot shifts that seemed to him barbaric.

One major challenge was, of course, translation from the adapted English texts to the decorum of elevated classical French. The first serious, if selected, translations of Shakespeare in French appeared in 1748. By 1778, the complete range of plays was translated by Pierre le Tourneur, who wrote in his preface that Aristotle would have changed the *Poetics* because Shakespeare was superior to Sophocles or Euripides (Pemble 2005). Le Tourneur translated into prose and removed passages that seemed part of the cruder Shakespeare in the literary and elevated social expectations of the day, though he included the removed passages in notes and translations that showed his informed awareness of much of the originals. Perhaps the classical decorum of French literature and drama was beginning to erode into energies that would lead to the revolution.

Le Tourneur's translations were surprisingly popular. The *Mercure de France* commented: "It's making a big impression ... It is therefore a good thing, and much needed" (Pemble 2005: 85). Voltaire was appalled at this new popularity, calling

Shakespeare a "provincial clown." He claimed in his later years that the age of reason had ended and France was becoming barbaric. Most galling was his own role in calling attention to what he saw as reasonable parts of Shakespeare in his early writing: "What makes the whole thing more calamitous and horrible is the fact that I was the one who first mentioned this Shakespeare ..." (Pemble 2005: 5). Voltaire's objections to Shakespeare were known well enough in England that as early as 1769 Elizabeth Montagu wrote *The Essay on the writings and genius of Shakespear*, a frequently reprinted defense of Shakespeare with specific responses to many of the Frenchman's criticisms. Her work was translated into German and even influenced the young Goethe.

The place of Shakespeare in Germany was far more extensive and deeply engaged than in France. There was a tradition of traveling players performing versions of Shakespeare in the seventeenth century, and scattered adaptations appeared in print through the eighteenth century. The critical essays and perspectives of Gothold Lessing and Johann Herder involved a search for a German aesthetic and literature in a challenge to French neo-classicism. Lessing's writings on drama included references to Shakespeare in large part as a counter argument to Corneille and Voltaire (Paulin 2015: 88). The problem of text and translation went through various phases in the 1760s. The struggle to develop more accurate texts in England posed questions of sources for translation into German. One path was the publication in English as well as German of anthologies of praised excerpts, such as Pope suggested in his highlighting of special passages in his edition.

In Germany, a variety of commentators like Lessing and Herder encouraged new translations and reflections on the plays. The idea of Shakespeare quickly became a major preoccupation in Germany. Shakespeare became so influential for German writers that in 1796 Schlegel proclaimed that "Shakespeare is completely ours" (Paulin 2015: 326). This was carried out in the work of Johann von Goethe and the translations of Friedrich Schlegel and Ludwig Tieck. As a German affirmation of these claims, the Deutsche Shakespeare-Gesellschaft was founded on April 23, 1864 as the first formal Shakespeare society in the world, and it continues to this day.

Herder's major essay on Shakespeare that reached its mature form in 1773 linked his sense of the historical folk traditions of culture with the plays. Herder translated scenes from Shakespeare and established a cultural connection between Shakespeare and emerging German literature (Paulin 2003: 114). The *Sturm und Drang* period, the beginning of the Romantic era, and the role of Goethe all drew on extensive contact and estimation of Shakespeare. Translations were attempts to bridge a sense of Shakespeare with the significant development of German literature toward the end of the century. Anthologies, partial translations, prose versions, and the development of German blank verse brought Shakespeare into greater prominence as well as stimulating new achievements in German literature.

Goethe's enthusiastic encounter with Shakespeare in 1770, the new and now classic translations of Schlegel, and the dramatic and critical achievement of Schiller all demonstrate the growing importance of Shakespeare to German culture. Partly stimulated by news of Garrick's Jubilee and the translation of Elizabeth Montagu's essays, Goethe began reading popular anthologized Shakespeare in Dodd's *Beauties of Shakespeare* (1752) (reprinted more than thirty times), and then complete plays in 1770. In 1771, at the age of twenty-two, he wrote and presented his first critical response in a speech delivered on October 14th in Frankfurt: "On Shakespeare's Day." The young Goethe found a world of discovery of character and self and a new vitality of creativity that stirred his own sense of language and meaning. His enunciation of his awakening through Shakespeare is well-known:

> The first page that I read made me his for a lifetime, and once I had finished the first play, I stood like a man born blind, to whom a wondrous hand gave the gift of sight.
>
> —Pascal 1937: 98, my translation

Goethe's early enthusiasm for Shakespeare influenced much of his creative work: his early play *Götz von Berlichingen* (1773) with its range of short scenes and shifts, *The Sorrows of Young Werther* (1774) with its many echoes of *Hamlet*, and *Wilhelm Meister's Apprenticeship* (1796), which includes extensive discussions about Shakespeare. Goethe's engagement with Shakespeare continued throughout his work and life. In addition to essays and influence on many of his major works, Goethe continued commenting on Shakespeare in his famous conversations with Johann Peter Eckermann in the last years of his life.

By the turn of the nineteenth century Shakespeare's influence and presence in the German speaking world was extensive in many of its greatest writers and through enduring classic translations and a growing history of performance. The expansion of Shakespeare's role in German culture continued through institutions, criticism, and performance. In the early twenty-first century more Shakespeare plays are produced in Germany than in England.

CONCLUSION

The history of the development of Shakespeare's reputation and commemoration in the eighteenth century is a unique case study in the nature of cultural memory. In a variety of areas, the very fluidity and adaptability of Shakespeare as writer and dramatist allowed the multifaceted development of his reputation and influence. Certainly, the vividness and variety of character, language, and story in his work, as well as popular appeal, give him a range and fascination almost unique in artistic culture. In the eighteenth-century Shakespeare was seen to be central to the shifts of the age: performance, adaptation, the growth of literacy, popular and scholarly publication, economics, national identity, and extension into other language cultures. Shakespeare is protean in his work and in his place in cultural memory. Goethe might well deserve the final word from the 1813 title for the beginning of his series of essays on Shakespeare:

Shakespeare und kein Ende   (Shakespeare and no End)

CHAPTER FIVE

Ideas: Philosophy, Religion, and History

PATRICK H. HUTTON

THE ROLE OF MEMORY IN THE EIGHTEENTH-CENTURY HISTORIOGRAPHY OF THE ENLIGHTENMENT

The eighteenth century in Europe and the Americas was a time of widening horizons and transformative change in historical understanding, and so of ideas about the relationship between memory and history. At the beginning of the century, history and memory were naively allied. Historical scholarship was largely devoted to promoting the memory of edifying lives of personalities of legendary stature and signal events that stood out as times and places worthy of remembrance, islands of memory in the otherwise coursing stream of history that held no larger meaning. Such history placed emphasis on the timelessness of the human condition. The wisdom that history might teach lay in the exposition of eternal verities. Such history was didactic, providing lessons for the instruction of youth, often as cautionary tales. Plutarch's *Parallel Lives*, written deep in Greco-Roman antiquity, still served as a model and widely read resource for reflecting upon memorable heroes out of the past. But in time-traveling to century's end, one finds that history and memory had gone their separate ways. Each had acquired a vocation of its own. History had become an autonomous field of scholarship that looked for patterns of change as these inhere in the findings of documented research (Koselleck 1985: 27–38). Such scholarship was based on the premise that humankind creates its own history and so can reconstruct it, a doctrine that would come to be characterized as "historicism" by the late nineteenth century (Kelley 1998: 266). It was put to use in grand narratives of national history, crucial to civic education. Just as history was turning outward upon a wider world, memory was turning inward as a search for truth within the self, notably in the reinvention of autobiography as a genre for soul-searching.

My interest in this chapter concerns the time in between—the eighteenth century conceived as a transitional era between ancient and modern ways of thinking about history, and more specifically for its uses of memory during that interim. My general line of argument is that issues about memory continued to wax large in historical interpretation, but in new ways. I address these as they came to the fore in the historiography of this era: mnemonic schemes in the philosophy of history; research on the workings of memory in oral tradition; the reinvention of autobiography as a method of self-discovery. I draw out contrasts in interpretations offered by scholars who exemplify opposing positions: churchman Jacques Bénigne Bossuet and savant Nicholas de Condorcet for their mnemonic schemes of history; rhetorician Giambattista Vico and philosopher David Hume on memory in preliterate societies. I close with a coda concerning the affirmation of memory's therapeutic value in Jean-Jacques Rousseau's search for the self.

MNEMONIC SCHEMES IN THE PHILOSOPHY OF HISTORY

From a historiographical perspective, the philosophy of history may be interpreted as a transitional genre between histories of the lives of legendary personalities and history as the story of nation-building. Situated between them, the philosophy of history developed its own protocols. Not the memorable past but the anticipated future lay at the heart of this enterprise, a kind of modeling that lent coherent structure to the timeline of history. The eighteenth century is remembered today as its golden age. It was among the most popular fields of scholarly inquiry during that era. As visionary writing about the past, the philosophy of history was neither philosophy nor history, but a laminated hybrid—a "centaur" in the words of historian Vincenzo Ferrone—that did not quite fit either category (Ferrone 2015: xv). In its resources, it owed something to both, and even more to memory in its imaginative reach at once into a remote past and toward a beckoning future. Philosophers of history wrote grand narratives. Their popular appeal lay in their claims to present a unified history, one that told the story of humankind's advance from benighted ignorance into rational understanding. In sweeping outlines, they affirmed the faith of the Enlightenment that humankind was proceeding toward the scientific mastery of nature and the perfection of social and political institutions. In this venture, they aspired to signal a direction of moral intention inherent in the pattern of historical change. Memorable events and prominent personalities were fitted to this preconceived plot line. Progress was its defining theme, from obscure beginnings tending toward a presumed destiny. Paradigmatic in nature, the philosophy of history lent itself readily to programmatic design. History was being reconceived as a mnemonics of time (Zerubavel 2003: 14–15).

During the eighteenth century, nearly all of the leading philosophers tried their pens at composing such ambitious works of historical imagination. The illustrious gallery included such luminaries as Giambattista Vico, Jean d'Alembert, Voltaire, Johann Herder, Nicholas de Condorcet, and Immanuel Kant. Long after the philosophy of history had fallen into disrepute among professional historians for its determinist designs, writings in this genre would continue to be read by posterity for their rich excursions into the thinking of the age of Enlightenment, and at a more profound level for their insights into the timefulness of the human condition. The philosophy of history was based on the idea of humankind's self-transforming powers, and in light of these, the expectation of an ongoing trend toward the mastery of nature and the refinement of human institutions.

Philosophers of history stood in opposition to the medieval teaching that the human condition is fixed. Change, they argued, is inevitable, and they held rising expectations about its direction as the century progressed, dramatically so with the coming of the French Revolution. They aspired to write histories that were universal and cosmopolitan. They were universal in their belief that the meaning of history could be found in a grand narrative common to the development of all nations. They were cosmopolitan in that they acknowledged cultural differences among them. Typically, they included a tour of the world, identifying innovative thinking in a given epoch with one of the nations of the world. As Voltaire famously remarked, the mores and manners of humankind may vary, but human nature is everywhere the same (Voltaire [1756] 1963: 2: 810). The philosophers also saw parallels between the social and the natural sciences. Science was guided by uniform patterns in nature, therefore why not human history? They punctuated their narratives with stages of development. As mnemonic schemes, their temporal designs marked a departure from the spatial ones of sixteenth-century cosmology, designed by the Renaissance magi in the form of wheels, circles, and theaters (Yates 1966: 368–89). By contrast, the philosophies of history of the eighteenth century were cast as linear timelines foretelling a more auspicious future. The progress of humankind into rational understanding was ongoing but uneven, marked by periodic reversals of fortune and even of decline. Each epoch along the way displayed its own characteristics, reflecting its particular concerns. Known history constituted a solid middle ground between hazy horizons—a primordial past still enshrouded in shadows and a future conceived only as an imagined destiny. Speculation about what lay beyond them emerged out of interpretations of the middle of the story, whose patterns permitted speculation about these hidden domains.

The authority of religious teaching about history played a waning role in this enterprise, given an accelerating trend toward the secularization of knowledge about the human condition over the course of the eighteenth century. Still, the idea of providential guidance exercised a lingering effect upon this newly formulated conception of history, for most philosophers of history continued to identify some transcendent principle that informed its course. For some, the idea of Providence maintained an inertial appeal as a metonym for an increasingly abstract conception of a guiding force in history. Once conceived as a deity that intervened directly in human affairs, the idea by the eighteenth century had come to be reconceived as one that set the process of history in motion without further intrusion into human affairs. Accordingly, the philosophers bracketed the concept of God as a trinity as a theological proposition irrelevant to human need, and so set aside consideration of its implicit soteriology of redemption. The historical concept of Providence proposed a hidden God, one that correlated with Deism in eighteenth-century theology (Goldmann 1964: 36–7, 303–9). Reference to the term followed from the philosophers' conviction that the transcendent meaning in history becomes visible only over the long run.

It is interesting to note how many of the eighteenth-century philosophers invoked the term Providence in their writings. Voltaire referred to Providence as a supernatural reality his heart could not deny. Herder, too, frequently invoked Providence as a benign overseer. The role of Providence was a central proposition in Vico's theory of history, based on his notion that the short-term pursuits of humankind fulfill a long-term divine plan. Eventually, however, the idea surrendered its theist label for secular equivalents, as in Immanuel Kant's "unsocial sociability," Hegel's "dialectic of reason," or Jules Michelet's spiraling gyre. Modifications in the understanding of the idea of Providence, therefore, provide an index to the way in which the philosophy of history over the course of the century shed its theological trappings. Providence was reborn as Reason. God's purposes in history gave way to those of humankind.

Even in these secular versions, however, faith remained a motivating force. Like their theist predecessors, philosophers of history affirmed their conviction that the meaning of history might be unlocked with reason as the master key to its workings. As German philosopher Immanuel Kant remarked, belief in the power of reason is an affirmation of the human will to fashion its own destiny. As the century proceeded, philosophers became more radical in their expectations, notably with the coming of the French Revolution. Therein the concept of ideology was born, with its explicit linking of theory and practice. Radical expressions of the philosophy of history, as envisioned in the schemes of Henri de

Saint-Simon and Charles Fourier, placed a utopian accent on the notion of social planning. All this gave new moment to the role of revolution in accelerating advance into a new age. Considered in its ensemble, the passage from theology to philosophy as the guiding principle of change over the course of the eighteenth century might be characterized as a move from prophecy to forecasting.

A critical interpretation of this infusion of faith into the philosophers' grand narrative of history was offered in a grand thesis of his own by American historian Carl Becker early in the twentieth century. In his *Heavenly City of the 18th-Century Philosophers* (Becker 1932), he put the genre in historiographical perspective with wit and irony. The philosophers of the eighteenth century, he argued, styled themselves as champions of reason and science. They railed against the revealed religion of Christianity as a medieval inheritance that should be banished from an Enlightened Age. Yet in their zeal to trace the rise of humanity in the name of reason they unwittingly reconstructed the Heavenly City of Augustine once more, this time as an earthly destiny. Speculation about the future of history may have changed, but the structural design in which it was given form remained much the same (Becker 1932: 28–31).

Becker composed his book during the early 1930s, an era of economic and political crisis in which the optimistic forecasts of the Enlightenment were visibly under attack. He sensed how different that time was from his own, for the idea of progress could no longer be so easily invoked as the watchword for the making of the present age. Intellectuals in the twentieth century no longer shared the naïve optimism of their eighteenth-century forbearers. Still, most recognized that the historical outlook of the Enlightenment philosophers was a legacy worth remembering, and their writings to be respected as source material for pedagogical reflection. How could it have been otherwise, he queried, for this was a history whose purpose was religious in a civic sense. The eighteenth-century philosophers offered new perspectives on imponderable questions about which humankind had ruminated since the emergence of its capacity for critical thought deep in antiquity: What is human nature? What role has religion played in addressing the relationship between the known and the unknown world? Does humankind have a destiny, and if so, how might it be conceived? What is the role of forecasting in historical thinking? While no one any longer expected definitive answers to such questions, the philosophers of history who addressed them remained thinkers with whom to reckon, and their writings continued to be assigned in philosophy, history, and religion courses in colleges and universities in Europe and the Americas throughout the twentieth century. For generations of educators, the future-oriented paradigm of the eighteenth-century philosophers of history was a model of hopes and dreams with which to nurture the idealism of the young.

The Theist Bossuet vis-à-vis the Humanist Condorcet

To look more closely at mnemonic overlay in the making of the genre of the philosophy of history, I compare two of its leading exemplars: its theist roots in the rhetorical piety of Jacques-Bénigne Bossuet (1627–1704) on the eve of the eighteenth century with its humanist affirmation in the philosophical speculation of Nicholas marquis de Condorcet (1743–94) toward the century's end. At the beginning of the century, the idea of a universal history remained deeply imbued with theology. For a Christian apologist such as Bossuet, Providence reigned over history, guiding its long-range course in the interest of sustaining humankind as His creation. By the end of the century, however, such theist speculation had all but disappeared. In the vision of philosopher Condorcet, writing in the midst of the French Revolution, history had cast off the mantle of theology in favor of that of philosophy, one that proclaimed humankind's rising confidence in its ability to shape its own future. Condorcet traced the moving story of humankind's discovery of its powers of reason deep in antiquity and their development over the following 2,000 years. In his own day, he remarked, statesmen of the Revolution were applying principles based on practical reason to refashion the political and social institutions of the French nation, precedents for further reform. He believed that their influence would soon spread to a wider world. The future of history, he opined, was henceforth open to the infinite ways in which humankind might choose to fashion its prospects. History so reconceived was humanist in inspiration and cosmopolitan in outlook.

Bossuet was a high prelate in the French Catholic Church. As bishop of Condom and later of Meaux, he enjoyed a reputation as one of the leading religious orators of his day. Renowned for his eloquent sermons, he was also learned in the humanities. For a time, he served as tutor to the Dauphin, the son of King Louis XIV, and it was in this calling that he wrote his *Discourse on Universal History* (1681) as a guide to his education (Bossuet [1681] 1976). Bossuet's religious teachings were orthodox, but his broad learning enabled him to place worldly knowledge in a religious context. In this respect, he epitomizes the religious thinking of the late Baroque era by seeking to deal with the modern secular world on its own terms. His prose is rhetorical and didactic. He used his vast learning to

FIGURE 5.1: *Portrait of Jacques Bénigne Bossuet*. Philosopher of history: the theist vision. Courtesy of Getty Images UK.

explain the meaning of history from a Christian point of view. His complex and ornate essay might be regarded as the supernova of Christian apologetics for divine guidance in human history. It had a remarkable staying power among the faithful well into the nineteenth century (Ranum 1976: xiii–xliv).

Bossuet's *Discourse* interested the humanist philosophers of the eighteenth century as a touchstone against which to measure their move into a secular view of history. Bossuet's scholarship was nonetheless distinctive for his blend of the sacred and the profane. Dealing with what he took to be the beginning of historical time in God's creation of Adam and Eve and proceeding in his narrative into the early Middle Ages, he integrated his account of Hebrew, Greek, and Roman history into a single storyline. He built his interpretation around the lives of memorable people, with little discussion of their social or cultural context. His account began with the Old Testament stories of Adam and Eve, Noah, Abraham, and Moses. But he then found a place for Romulus as the founder of Rome, Cyrus as a benefactor of the Hebrews in the making of his middle-eastern empire, and the Greek philosophers Plato and Aristotle. He devoted some attention to Alexander of Macedon, deflating claims to his greatness. The coming of Jesus Christ was of epochal importance in his account, though he did not conclude his history there. He continued with discussion of Paul of Tarsus, Constantine, and other leaders of the late Roman Empire, concluding with Charlemagne well into the medieval era. In this sense, Bossuet's history, while proclaiming divine guidance, avoided apocalyptic pronouncements. He likewise eschewed stories of miraculous happenings. His purpose was to show how the pageant of history itself reaffirms Christian faith, much as had Augustine of Hippo during the late Roman Empire. Regimes rise and fall, as do the fortunes of prophets and kings. But the changing course of historical events does nothing to alter the human condition. Under the aegis of Providence, humankind thrives, thanks to His will.

Bossuet divided his history into twelve epochs, each of which featured exceptional leaders in distinctive settings. In this respect, he provided a travelogue of ancient Mediterranean history, the only "world" that mattered in his account. He dated these with chronological precision, as if all of history could be localized as events within the timeline that he sketched. His display of learning was intended to lend authority to his stature as historian. At the same time, he accepted the calculations of Eusebius of Caesarea in the fourth century CE about the age of the world in which no savant in his own age any longer believed. But Bossuet was writing for the faithful laity, not the intellectuals. His interpretation stayed close to popular devotional literature. His account of sacred history enveloped profane history, rather than according it equal standing. Giving priority to the sacred history of the Bible, Bossuet accepted the fundamentalist teaching that the world was but 6,006 years old, a pious nod to the church fathers.

Bossuet presented his history in a manner analogous to the painting of a medieval triptych. The first side panel provided a concise review of the story of history noted above. The opposing side panel concerned the uncertain political fortunes of empires. It was specifically devoted to the practical education of the Dauphin in his training to enter public life, for it revealed the limitations and errant ways of imperial rule. The hubris of Alexander of Macedon received particular attention, for the reign of no other ancient ruler was so grand yet fleeting. His argument is reminiscent of Augustine's characterization of the City of Man vis-à-vis the City of God. Empires rise and fall; the City of God endures.

The center panel contains the crux of Bossuet's interpretation. The continuity of history, he argued, lies in the continuity of the Judeo-Christian tradition. Through its sacred books—the Old and New Testaments—the course of history may be traced in its entirety. No other religion can make that claim. Some of the sacred books of the Romans and the Egyptians have survived, he remarked, but most have been lost. These accounts are restricted to specific times and places and provide no basis for a universal history. It is in their continuity as a written history that the sacred books of Christianity reveal God's plan for humankind. Building on Jewish tradition, Bossuet nonetheless made his case for Christianity as a catholic faith. He distinguished the Old and the New Testament on the basis of their propagation. The Old Testament, he commented, was publicized among the Hebrews alone. The New Testament was broadcast by Paul of Tarsus to the world at large (Bossuet [1681] 1976: 289–95).

Condorcet was a leading French philosopher identified with the late stage of the European Enlightenment. A protégé of the Encyclopedist Jean Le Rond d'Alembert, he excelled in mathematics, with a particular interest in practical application of the calculus to the social as well as the natural sciences. Moving in high political and intellectual circles, he was appointed Director of the Royal Mint of France during the waning days of the Old Regime. With the coming of the French Revolution, he became a leading figure in its politics. He was elected to the Legislative Assembly in 1791 and to the Convention in 1792, where he was assigned to the committee for drafting a constitution for the new

FIGURE 5.2: *Portrait of Nicholas, marquis de Condorcet*. Philosopher of history: the humanist vision. Courtesy of Getty Images, UK.

Republic. Even among republican revolutionaries, Condorcet held particularly progressive political views. He advocated the abolition of slavery, independence for the French colonies, and equal rights for women. Caught up in the factional rivalries of the early days of the Republic, he sided with the soon to be outlawed Girondin faction and went into hiding. Captured and arrested, he died in prison, but not before he had written his remarkable *Sketch* (1793), drafted as a prospectus for a proposed *Historical Tableau of the Progress of the Human Spirit*. He never had the opportunity to develop this larger work, but his *Sketch* provides a précis of his design of a universal history and is exemplary of the philosophy of history as a vehicle for affirming the values of the Enlightenment. Lucid, concise, and carefully organized, its broad outlines were conceived in the manner of a mnemonic scheme (Condorcet [1793] 2012: 1–147).

For Condorcet, history is the story of human progress through the use of reason. In his *Sketch*, he highlighted significant moments of consciousness-raising. He portrayed history as a continuous storyline, a pageant that he divided into ten epochs. The tenth was his own contemporary age, in which he looked toward future possibilities for the perfection of the human condition. He conceptualized his history as interplay between the advance and retreat of the cause of reason. There were exemplary uses of reason in antiquity, notably among the Greeks, and again in modern times. In between intruded a middle age, a dark era of superstition in which a priestly class gained authority. As reason's adversary, organized religion presented an obstacle to scientific research and learning.

Condorcet was keen on pointing out the networks through which new ideas traveled. Critical to his argument were advances in the technologies of communication, analogous in a way to Bossuet's ideas about publicity in the dissemination of religious teaching. The invention of manuscript literacy in Greco-Roman antiquity made scientific achievements possible. Restricted to an intelligentsia, he maintained, literacy was too rare among the public at large and the archiving of knowledge too haphazard to sustain progress in science. In the Middle Ages, therefore, Europe lost its intellectual edge and receded into ignorance under the priestly claims of religious dogma. The learning of the ancient Greeks was saved from oblivion by Islamic sages, who preserved this inheritance in their libraries in North Africa and Spain as an essential conduit between the learning of the ancient Greco-Roman world and Europe in the age of the Renaissance.

The invention of print literacy during the European Renaissance made possible the renewal and ongoing advance of scientific knowledge. Censorship became increasingly difficult to impose, and literacy spread rapidly among ever larger elements of the population. By the eighteenth century, scientists and philosophers had come to enjoy the support of a reading public. Not only would learning be sustained, its propagation would accelerate. For Condorcet, the French Revolution marked humankind's crossing into a culture based upon rational methods of inquiry and humanist ethical ideals. He noted the principles enunciated in the preamble to the French republican constitution that he himself had helped to draft: equality before the law, representative government, popular sovereignty, careers open to talent, religious toleration, and respect for the advancement of humane learning (Condorcet [1793] 2012: 105–7, 126–7).

The contrast between Bossuet at the beginning of the eighteenth century and Condorcet at the end may be dramatized in the contrast between their visions of history: theology vs. philosophy; theism vs. humanism, divine guidance in the preservation of humankind vs. self-transformative human development, prophecy vs. forecasting. At the same time, there were similarities in the way their histories were structured. Both aspired to write a grand narrative of history; both were linear in their conception of historical time; both punctuated a continuous storyline by highlighting particular epochs; both envisioned culminating moments in the story of humankind; both were imbued with faith, if of a different order. Most significantly, both believed in the possibility of a metahistory whose meaning lay in a process rather than a simple narrative of events. As paradigms of historical change, their conceptions of history envisioned an imaginative role for memory in shaping a narrative for the interpretation of events. In its theist as in its humanist vision, memory inspired the historians' frameworks for interpreting the past in readily perceived mnemonic designs.

PROBING THE DEPTHS OF TIME IMMEMORIAL

Little in what we have since come to regard as serious historical research in the eighteenth century was guided by such great expectations. Whereas philosophers of history looked expectantly toward a beckoning future, other scholars harked back out of intellectual curiosity into the deep recesses of the past. Painstaking research into their realities was underway in a variety of scholarly undertakings, and their cumulative effect prepared the way for historians to push back the horizons of antiquity. In its ensemble, their honest labor, cautious in expectation and careful in research, elaborated a historical record that philosophers of history had been obliged to leave to speculation. They were a heterogeneous lot—art collectors, archaeologists, geologists, naturalists, and folklorists who worked alongside those who styled themselves historians. What unified them was a focus on concrete evidence, documenting their findings along the way (Grafton 1997: 1–4, 220–2).

There had long been scholarly interest in Greco-Roman antiquity, prized as the ancient foundation of modern education. It was a tradition of high culture and advanced learning in the humanities. Modern scholars especially admired the philosophers of antiquity, particularly among the Greeks and especially the towering intellects of Plato and Aristotle. Significant discoveries in the antiquities of Greece and Rome inspired critical interest in the history of art and archaeology. The eighteenth century would witness the beginnings of the reconstruction of the Parthenon atop the Acropolis in Athens; in Italy, the ancient cities of Herculaneum and Pompeii were unearthed. Johann Winckelmann, a German connoisseur of the artwork of antiquity, acquired a scholarly reputation as the first art historian (Moatti 1993: 74–85). There were as well great strides among students of natural history. The geologist James Hutton argued for a vastly older world, an earth that was not thousands but millions of years old. Fossil finds of giant reptiles gave evidence of a living past so immeasurably different from the modern world that it defied the imagination (Rossi 1984: 3–120). Such new directions in scholarship were as yet carried out on the margins. Developing independently, they converged by the end of the century, preparing the way for the emergence of history as a professional enterprise. Distancing itself from philosophical design, history was becoming an autonomous discipline of its own.

The written record of the Greco-Roman era may have been abundant, but evidence of a deeper past was practically non-existent, a realm that historians thought of only as "the dark abyss of time" (Rossi 1984: 107–12). Serious inquiry into that past faced a major obstacle in the teachings of sacred history. Relying exclusively upon the Old Testament, church authorities compressed human history into some 6,000 years (Rosenberg and Grafton 2010: 26). In a culture still deeply devoted to Christian teaching, there was much at stake for the Church, for sacred history as a tradition of collective remembrance was a

FIGURE 5.3: *Discovery and excavation of the Temple of Isis at Pompeii*, 1776. An archaeological inquiry into the culture of the ancient Roman world. Courtesy of Getty Images, UK.

foundation of popular piety. How were historians to break through this barrier without rousing the ire of ecclesiastical authorities or inviting political censorship? Political theorists circumvented the problem by making references to speculative, as opposed to chronological origins. Imagining passage from a state of nature into civil society, Thomas Hobbes, John Locke, Jean-Jacques Rousseau, and Immanuel Kant postulated a primordial social contract without localizing it in a particular historical context. But the prospect of investigating the realities of a pre-Adamite past could not help but intrigue humanist scholars in an age of Enlightenment. Even biblical scholars were beginning to research the historical context in which the books of the Bible had been composed, permitting a profane historical reading of texts long considered sacred (Funk and Hoover 1993: 2).

For would-be students of early human societies, therefore, the challenge was to separate profane from sacred history. In an age of cosmopolitanism, with its rapidly expanding knowledge of cultural diversity in a wider world, it had become obvious that the sacred history of the Hebrews as recorded in the texts of the Old Testament could not encompass the past of all nations of the world. Each possessed its distinctive culture, its genealogies devolving toward origins too remote and diverse to absorb into the Christian calendar with any credibility. As early as the mid-seventeenth century, Isaac de Lapeyrère proposed that it was time to accept the reality of multiple chronologies for dating the human experience (Rossi 1984: 136). The call for such latitude suggests how tenuous had become the hold of religious teaching upon the writing of profane history. Theology was losing its claim to speak with authority about history, as it already had about cosmology.

The chronology of sacred history, moreover, was based upon a tradition of literacy that took the scripted text as a point of departure. The breakthrough in understanding the pre-Adamite past, therefore, would come rather through the study of oral traditions. These were living traditions of storytelling for the majority of the European population,

FIGURE 5.4: *Portrait of Giambattista Vico*. Historian of the poetics of language in preliterate societies. Courtesy of Getty Images, UK.

remodeled through the ages but with ancestral connections to a preliterate past. Scholarly interest in the folktales and folklore of oral traditions sprang up everywhere in Europe during the eighteenth century. Collectors included Thomas Percy in England, James Macpherson in Scotland, Jacob and Wilhelm Grimm in Germany, and Johann Herder in Latvia (Ong 1982: 16–17). Most important for our purposes, however, was the research and writing by the Neapolitan rhetorician Giambattista Vico, who inquired into the etymological origins of the Latin vocabulary. What he discovered among them were primordial powers of memory that governed a way of thinking that was poetical and laden with emotions. His research would lead him into an interpretation of memory as a matrix for the development of human resources for reasoning, a position that set him at odds with the mainstream of Enlightenment thought.

Vico on the Inspiration vis-à-vis Hume on the Habit of Memory

I contrast two mid-century philosophers who addressed the nature of collective memory in their writings about the origins of civil society: Giambattista Vico (1668–1744) from the standpoint of the evolution of language in preliterate societies; David Hume (1711–76) from that of religious ideas during that era. Their writings on such subjects appeared at roughly the same time. Vico was a Neapolitan professor of rhetoric, Hume a Scottish philosopher. Vico has since come to be recognized as one of the most original cultural historians of the eighteenth century, and a harbinger of late-twentieth century historiography for his interpretation of the dynamics of cultural and social processes. In Vico's writings, one espies the beginnings of a cultural history of memory (Hutton 1993: 32–51). Hume is remembered today as an eminent figure in the development of modern philosophy for his contribution to an understanding of empirical method in formulating a theory of knowledge. Long a staple of introductory philosophy courses, his writings have enjoyed a revival, given the urgency of grounding knowledge in demonstrable evidence in the face of the blurring of reality and fantasy in today's digital-age culture. To my knowledge, Vico and Hume never exchanged thoughts, and appear to have been unaware of one another, yet they led surprisingly parallel lives in their pathways to scholarly accomplishment while suffering disappointments along the way. Vico failed to win the chair in jurisprudence that he coveted. Hume's philosophical skepticism, particularly on matters of religion, was too controversial to permit his appointment to a university chair in philosophy. During their mature years, each turned to history. For his theory of history in his *New Science* (1744), Vico was to receive ongoing posthumous fame. As for Hume, he earned recognition in his own day for his *History of England* (1762), a pioneering venture in national history that would come to dominate nineteenth-century historiography.

More importantly, there are uncanny similarities in their interpretations of the origins of the civilizing process. Vico and Hume shared an interest in the emergence of consciousness among preliterate people, and they arrived at many of the same findings (Haddock 1986: 195–7). Both agreed that human consciousness emerged out of sense experience, and that humans relied upon memory because of the frailty of their capacity for reason. Both argued that the first religions were polytheistic, wondrous magnifications of human traits and powers born of fear of an unfamiliar world about which they struggled to make sense. Both noted that memory gives flight to the imagination, eventually to be reined in by the birth of reason. At the same time, they put their findings in vastly different perspectives. Vico was in some esoteric sense a believer in the reign of Providence over history. Hume was a religious agnostic. He did not deny Providence but bracketed the question of spiritual transcendence as beyond the ken of human understanding. Despite similar findings of fact, they arrived at opposing views about the significance of the role of religion in the making of ancient civilizations.

Vico came to history by way of his training in rhetoric and law. While respectful of the growing importance of the modern sciences, he wished to reaffirm the enduring value of the ancient tradition in which he himself had been educated. As an orator, he had particular respect for the power and resources of memory. In his early writings, devoted primarily to pedagogy, he emphasized the importance for the young to develop their powers of memory before turning to more abstract ways of learning. In the famous quarrel of the day between Ancients and Moderns over approaches to education, he aligned himself with the former (Levine 1999: 137–9, 147–53). That stance would lead him eventually into study of the evolution of thought among the ancients, and through it into the formulation of a "new science" of history. Fathoming the "wisdom of the ancient Italians" became the passion of his research during his mature years. As early as 1725, he wrote a preliminary tract on their thought, then worked his way through successive versions of his *New Science* (Lilla 1993: 106–7). In the third edition, published in 1744, he remarked upon his belated breakthrough to the "master key" of his inquiry—that among the ancients in preliterate societies, knowing and doing were coeval, reverse sides of the civilizing process. In decoding their poetical language, the modern-day historian could ascertain not only the nature of the challenges they had faced, but also the foundational institutions they had created to cope with them—for Vico, marriage, burial, and religion.

Vico's forays into the cultural history of the primordial world of preliterate societies set the stage for his distinction between sacred and profane history. He put the matter this way: God has created nature, and so only God can understand the ultimate source of its workings. But humankind has created its own history, and therefore can reconstruct it. It was a preliminary proposition for his interpretation of the development of profane history apart from the biblical record. He bracketed discussion of sacred history so as to ward off political controversy. As God's people, he argued, the Hebrews possessed a sacred history that was exceptional, one apart from the profane history shared by the rest of humanity. The origins of thought among these "gentiles" followed a common pattern emerging out of pre-literate oral traditions. It was that process that he proposed to interpret.

There were two sides to Vico's inquiry, one philological, the other philosophical. His method of research was philological. He recognized that the use of language is dynamic and evolves over time from poetical metaphor, the idiom of preliterate people, toward abstract irony, the refinement of rational critical thought. The original meaning of their poetical language was over time forgotten, and the logic of linguistic development never properly understood. He concluded that modern uses of language contain hidden origins, whose meanings were modified before being lost along the way. He therefore worked at the threshold between orality and literacy to decode the meaning of oral residues within the texts of ancient Greek and Roman literature.

Vico argued that the preliterate Greeks conceived of memory as mimesis, originally the imitation of nature by literally mimicking its sights and sounds. Mimesis had a creative and a preservationist side, reflecting the ambiguity of the relationship between imagination and preservation within memory's resources. Memory was creative in that it imagined the world of nature in anthropomorphic forms. It was preservationist in that knowledge of the world so conceived provided a structure for interpreting human experience. All human language, Vico proposed, was originally metaphorical, and all storytelling mythological. Memory and myth were therefore integrally allied in that myth was a poetical way to recollect humankind's confrontation with the challenges of fashioning a human world of its own. The storyline of mythic narrative provided a sense of sequence in the time it took for humans to meet the fundamental challenges of creating civil society. In that sense, mythology was an archive of remembrance of the way humankind first forged its understanding of the world. Vico's project was to de-mythologize these ancient traditions of storytelling.

Vico's key point is that memory is a matrix. In the primordial rise of human consciousness, development of the faculties of memory was a precondition for the birth of reason. Only over time would poetical language be modified into forms that permitted rational abstraction. In the same way, the storyline of mythic narrative was a primitive method of time-factoring. Recourse to collective memory in interpreting the relationship between past and present, Vico explained, ran in cycles. In preliterate societies, the trend toward abstraction was accompanied by a loss of the passion that new challenges had once inspired, and as precedent gave way to custom, forgetfulness about the sources that had initially inspired poetical creativity. History, as understood by the ancients, followed the logic of memory as an eternal return to the sources of human creativity in cycles of remembering and forgetting. Critical historical understanding, therefore, was Vico's way of putting the dynamics of collective memory in a different kind of temporal perspective, and his *New Science* his way out of the logic of memory's imaginative poetry into history's mode of rational understanding. The move from antiquity into modernity was linear rather than cyclical and the way toward intellectual enlightenment. The poetical birth of knowledge had permitted the rational flourishing of the tree of knowledge. Vico reviewed in detail the poetical origins of all of the modern sciences that humankind had invented and through which its powers of reason had developed (Tagliacozzo 1993: 1–3). As he remarked, the ancient Greeks venerated memory in the guise of the goddess Mnemosyne, imagined as the mother of all of the arts and sciences. She was "the daughter of ignorance and the mother of knowledge" (Vico [1744] 1968: para 189, 819).

In the dawning age of Enlightenment, Vico was asserting history's mastery of memory, for his "new science" gave his generation critical insight into its workings. He noted two ways in which reliance on collective memory in his own day had led to misunderstanding of the mindset of preliterate people. The first concerned the idea of anachronism, which he characterized as the "conceit of scholars" who believed that the human use of language had changed little through the ages and so paid homage to the "matchless wisdom of the ancients." For evidence, he decoded the original meaning of the poetical epics of Homer. Homer was not a single author, he argued, but a tradition of storytelling carried on by a cohort of wandering rhapsodes, the *hómēros* of preliterate Greek society. The second concerned the idea of exceptionalism, which he labeled the "conceit of nations." Here he explained that the Law of the Twelve Tables, the first recording of written law among the Romans, was not a borrowing from Greek jurisprudence, but a democratization of the law that developed autonomously in the move from oral into literate culture. There were no unique founding fathers.

If Vico's method of historical investigation was philological, his vision of history was philosophical. Here he attributed the course of history to Providence, conceived as a hidden god. There are two ways, he maintained, in which his idea of Providence may be understood as presiding over human history. In the first, God created humans in a way that they would in time come to a rational understanding of a world they had first defined poetically. To put it differently, in dealing passionately with immediate challenges in their early struggles to survive, they unwittingly began their journey toward the fulfillment of God's long-range plan for their destiny—the discovery of their rational humanity. In the second, Vico is more theological. Humans discovered God, he argued, in their creative effort to "divine the unknown," that is, to grasp the meaning of the world of experience in which they were immersed. In that sense, human creativity is a divine activity, and as such a mimicking of God's creativity. Vico's argument is akin to Plato's account of Socrates's self-defense of his inquisitiveness as a divine activity. As historiographer Karl Löwith has pointed out, Vico in the ambiguity of his argument about Providence provides a mid-eighteenth-century mediation between the theology and the philosophy of history (Löwith 1949: 124–36).

Hume turned to the anthropology of religious origins as evidence of the limits of human understanding in antiquity. To that end, he wrote a tract entitled the *Natural Origins of Religion* (1757). Like Vico, he characterized religious belief among ancient preliterate people as a predictable response to the conditions in which they lived and about which they understood so little. Their powers of reason were weak, and so they perceived the world with fear and wonder. In such circumstances, they imagined the forces of nature to be deities and ascribed to them human characteristics. The first religions of humankind were accordingly polytheistic. As a religious expression whose lexicon was anthropomorphic, polytheism was easily integrated into human understanding

FIGURE 5.5: *Portrait of David Hume*, 1767. Historian of the origins of religious ideas in preliterate societies. Courtesy of Getty Images, UK.

as benign fantasy. As the apotheosis of great men and women, it was a form of hero worship. Vico's accent had been upon the formative power of poetical wonder; Hume's upon the passive acquiescence of religious belief. Far from being the Vichian mother of knowledge, "ignorance is the mother of devotion" (Hume [1757] 2008: 185).

Hume, moreover, went on to explore a second stage in the development of religious understanding beyond Vico's analysis, wherein his interpretation took a polemical turn. During the Hellenistic Age, he argued, polytheism was superseded by monotheism, conceived as disembodied spiritualism. Monotheism was at once superstitious, dogmatic and intolerant. Its tenets were based upon metaphysical claims that have no foundation in human experience. Humankind cannot know anything about such a transcendental spiritual realm. He challenged the idea of Providence as a code word for divine guidance of which there is no evidence. Providence may exist, he allowed, but one cannot conjure up a creator from a perceived design in the world, for one cannot infer cause from effect. The idea of a benevolent deity that reigns over human experience is a proposition that cannot be verified. As such, it may be judged a phantasm irrelevant to any inquiry into the nature of the human condition. Hume made this point provocatively in his critique of miracle. The idea of a miracle requires a suspension of what humans expect of experience in the natural order. Without denying the possibility of miracle, Hume argued that it is based upon credulity, and as such highly improbable. It is an impediment to rational understanding of the phenomenal world in which humans actually live.

It is here that Hume introduced his interpretation of memory, in which he emphasized its imitative function and downplayed its imaginative one. Memory is a human faculty that builds the perception of experience into habits of mind. Habits are elemental forms of remembrance from which humankind derives its understanding of the world. Human knowledge, therefore, is based on the constant conjunction of experience and perception. The limits of knowledge are transgressed when humans engage in speculation about a disembodied metaphysical realm that hovers over the phenomenal world. The imponderable questions about the human predicament that so preoccupied the philosophers of history, therefore, must be consigned to a realm of conjecture in which there can be no expectation of resolution. What religious thinking has bequeathed to the age of Enlightenment, Hume suggested, is stimulating, even entertaining conversation, in which he himself indulged in his construction of an imagined debate between skeptics and believers in his *Dialogues concerning Natural Religion* (1779). Hume's skepticism is akin to the agnosticism of the ancient philosophers of consolation, such as the Stoics or the Cynics (Hecht 2003: 348–52). Sense experience, whatever its limitations, provides a better guide to human understanding than fanciful flights of imagination. The power of humankind lies in its capacity for rational critical thought, to which memory is ultimately subordinate. In antiquity, such reasoning powers were undeveloped, but they waxed larger along the way to the age of Enlightenment. Hume therefore set limits to unbridled skepticism (Pyrrhonism), for what we can know of the world based upon empirical evidence is considerable. For human knowledge, the everyday realm of experience matters. We can learn from it and use it to practical advantage. The common sense of habit stabilizes our lives.

It is no surprise that Hume never attempted a philosophy of history. Instead, he turned to history itself and acquired fame among contemporaries for his *History of England* (1762), which along the way catalogued the strife and cruelty committed in religion's name. As historian, Hume subjected evidence to rigorous scrutiny. He was among the first historians to address topics of manners and morals, opening a pathway into cultural history. Among issues concerning oral tradition, he exposed the poetry of the Scottish bard Ossian to be a fabrication, for it did not reflect the temper of the times in which it was supposedly composed. Ossian as an ancient epic, he explained, is improbable. The mores of generosity and civility that it conveys were unknown to the barbarous societies of those times. Nor does the epic mention religion, which was an impossible omission. Ancient preliterate societies had no choice but to be religious (Hume [1775] 1965: 390–400).

In their studies of religious origins, Hume and Vico arrived at many of the same findings as they probed time immemorial. Human consciousness emerged as a response to sense experience. Primitive humans were ignorant and credulous; their religious beliefs were reflections on their own vulnerability. They transformed their inadequacies into powerful deities in their own image. Their differences turned on the interpretations in which each had invested his commitments. Whereas Hume stressed the weakness of mind of humankind in its origins, Vico emphasized the power of memory to inspire the human imagination. Whereas Hume saw literacy as a bridge from polytheism to monotheism, Vico circumvented that discussion, and treated monotheism only in the guise of Providence, and then as a benevolent overseer. Hume presented memory as passive and reason as frail. Vico portrayed memory as an active precondition of reason. For Hume, memory is formed as a habit of mind through constant repetition, leading to a common-sense view of the foundations of human knowledge. Memory, moreover, inspires flights of imagination that can lead humans astray. Vico, by contrast, characterized memory as the source of human creativity. For Hume, reason is our consolation. It enables us to acquire practical knowledge of the world so as to deal effectively with life's challenges. For Vico, reason has its limitations. In its abstractions it can lose touch with memory's creative resources, for its power emerges out of the passion of primitive poetical thought. In the end, differences between Hume and Vico reflect tensions within the Enlightenment about the relationship between mind and heart.

MEMORY AND THE SEARCH FOR THE SELF

If history by the end of the eighteenth century laid claim to the exposition of public truths, memory delved into private ones. The search for the particular qualities of character of each individual opened a new vocation for memory in the guise of autobiography. Autobiography was, of course, a literary genre of long-standing as the exposition of one's accomplishments in a narrative of the principal events of a lifetime. Both Vico and Hume wrote autobiographies in this style. Autobiographies so conceived paralleled the biographies of edifying lives. In the late eighteenth century, however, autobiography was reinvented as a technique for discovering private truths within oneself. It is not that soul-searching was hitherto an unknown exercise. Such explorations dated from antiquity in the examination of conscience as an exercise in religious piety. Augustine's *Confessions* (400 CE) was its prototype. The difference is that in the late eighteenth century, autobiography was recast as a humanist genre. So reconceived, it paralleled the rise of the modern novel as an exploration of the psychology of feelings. Johann Goethe's *Sorrows of the Young Werther* (1774) is exemplary, as is Jean-Jacques Rousseau's *Nouvelle Héloïse* (1761). Rousseau taught his contemporaries how to read a novel as a way of drawing out a critical perspective on their own emotions (Darnton 1984: 231–2). These literatures marked the emergence of a new sensibility, an intimate realm of private reflection apart from commentary on one's public life.

The autobiographical writings of Jean-Jacques Rousseau (1712–78) epitomize this new kind of psychological reflection on the interior history of life's journey. He claimed that his public life held little importance by comparison. There is a certain irony in his self-deprecation, for he led a remarkable life and may have been the most famous intellectual celebrity of the eighteenth century (Lilti 2017: 109–59). His life, moreover, served as an unusual story for that era. He hailed from modest origins in Switzerland and set out on his own in early adolescence. During his youth he was a wanderer. He survived misfortune thanks to the largesse of wealthy women. Largely self-educated, he was a gifted writer, a musician of some talent, and a polymath who epitomized the broad learning of the eighteenth-century philosopher. His prize-winning essay for a literary competition sealed his fortunes. Taking advantage of his opportunities, he found his way into high places in both governmental positions and literary circles. As a writer, he received particular attention for his ideas about a social contract in which individuals would be reborn as citizens within a free society. Literary fame, however, did not provide the personal fulfillment he wanted. Or so he claimed.

In mid-life, Rousseau turned to a more personal kind of writing. Searching for authenticity that he could not find in public life, he looked inward in search of truth about himself as it emerged out of the depths of his psyche, an inner sanctum in which he sought a different meaning for his life history. One might say that such soul-searching was his reply to the vanity of the age. The social life of the salons to which he was invited made

FIGURE 5.6: *The Elderly Rousseau, Walking*. Soul-searching as an art of memory. Courtesy of Getty Images, UK.

him uncomfortable for its intellectual pretense. He despised the formal manners of high society. He had no patience for small talk. To reason he opposed sentiment, to irony transparency. His radical renunciation of what he perceived to be the false values of the well-born roused interest among admiring readers. As novelist and as autobiographer, he inspired them to reflect on their own lives. Many wrote to him, wishing to explain the difference his method of self-analysis had made in their lives (Darnton 1984: 242–9).

During his mature years, Rousseau wrote three works of self-analysis: his *Confessions* (1766–70), his effort at a transparent presentation of the vicissitudes of coming of age; his *Dialogues* (1772–6), an attempt at assessing his bad behavior along the way; and his *Reveries of the Solitary Walker* (1776–8), his late-life assessment of his project at self-analysis (Grimsley 1969: 225–67). The last is the most important for our purposes because herein he summarized his assessment of the problem of recollection as method in this kind of writing. He addressed a number of key issues, generated by further reflection on his earlier autobiographical writings. Feeling the effects of aging and battered by a bitter public quarrel with David Hume, he sought solace in solitude. One thing he had learned was how provisional were the truths one can learn about oneself. The search for the self, he recognized, is a never-ending story. Though he sensed that he was nearing the end of his life, he affirmed that there was still something that he could discover about himself as he recycled his recollections once more. Autobiography was open to perpetual revision as long as one had the power to engage personal memories. Searching among them was the primary resource of his old age.

Rousseau plotted *Reveries* in the manner of the classical art of memory. He created a structured mnemonic framework, and localized topics therein. His framework was a succession of ten walks from his home in Paris. These were places for the topics on which he meditated. If his reveries while walking did not measure up to the ideal of disinterested contemplation, his indulgence in them was more serene than it had been in his earlier self-portraits. He noted the preconditions he had established so that he might pursue this exercise: retreat from public life (its society as well as its politics); the search for solitude in natural surroundings, the pursuit of simple pastimes. Rousseau never succeeded completely in establishing these preconditions. His sense of persecution, rife in his earlier autobiographical writings, continued to surface, but only now and then. He claimed to have acquired greater equanimity, and so was able to probe his reminiscences with greater critical acumen. On these walks, he pondered a number of problems that nagged at his psyche. Among the themes that he developed, the following are of particular significance for his ideas about personal memory in the service of soul-searching.

The theme of Rousseau's first walks concerned the art of aging gracefully in the face of one's mortality. The art involved the techniques required to become contemplative. He pointed to the significance of middle age in his journey toward that state of mind. "At forty," he remarked, "I quitted the world and its vanities" (Rousseau [1782] 1979: 51). Rousseau would not have been able to use the modern term "mid-life crisis," now commonplace in ego-psychology. But his description of his mindset at this juncture in his life bears all of its hallmarks. Weary of the bruising intrigues of public life, he turned to the privacy of his own reflections as a refuge. It was the kind of meditation that enabled his spirit to soar. His search for the self was therapeutic, for it warded off depression.

Rousseau's *Reveries* also provided a nuanced assessment of what autobiography as soul-searching could convey about one's interior thought processes. He had come to recognize that complete transparency in writing about one's inner life is neither possible nor advisable. The worthiness of the quest to know oneself depends on the integrity with which it is pursued. His meditation raised the question of the nature of lying, and he explored its varied expressions. Harmful lies are reprehensible, but white lies, he allowed, are often innocuous. He admitted that in his autobiographical narratives he sometimes confabulated to fill gaps when his memory failed him. "I have often made up stories," he confessed, "but very rarely told lies" (Rousseau [1782] 1979: 79). Sometimes, he admitted, lying was preferable to truth-telling in situations in which the truth boldly stated might bring unhappiness or harm to another without purpose. He also admitted his guilt for lies about misdeeds in his youth. He repeated a story told in his *Confessions* in which his lie to cover a minor theft led to the dismissal of a fellow servant. He claimed that the incident had tormented him for fifty years, and so confessing to it in his autobiography alleviated a psychological burden. Yet in acknowledging the more egregious act of abandoning his children to a foundling home, he resorted to rationalization. Rousseau was determined to reaffirm that innocence and goodness lay at the heart of his soul whatever his transgressions along life's way.

The purpose of self-reflection, Rousseau believed, is to pursue happiness conceived as tranquility of mind. But such tranquility is an altered state. It tends to be short-lived, and its maintenance requires constant repair. He referenced two episodes. He recalled the solitude of a brief sojourn on a sparsely populated island in a Swiss lake as the happiest moment in his life. But he found more enduring contentment in his stay of some five years with Madame de Warens, a directress of a spiritual retreat house, for what he claimed was "perfect indolence." This beloved friend ten years his senior taught him the art of loving through the gift of her mentoring. He remembered her as "the most gentle and indulgent woman." She taught him how to love in a way that inspired others.

Rousseau's late-life retreat into a private world sustained by reminiscence might appear to be a far remove from his epoch-defining contribution to political theory some fifteen years before. But his late-life thoughts on the way individual autonomy plays into the social contract helps us to understand what he had in mind. In one of his last walks, he revisited his distinction between two kinds of self-love: within community (*amour propre*) and within one's own mind (*amour de soi*). The former involves self-respect in the eyes of others; the latter self-acceptance (Grimsley 1969: 262). The paradox of citizenship is that it is a social obligation among equals freely undertaken. In this way, he linked the pursuit of personal happiness with his social ideal. Rousseau, in his search for the self through practices of recollection, reaffirmed the autonomy of memory vis-à-vis history and set an agenda for its modern psycho-analytic vocation.

CHAPTER SIX

High Culture and Popular Culture

FIONA McINTOSH-VARJABÉDIAN

Literature can be considered as a *lieu de memoire* in the sense that it shapes collective memory and offers a "repertoire of stories about the past or images of the past available in a given culture" (Burke 2017: 20). Traces of historical events or figures were more or less developed in eighteenth-century literary works according to the genre to which they belonged. Whether appearing as mere allusions or as main arguments in the plot, historical references to events were refashioned to suit the story being told. They could draw images out of the past that, to a certain extent, diverged from historical accuracy in favor of verisimilitude. The weight of Aristotelian poetics was still strong in the tradition of *belles lettres*. Verisimilitude was considered as more apt to convey a moral meaning than a whole string of real but untidy events (McIntosh 2002: 15–26). A classical conception of history still predominated: Jean-François Marmontel (1723–99) quoted Cicero (*De Oratore*) at the beginning of his article on History and described the genre as *"testis temporum, lux veritatis, vita memoriae, magistra vitae, nuncia vetustatis"* (the witness of time past, the beacon of truth, the life of memory, the guide of life, the herald of antiquity). He stressed its collective and moral aims, for history "links generations and ages together through remembrance" (Marmontel [1787] 2005: 610). Finally, the goal of the historian was to establish what was worthy of remembrance by posterity ([1787] 2005: 612) and consequently to choose what should be told.

This form of hindsight built both national and transnational traditions. Antiquity still provided the main models in all of Europe, but national histories became more influential during this period. British drama was well known for its plays based on historical events in England's past. On the continent, this interest in national history was considered an exception (Voltaire [1732] 1974: 689). In France, remembrance of the past was transposed to other traditions, with mainly English or Oriental subjects, at first as a means to stimulate public interest, and at a second stage to promote other national traditions, notably German, French, Spanish, and Portuguese, so as to suggest implicit parallels with French political events. History as a guide to public life and a repertoire of great passions appeared as the prerogative of high culture. The examples it offered were shared among members of the same privileged background. However, a growing interest in popular culture was also justified by its capacity to depict the manners of the past and to recapture lost traditions. Hence, history became less and less a distinctive discipline and led to fuzzy boundaries in which collective memories issuing from oral popular culture were recuperated and assimilated into written and scholarly works (McNeil 2012: 23).

HISTORY AND THE DEFINITION OF HIGH CULTURE DURING THE EIGHTEENTH CENTURY

High culture encapsulates the genres that belong to the literary canon. These genres are hierarchized: epic poetry, tragedies, and some forms of historical writings come first, whereas comedies, novels, tales, occasional and circumstantial poetry, as well as other forms of history such as annals, chronicles, and memoirs belong to a lower sphere in the realm of literature. By choosing the former instead of the latter, the writer signified his wish to emulate the ancients and those modern writers well-remembered by posterity. As such, high culture belonged to the cultural memory of the elite. It provided its members with "elevated sentiments and high examples," nourished "public spirit, the love of glory, contempt of external fortune, and the admiration of what is truly illustrious and great" (Blair 1853: 15). Great works are supposed to have a clearly epideictic function, presenting lasting models of what should be blamed or praised by posterity. As they are mainly founded on ancient figures such as Cato, Brutus, the *Horatii* or Alexander, and on the narrations by Livy, Diodorus Siculus, Plutarch, and Appian, the examples are largely transnational, as exemplified in Johann Christoph Gottsched's *Sterbende Cato* (Dying Cato) (1732) or Colley Cibber's *Caesar in Aegypt* (1725), or Friedrich Schiller's essay on tragedy, *Über die Tragische Kunst* (About Tragic Art) (1792).

Whatever the genre, the prestige of classical historical figures resided in their universality, even though they may have illustrated more local political concerns (Bevis 1995: 203; Briant 2012: *passim*). Indeed, Marmontel, author of many articles on literature for the *Encyclopédie* of Diderot and d'Alembert (1751–72), defined epic poetry as "the imitation in a narrative of an interesting and memorable action" (Marmontel [1787] 2005: 509). Memorable does not mean *stricto sensu* historical, for it denotes the idea that many things that actually happened have been forgotten and need to be forgotten. Voltaire (1694–1778) considered that Homer transcribed "part of the history and fables of his time." He argued that, thanks to the versified form (understood here as a kind of obstacle to easy literary productions), only the greatest events were saved in collective memory, as if the poetical form acted as a kind of sieve and selected only what was most important. (Voltaire [1728] 1816: 310).

Since the Renaissance, the critical inheritance of Joseph Just Scaliger (1540–1609) and of Ludivico Castelvetro (1505–71) enabled writers to choose real events instead of myths to serve as an outline on stage. Pierre Corneille (1606–94), who was still considered in eighteenth-century Europe as a model for tragedies together with Jean Racine (1639–99), gives a few clues about the constraints historical facts had on plots, but also about why they were considered a main ingredient in tragedies. He puts forward the argument that they were largely accepted by the public as plausible. In this sense, they do not differ from mythological plots because tradition as such enables the poet to justify abhorrent and abnormal behavior such as parricide or infanticide, which otherwise would seem too unbelievable to be accepted by the audience (Corneille [1660] 1987: 118). The destructive passions of great families are represented on stage. They combine both the individual jealousies and motives that can be recognized by the public, as well as the political ambitions and concerns that trouble the public sphere. The historical framework can be adapted to the needs of the tragic form. For the action must have a beginning, a middle, and a clear-cut ending (Corneille [1660] 1987: 125). Historical circumstances may be added or modified in order to reinforce understanding of the chain of events; but Corneille is careful not to disturb the public's preconceptions, and poetic inventions can only take place in the blanks left by general historical knowledge (Corneille [1660] 1987: 167–8). Despite his criticisms against Corneille (and especially his *Rodogune*), Gotthold Ephraim Lessing (1729–81) does not fundamentally question the fact that tragedies founded on history have to be exact only to a certain point (Lessing [1767–9] 1981: 154). Characters are a more important element on stage than the historical outline itself ([1767–9] 1981: 125). This is the reason why eighteenth-century writers still debated whether poetic distance of the plot was necessary, and whether it was possible to represent recent events on stage. Indeed, they might be more widely known and therefore more difficult to transform poetically.

For that matter, geographical distance was sometimes equated with historical distance (Postert 2010: 61); hence the relative success Oriental subjects had on the French stage under the influence of Jean Racine's *Bajazet* (1672). Voltaire's *Mahomet* (1736) and his Byzantine *Irène* (1778) extended the influence of these oriental settings on the European stage and more especially in London, where both plays were adapted (Bevis 1995: 201). Lessing's *Nathan der Weise* (Nathan the Wise) (1779) borrowed elements from the positive image of Saladin in the *Decameron*. British history also established a kind of geographical distance for the French playwrights. Thomas Corneille's *Le Comte d'Essex* (1678) was regularly played during the eighteenth century in Europe, among the much larger bulk of plays still based on ancient history. The core references of the European elite and, in some cases, of the European bourgeoisie (Bevis 1995: 117), were expanded. Voltaire's *Zaïre* (1732) was a huge success, which mixed both an Oriental setting and French characters during the Crusades. It was adapted in English by Aaron Hill three years later. The appeal of these new subjects was truly transnational, as exemplified in Jan Frans Cammaert's (1699–1780) Dutch version of Thomas Corneille's play in 1750 *Doodbaerende stantvastigheyt in den graeve van Essex onder Elisabeth, koninginne van Engeland* (the steadfastness of the earl of Essex before his death under the reign of Elizabeth, queen of England). However, a more national justification of modern subjects emerged gradually during the long eighteenth century. Still, on the English stage the French influence was perceptible: John Banks' *The Unhappy Favourite, or the Earl of Essex (1682)* was influenced by La Calprenède's play of 1632, and Henry Brooke's version published in 1761 followed Banks (Marshall 2008: 196, note 42).

The key role of history in the definition of high culture is all the more important as the theoretical arguments on the use of historical outlines in epic poetry evolved toward resembling those developed for tragic plays (Taylor 1970: 105). *La Henriade*, published in London in 1728 with a summary of the events, was centered on the accession of Henri IV to the French throne. It rejected all marvelous ingredients, imitating Lucan's *Pharsalia*, even though some contemporary literary critics considered the mythological and extraordinary elements essential to the epic form. The hero's actions should give an impression of psychological necessity and verisimilitude, although they should not be devoid of a certain form of grandeur (Taylor 1970: 131). The narrative should not be encumbered with useless detail or obtrusive erudition. Concerning emplotment or antiquarian details, Voltaire had the same ideal of conciseness and necessity for his nonfictitious historical narratives (Taylor 1970: 139). But this similarity in style does not mean that the poet should, like the historian, stick to the facts in all circumstances. Just as tragedies based on Mary Stuart forged a meeting between the Queen of Scots and the Queen of England for the sake of a stronger dramatic effect, Voltaire imagined a meeting between Henry of Navarre and Elizabeth I in order to imitate Virgil's representation of the vicissitudes of Aeneas' treatment of Queen Dido.

Contrariwise, plots in comedies were supposed to be invented, although some exceptions can be noted, such as Charles Collé's *La Partie de Chasse de Henri IV* (1768) in which the figure of Henri IV appears on stage. But the author himself underlines that it is an exceptional feature and justifies his choice by the living and loving memory of the King and his minister, the Duc de Sully (Collé [1768] 1974: 599). The emphasis on invention can be explained by the fact that comedies generally represented low characters (peasants, valets and bourgeois), who were generally left outside of the interest of history. Collé explains he is giving an insight into the private life of a king who was known for his good and simple nature ([1768] 1974: 600). Because of the conventions concerning the characters and the genres in which they were likely to appear, even dramas such as bourgeois tragedies were played on a lower key, despite the fact that some reinterpreted classical plots, such as Lessing's *Emilia Galotti* (1772), inspired by the Livian Virginia.

The situation is more complicated for novels and prose narratives because they played on a conscious generic blur. Some authors justified novels as a genre by virtue of the uncertainties of the historical record, or by the knowledge that its storylines were fictitious (Lenglet Du Fresnoy 1734: 59). However, such a move was not widespread. Walter Scott (1771–1832) made fun of this propensity to mix genres when describing Waverley's faulty education: "The French had afforded him an almost exhaustless collection of memoirs, scarcely more faithful than romances and of romances so well written as hardly to be distinguished from memoirs" (Scott [1814] 1986: 14). But of course, he himself played with generic boundaries in his historical novels. Long before Scott, Pierre-François Guyot Desfontaines (1685–1745) presented his story of John of Portugal as a historical novel (*roman historique*), a genre he considered both superior to the epic poem (because it was devoid of supernatural intervention), and to non-fictional historical narratives (because they contained marginal elements of fiction that embellish the composition) (Desfontaines 1724: preface). Once again, the tragic model and its justification are extended to the narrative form.

The mode of narration in the first person singular frequently creates a sort of indeterminate zone between facts and fiction, for the novels and the romances resemble memoirs. The Abbé Prévost (1697–1763,) like Daniel Defoe, shared his time between novelistic and journalistic writing (Bloom 2009: *passim*; Peraldo 2010: 21). *Le Philosophe anglais ou Histoire de M. Cleveland, fils naturel de Cromwell* by Prevost first appeared in French between 1731 and 1739, before it was translated and edited many times in English, nearly immediately after the French edition. Notwithstanding the starting point of Cromwell's imaginary bastard who helped Prevost denounce the Protector's hypocrisy, many allusions are made to historical figures, such as Henrietta of England, or the Duke of Monmouth. A few elements, either of their real stories or of facts imputed to their lives, appear in the narrative and create a form of connivance. The Protector's hypocrisy was a popular theme in France, the possible murder of Henrietta too. As for Monmouth, he is depicted as arrogant, violent, and inclined to follow his passions at all costs; Clarendon appears in his French exile as a symbol of the vicissitudes of Fortune, one of the major themes in the novel. All these depictions of their traits belonged to common knowledge in France and were intertwined in fiction with an all-encompassing judgment about English revolutions (Goulemot 1996: 99–126).

It would be impossible here to allude to all the fictional narratives that refer to real events or to real persons. Since Ian Watt's *Rise of the Novel* (1957), these are generally linked to a growing realism, and to an effort to curb the fantasies of the Romance as a genre, for the "'marvellous' [was dismissed] as unworthy and inappropriate" (Beasley

1976: 444). Thus, the plot in *Tom Jones* (1749) is "placed alongside the events of the '45 Rebellion" (Brown 1979: 209), leading to many possible and disturbing parallels. *Roderick Random* (1748) gives the reader a short insight into the Battle of Dettingen of 1743. *Candide* (1759) alludes to the earthquake of Lisbon about which Voltaire had written a poem in 1756, a year after the catastrophic event. *Delphine* (1802) by Germaine de Staël (1766–1817) represents the French Revolution as a background to the love story between Delphine and Léonce. Strangely enough, considering both the literary and the historical context, the readers of Goethe's *The Elective Affinities* (1809) receive no details concerning the battles where Eduard, one of the main characters, has fled to escape from his bungled family affairs; the novel merely alludes to wars that might possibly be the Napoleonic Wars in Germany, with no further identification. Even though his epic poem, *Hermann and Dorothea* (1797) refers directly to the French Revolutionary Wars, Goethe seems intent upon keeping a more universal and impersonal viewpoint by not alluding too directly to contemporary events (Boucher 1954: 134); Eduard is just an unspecified Baron in the prime of life. *Wilhelm Meisters Wanderjahre* (Wilhelm Meister's Journeyman Years) (1796) also aims at the symbolical and requires the readers' initiation (Redfield 1996: 19). The historical circumstances of the plot are fuzzily depicted. However, the popularity in Europe of most of the novels that deal explicitly with contemporary or historical events publicize them (if not in detail) outside the national boundaries of the work itself. News has a transnational impact and novels mirror this new interest.

However, this historicism does not change the lowly status of the novel as a genre fundamentally. Indeed, recent history and real events were perceived to be anecdotal, as they had been for the ancient writer Procopius, containing secret and scandalous accounts of the lives of famous characters, or mere contingent facts with little universal appeal. In a system still attached in the arts to the ideal of *belle nature* or to the *beau idéal* (Beasley 1976: 439) or to the *Grand Beau* (Becq [1984] 1994: 515–17), to quote the most frequent expressions, they belong to the background of history, together with memoirs and chronicles, however widespread they may have been. In his narratives, *Nouvelles Françaises* (1772–5), Louis d'Ussieux popularized stories of the Crusades and of the religious wars, supplemented with anecdotes extracted from his travels; they were translated into German from 1777 onwards (Moser 2015: 304), first for the Swiss public, then for the German and the Imperial readership. Before that, from 1734 to 1743, François Gayot de Pitaval published his *Causes célèbres et intéressantes avec les jugemens qui les ont decidés* (*Famous and Interesting Cases with Judgments about Them*), true judicial stories that were supposed to compete with the growing taste for novels. His success and influence lasted a century, since Walter Scott alluded to the work in *The Heart of Midlothian* and presented it as a source of inspiration. There were many editions and translations of these collections. In Britain, Charlotte Smith chose a title (*Romance of Real Life*) in 1787 that expressed the ambivalence of the form. On the contrary, in Germany, Schiller translated it in 1792 under the title *Merkwürdige Kriminalgeschichten und Rechtsfälle* (*Remarkable criminal stories and law cases*), whose subtitle: *ein Beytrag zur Geschichte der Menschheit* (*a contribution to the history of Mankind*) lent a universal allure to the affairs. Indeed, Schiller's preface underlines the transnational and moral value of this vast collection extracted from Pitaval and completed it with affairs from other countries and other authors (Schiller 1792: n.p.). The chronology of this translation from 1773 onwards, together with the publication of another work called the *Causes célèbres* by Des Essarts (1744–1810), indicate that there was an important reflection on the aesthetic effect of criminal stories and on the significance of their remembrance. To recall recent cases, instead of older ones, meant that the events were still known and that there were still living witnesses. According to Des Essarts, the illusion created by the narrative was stronger and the readers were more engaged in the story. The facts were true instead of being mere possibilities, and the readers could imagine that the events could have happened to them (Des Essarts 1773: 5–6). The new prestige of novelty did not exclude parallels with the legislation and the crimes of the ancients (Des Essarts 1773: 52–3). The comparisons and learned disquisitions on Charlemagne or on Louis IX for instance (Des Essarts 1773: 58–9) show that popular culture from the gazettes was assimilated into a more scholarly framework, a phenomenon that can be observed in forms of low culture too.

Such works show that the material deemed memorable was extended; these criminal stories not only depict the destructive passions of the elite but also those of everyday men and women. The defense of these moral cases is similar to the justifications for tragedies and stresses the moral value of the spectacle offered by reversal of fortune. These similarities between the representation of the elite and of the lower classes can be compared to a larger change in historical writing itself and to a certain number of attempts to depict the people and the customs of an age, instead of focusing on the great and powerful only.

ELEMENTS OF CHANGE: REMEMBERING THE PEOPLE

Behind the more traditional epideictic function of historical writings that is regularly expressed by eighteenth-century historians and authors, new concerns emerged. On the one hand, Charles Rollin's (1661–1741) influential work was centered on examples of revolutions within states that he attributed to the pride of princes or the faults of nations (Gribbin 1972: 616); on the other, he expressed a strong interest in the manners of the age, that is in a more collective form of history. His *Histoire ancienne des Égyptiens, des Carthaginois, des Assyriens, des Babyloniens, des Mèdes et des Perses, des Macédoniens, des Grecs* (1730–8), was translated into English and Dutch and also into German by Gottfried Ephraïm Muller. His *Histoire romaine* (1738–48), completed by Jean-Louis Baptiste Crevier (1693–1765), was translated many times into English. Abridged forms were studied in schools up to the mid-1850s. Although his work contributed to keeping alive famous ancient historical figures in public memory, Rollin emphasized that this aspect of history was less useful than understanding why empires disappeared or knowing about the manners, the customs and the laws of these ancient peoples (Rollin 1740: viii). These ancient nations were to be judged according to their virtue, or their patriotism and spirit of honor, themes that informed the rhetoric of politicians during the French Revolution under Rollin's enduring influence (Rollin [1738] 1823: 29).

Interestingly enough, what Rollin meant by manners included the principles of government, the religion and beliefs of the people, the organization of the army, the sciences and the arts and the trades (*métiers*) (Rollin 1740: 33). Whole chapters were devoted to these topics, instead of focusing exclusively on dates and chronologically ordered events. The French have a specific word, *tableau* (picture), to designate a mode of narration in which a general overview is given. In modern history, a more modest attempt can be found through David Hume's remarks on the state of the arts and sciences in his *History of England* (1762).

These writings epitomize an important shift in both historical writing and cultural memory during the eighteenth century. They also entail an epistemological challenge for the historian, especially when these descriptions concern ancient history or peoples with no written history as such or with un-deciphered written inscriptions. Archaeology was at its very first steps with the development of antiquarian studies and societies. The *Académie des inscriptions et belles-lettres*, founded in 1663, was one of the most prominent in Europe. Textual sources still had the highest authority compared to material artifacts. For that matter, Edward Gibbon's *History of the Decline and Fall of the Roman Empire* (1776–88) was exceptional, considering the number of notes that referred explicitly to the *Académie*'s findings. So how could a historian write about nations and peoples without relying on written history? Critical history, of which Pierre Bayle (1647–1706) is one of the first proponents, developed the idea that myths and legends were founded on facts that had been corrupted by time. This critical interpretation of the meaning of mythology helped justify oral traditions or popular narratives and poetry far beyond the field of classical studies, since all myths could be pruned and all legends could be collated and rationalized in order to recapture past events. Finally, manners could be deduced from the details of the narratives themselves.

During the second half of the eighteenth century, the attempt to reconstruct the past had a special appeal in areas where oral and popular culture was particularly vulnerable, such as Scotland and Ireland, but also in Latvia, as Johann Gottfried Herder's (1744–1803) "experiences with Latvian folk culture served as an impetus to his research on folk culture generally" (Tantillo 1999: 32). In 1765, under the influence of Thomas Blackwell's admiration for primitive free societies and poetry (Stafford 1996: x), James Macpherson (1736–96) created a "strange Celtic past" (Stafford 1996: v) that seemed to compete with Homer's Greece. Of course, Ossian was partly Macpherson's invention; but the Ossianic poems were inspired by "the very antiquarian spirit of the classicists, who sought to reconstruct lost societies through careful scholarship" (Stafford 1996: xi). Indeed, the way Macpherson justified his work is telling, for it shows how modern societies could lift the veil of obscurity and fix elusive traditions. As he explains:

> Inquiries into antiquities of nation afford more pleasure than any other real advantage to mankind. The ingenious may form systems of history on probabilities and a few facts; but at a great distance of time, their accounts must be vague and uncertain. The infancy of states and kingdoms is as destitute of great events, as of the means of transmitting them to posterity. The arts of polished life, by which alone facts can be preserved with certainty, are the product of a well-formed community. It is then historians begin to write, and public transactions to be worthy remembrance. The actions of former times are left in obscurity, or magnified by uncertain traditions. Hence it is that we find so much of the marvelous in the origin of every nation; posterity being always ready to believe anything, however fabulous that reflects honor on their ancestors.
>
> —Macpherson [1765] 1996: 43

Macpherson's rhetoric is in tune with parallel attempts to recapture the past. Even if some proved to be more trustworthy and more faithful to the original sources than others, the process by which oral traditions were supposed to be fixed by scholarly endeavors were strangely similar. Fabliaux were neglected because the sublime and the heroic were being promoted, whereas farces and comic narratives were rejected as giving too coarse an image of the people and of its manners (Fink 2002: 234). The so-called people's voice had to be separated from the outcries of the populace (Mondon 2007: §6). As Groom demonstrates, Thomas Percy's (1729–1811) emphasis on a national past (during the same

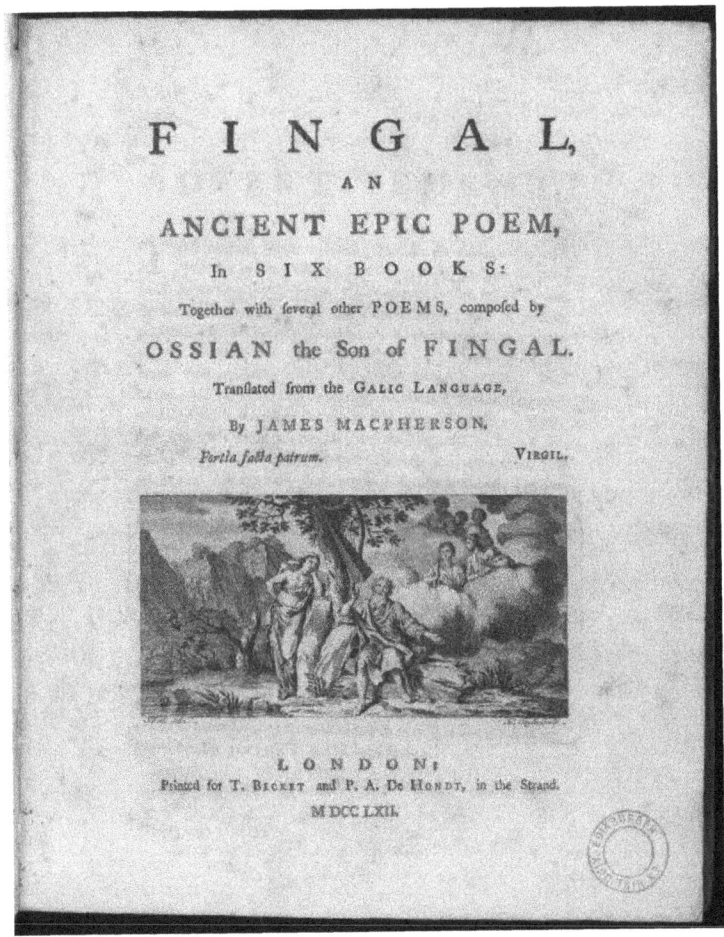

FIGURE 6.1: Title page of a poem published by James Macpherson, 1789. Courtesy of the University of Edinburgh.

period as Macpherson) was a "conservative tactic to circulate 'ballads of a proper tendency'" (Groom 1996: 56). It meant a form of selection and an "editorial fiddling" (1996: 57) of old ballads that were reconstructed by Percy's collations. Introductions to each poem and notes demonstrate the weight of erudition. The introductions, together with the "Essay on the ancient English minstrels" inspired by Paul-Henri Mallet's *Histoire du Dannemarc* (1758), point out the possible historicity of the poems. Percy not only refers to battles such as Otterburn and to Jehan Froissart, but also to the manners of the time, judging, for the tale "Sir Cauline," that the practice of healing and of surgery was common "among all the Gothic and Celtic nations" (Percy [1765] 1996: 36).

In 1819, a similar "editorial fiddling" can be traced in Germany. In their preface, the Grimm brothers also justified the way they selected the supposed right variant that should prevail over other corrupted forms of the tale, thanks to their philological methodology. Hence, they chased interpolations and embellishments that, according to them, tampered with the original spirit of the tale and promoted German regional versions together with Austrian ones. Hence, the tales were supposed to represent what they considered to be pure German behavior and morals. By reconstructing the original form, the Grimm brothers believed they could recapture the epic quality of the narratives and the strength of their mother tongue. Moreover, they thought they could defeat the inevitable corruption of time (Grimm [1819, 1857] 1980: 21–2) by promoting German simplicity against French artificiality, just as Herder had done in his *Volkslieder* in 1778 (Fink 2003: 76).

Nationalistic strivings combined with new ways of envisioning both the past and the people. These scholarly editors decided to keep as precious tokens of disappearing manners and beliefs what had been rejected by the older generation of writers as mere superstitions or as stories that were best forgotten. According to Herder, language itself keeps alive traces of the past and "mirrors the beliefs and the manners, the experiences and the History of the Nation" (Kim 2002: 25). Orality could both point out dialects which had to be purged from polite speech and more positively, affirm national identity, enabling the poet to "replicate the collective folk memory to the listeners" (McNeil 2012: 25).

Some of these collections of old ballads and folk tales answered to more conservative ideologies, others to more radical ones. The difference in political treatment is reflected in the image of the people that they convey (Mondon 2007: §9–13). Joseph Ritson (1752–1803) put forward how paradoxical it was that a twelfth- or thirteenth-century outlaw, Robin Hood, could still be sung in ballads and remembered in his times. This fact had excited his curiosity and justified his endeavor to retrieve old fragments of these popular songs (Ritson [1795] 1883: preface, xii). Solid evidence was scanty, according to Ritson, but he wished to promote the image of a pious and heroic outlaw, comparable to William Wallace (Ritson [1795] 1883: ix), known for his "spirit of freedom and independence which has endeared him to the common people, whose cause he maintained" (Ritson [1795] 1883: xi). He professed greater trustworthiness than Percy. However, "[i]t is illuminating to note the assurance with which Ritson cites these authorities. The Sloane MS Ritson admits to be of the sixteenth century; few of his other authorities are earlier; yet not for a moment does he hesitate over their verity. He takes whatever will support his theory, and quite guilelessly asks us to believe whomever he chooses" (Moreland 1935: 523). Hood is treated as a genuine historic figure, despite conflicting traditions that are inherent in legends (Simeone 1953: 305).

Whether these heroes of ballads or popular songs were historical or mainly legendary like William Tell and Robin Hood, they played an important part in the emerging consciousness of the people and in their collective memory. They also testify to a long-lasting change in what was to be considered a memorable figure: it had to encapsulate the spirit of the people, to carry its ideals and its aspirations, instead of epitomizing a more abstract form of political virtue. The figure of the outlaw emerged in France, and even in Holland, Germany, and Italy from the middle of the eighteenth century onwards, with the multiplication of stories on the smuggler Louis Mandrin. But whereas Robin Hood was idealized as a good outlaw who protected the poor and the destitute, the first narratives on Mandrin underlined his cruelty and announced a lurid interest in his ordeal and execution in their book titles (Maignien 1890: 2). Although he was popular, he did not acquire the symbolic value of Robin Hood, William Tell, or Rob Roy, probably because his stories, such as l'abbé Regley's *Histoire de Louis Mandrin, depuis sa naissance jusqu'à sa mort, avec un détail de ses cruautés, de ses brigandages et de son supplice* (History of Louis Mandrin from his birth to his death with a detailed account of his cruelties, his robberies and his execution) (1755) were told so as to denounce the outlaw's cupidity and

FIGURE 6.2: *Portrait of Louis Mandrin in the prison at Valence prior to his execution in 1755.* Courtesy of the Bibliothèque Nationale de France.

brutality rather than to glorify him. Mandrin is treated more as an individual case than as a symbol of the French people or of the oppressed. His vices make him a self-serving criminal. Other ingredients are therefore necessary so as to endow the figure of the outlaw with greater luster. Both Robin Hood and Goethe's unlikely historic hero, Götz von Berlichingen (1773), the knight, or in reality, the mercenary with the iron-hand, become rebels because of unjust laws or oppressive and illegitimate power. Götz in particular represents the old medieval order in the play, against new foreign laws that curbed the Germanic freedom. To the end, he decides that he must stay faithful to the emperor, just as Robin Hood remained faithful to Richard the Lionheart. When the knight sided with the rebellious peasants, it was to limit their most disruptive instincts, though in vain. Justice is paradoxically essential to the building of the outlaw legend in collective memory.

Through these figures, the relationship between the people and the representation of its aspirations is regularly questioned. The debate Ritson hints at concerning Hood's nobility and titles in his introduction can indeed be understood politically: can the people act for themselves with one of its members at its head, or do the people need a leader from a higher class to inspire them? To what extent can popular rebellion be considered legitimate? The onstage adaptations of Robin Hood made clear that he was "agitating against the misrule of King John" (Burwick 2011: 120). However, the French Revolution and Bonapartism gave a new turn to the debate and to the idea of popular action during the nineteenth century. Indeed, the figure of Robin Hood had a strange aftermath under the pen of the French radical historian Augustin Thierry. Thierry had read with keen attention Walter Scott's *Ivanhoe* (1819) in which Locksley/Hood appeared, underlining the key role of the momentous political and social conflict between the oppressed Saxons and the aristocratic and haughty Normans for understanding modern politics (Simeone 1953: 306).

The melodramatization of some of these figures made them more popular and demonstrated constant shifts between high and low culture. Erudite scholars and antiquarians had refashioned oral sources, and in turn, the ballads inspired melodramas or novels such as Scott's *Ivanhoe* and *Rob Roy* (1817). Such generic shifts were accepted in London because "the distribution of the classes had ceased to be as reliable a determinate in the theaters of the early nineteenth century" (Burwick 2011: 117). Hence, the same cultural references could be shared among a large spectrum of social classes under various guises and by-products. Circulating libraries, cheaper book editions, engravings, and artifacts, all contributed to keeping some episodes available to the imagination of the public and conferred upon legends the authority of genuine national history. These episodes could be reactivated and refashioned according to the circumstances and the audience, thus creating a kind of transferable culture both inside and outside national boundaries.

FLEXIBLE STORIES: LINKING HIGH AND POPULAR CULTURE

Cultural memory refashions events and figures out of the past. It verges on the legendary, hence its lasting power. It also mirrors changing attitudes and questionings concerning history itself, for the dramatization of the plot and the reorganization of the outline enable the writer to mediate the various and possibly conflicting interpretations of historical facts. The case is obvious for Mary Stuart, who was deemed both responsible for and victim of her actions. Thus, writers identify and play with the aesthetic potential of past situations in order either to embody contemporary political and religious debates or to overcome them. Cultural memory can offer a form of social healing by making all audiences identify with the characters. National figures such as Rob Roy, Robin Hood, and William Tell emerged, and their appeal depended on their capacity to unite high and low audiences. In a period in which cultural boundaries were becoming less clear-cut in light of the growing success of melodramas and novels, authors such as Walter Scott proved that reconciliation between high and popular culture was possible.

The Case of William Tell

The success of a historical or a semi-historical figure or story can be measured by its capacity to be remodeled, according to the events and the circumstances in which it is told or represented. Despite multiple reinterpretations of the William Tell story, the main outlines are stable: civic virtue and defense of liberty are the most constant features of the plot. The variations are due to the role that has been imparted to this figuration of liberty: the more heroic he seems, the more fictionalized is his story. Other discrepancies appear concerning the aftermath of the revolt and give the audience a clue about how popular action is legitimated or repudiated in the play.

When Antoine-Marin Lemierre's (1733–93) play *Guillaume Tell* went on stage for the first time on December 17, 1766, it was criticized because it transgressed the rules of French classical tragedies and the literary canon by representing peasants and primitive populations as heroes—for the Swiss were considered as such common social types

(Lemierre 2005: 21). The play, which at first had aimed to renew the French stage with fresh subject matter in the same spirit as Voltaire, was more successful twenty years later (1783–6), and before the French Revolution, for two reasons. Firstly, the American War of Independence had given a new significance to the play. Secondly, Lemierre rewrote part of the play in order to satisfy the demand of the audience for more spectacular effects on stage. Instead of the form of the dramatic narrative used by Corneille and Racine, Lemierre represented the scene in which Guillaume Tell had to shoot an arrow on a fir cone (*pomme de pin* in French) on his son's head on stage (Act IV Scene 2) to promote the greatest thrill for the audience (Marchal-Ninosque 2008: note 187, 236). However, the national uprising, which found echoes in the War of Independence, remains less important than the patriotic virtues the author wished to promote and to which he gives a more general meaning. Cléofé, Tell's wife in the play, reminds the public of Portia, Brutus's wife and Cato's daughter, enhancing the parallels between Brutus's or Cato's republicanism and Tell's defiance of Gessler's tyranny, in the same spirit as had Charles Rollin in his work. Indeed, the figure of the Swiss plowman was assimilated to that of his Roman counterpart, as depicted by Titus Livy (Marchal-Ninosque 2008: note 11, 191) and by Rollin. The play has a clear epideictic function and demonstrates the virtue and the simplicity of manners of Tell and the legendary Arnold von Melchtal. Lemierre follows Alexandre-Louis de Watteville's *Histoire de la confédération helvétique* (1754) in many instances. Watteville had already stressed Helvetic virtue, depicting its unheroic nature, in that it was founded not on individual military exploits but rather on collective acts of justice and equity (Watteville [1754] 1757: 2). The grand counselor of the city of Bern also points out the special privileges the emperor Rudolph had given to the Swiss, legitimating their revolt against a tyrannical power and stressing their liberty.

In his *History of the Helvetic Confederation* (1790), the German writer Johannes Müller (1752–1809) presents William Tell as a true historical figure of the fourteenth century. The events are dated from 1307. Müller, like his predecessors, underlines the virtue of Swiss men and women, who according to him have strong character because of the equality and simplicity of their manners. The picture before the Austrian oppression is idyllic and stresses the orderly happiness and activity of the peasants. William Tell is presented as a true hero but his function is mainly to epitomize the strife and woes of the confederates. On the contrary, Jean-Pierre Claris de Florian (1755–94) concentrates his narrative on Tell and the main characters are all related to him. Melchtal is both the hero's double and his future in-law, since the writer invented a romantic by-plot in which Melchtal's daughter, Claire, and Tell's son, Gemmi, fall in love and are affianced. The tone resembles that of an exemplary story or of a romance. William Tell designed the plot for the insurrection; the other participants have a subordinate role and obey his strategy. The story ends with the hero's harangue in which he proclaims the birth of the republic. The work was published posthumously in 1801, but the shadow of the French Revolution looms large on the hero's last words, even though the author had been imprisoned by Robespierre and most probably died because of his detention.

The French Revolution also had an effect on the reception of Schiller's play *Wilhelm Tell* (1804), because of the similarities in the uprisings and goals that had emerged during the previous decade. Lemierre's work also profited by the events, since it was edited seven times from 1789 to 1810, adapted as an opera in 1791, and staged in English in 1794. Its significance had changed once again because of this new context and seemed to have anticipated the Revolution as such. Florian's story also became the basis of a British stage production (Burwick 2011: 110). It is noteworthy, however, that the German play, when compared to Florian's narrative, hails the birth of a nation and not that of a regime. By linking the demands of the Helvetic cantons to those of other German principalities (such as Swabia and Rhineland), their political aspirations seem both similar and, to a certain degree, legitimate. In the French narrative, Tell seems to announce the coming of a providential leader, whereas Schiller represents a more collective uprising of the three Swiss cantons. Another major discrepancy can be noted between the two versions. In Florian's narrative, Tell and his wife are both convinced that their cause is just and that all sacrifices are necessary for the greater cause. Schiller gives a more nuanced view. Hedwig, Tell's wife, strongly complains about the predicament in which her husband's actions have put the whole family. Tell himself does not express the same kind of unhesitating confidence as his French counterpart. Finally, Schiller draws a possible and upsetting parallel between Tell's killing of Gesler and Duke John's murder of Albrecht, which is explicitly named a parricide. The new nation is proclaimed but the hero abandons his crossbow forever because of the stain of blood that has symbolically defiled it. Thus, the poet leaves room for a double reception: the predominate one celebrates old liberties and patriotic political action to defend the basic rights of the citizens (Mettler and Lippuner 1989: 92–3); the other under the influence of the French Terror questions the limits of violence and uprising (Krobb 2005: 286–7).

The Case of Mary Stuart

Compared to this widely accepted form of cultural memory, Mary Stuart represents a much more debatable figure. On the one hand, the Catholic interpretation of the events

FIGURE 6.3: *A party on Lake Urner-See, Switzerland, with the chapel of William Tell and the village of Brunnen in the background.* Courtesy of the Austrian National Library.

make the Scottish Queen the rightful heir to the English throne and a martyr; on the other, the Protestant account of the facts depict her as a false, intriguing woman.

The Scottish Queen inspired multiple plays, songs, ballads, and engravings. It is impossible to give an exhaustive view of the various works she inspired. For political and religious reasons, the two memories compete, firstly in histories, treatises, and apologies, secondly under various fictionalized forms. Jean de Bordes, a French Jesuit, first identified the tragic potential of the character in 1589 (Conroy 1999: 28). On stage, the *Queen of Scots* emerged in France in 1601 in a play by Antoine de Montchrestien, in 1639 by Charles Regnault, and in 1691 by Edmé Boursault. The last reflects contemporary controversies on women succeeding to the crown, a major issue that also appears in Samuel Jebb's collection of documents, *De vita et rebus gestis serenissimae principis Mariae Scotorum reginae* (On the life and acts of the most serene princess Marie queen of Scots) (1725). Boursault sticks to the French view and demonstrates the superiority of the Salic Law that bans women from power. Though patronized by James Stuart, John Banks' play *The Island Queens* (1684) was censured in England because the subject was still too contentious at the time. It appeared under a new title *The Albion Queens* in 1704 and was reedited successfully throughout the century until 1791. Strangely enough, the latter part of the century brought the Scottish Queen to the fore. The statesman John St. John wrote a tragedy that was represented on stage in 1789; in 1792, Mary Deverell, wrote and published a historical tragedy or dramatic poem, though it was never performed. Friedrich Schiller wrote his famous drama in 1800. The same year appeared an anonymous historical ballad, "written by a Lady."

The dark legend surrounding Mary was still alive under the lasting influence of George Buchanan's *History of Scotland*, reedited in 1733. Elie-Catherine Fréron refers to him as an elegant but untrustworthy historian in his *Histoire de Marie Stuart, reine d'Ecosse et de France* (1742). Those who opposed his negative view had to answer his charges about Mary's so-called wantonness and about Darnley's murder, as did the ballad. The image of Buchanan's misogyny imbued most of the representations of the Queen of Scots, particularly the *History of Scotland* written by William Robertson (1759). The historian stresses her many charms and explains how they not only roused Elizabeth's hatred but also contributed to her downfall. David Hume is more nuanced in his *History of England* (1754–62). Although he refers to the personal jealousies of both queens, he also criticizes strongly the bigotry of the Scottish Reformers who could not understand Mary's many accomplishments. The prologue by William Fawkener to the play *Mary Queen of Scots* by John St. John also points out the cultural backwardness of Scotland in order to explain why she was chased away and imprisoned in England. However, in the play itself, John St. John seems to stick to the darker legend, as Mary's power on men was directly felt by the Duke of Norfolk, her dupe. Schiller amplifies this theme by multiplying the number of noblemen ready to sacrifice their lives for her cause; he gives an extensive review of the plots against Elizabeth. Mary becomes an accessory to the murderous schemes.

Pity, a main ingredient in eighteenth-century tragedies, is generally used for more apologetic purposes. Mary Deverell depicts the Scottish Queen as a most vulnerable woman, who incidentally faints a lot. Men manipulated and wronged her. Her execution is considered by one of the characters, Burgyne, to be an immolation, thus waking up religious images of the *agnus dei*. Banks also conveys a pitiable image of the Scottish prisoner but applies this sentiment to Norfolk and to Elizabeth as well. For Norfolk is trapped by his own feelings of pity towards Mary, and Elizabeth by her status as a queen. All the main characters become victims of circumstances. For that reason, the play is among the most

FIGURE 6.4: *Portrait of Mary Stuart, Queen of Scots*, engraved by Jacobus Houbraken, 1738, after Hans Holbein. Courtesy of the Wellcome Collection.

many-sided. Even Schiller's Mary is not devoid of the sublime once she accepts her death (Field 1960: 337). Her decapitation is "mirrored step by step by Leicester" (1960: 339) The conclusion chimes with Boursault's interpretation, as the French playwright makes Elizabeth comment on Mary's horrendous execution. His play ends in her declaration that at least Mary will find a repose that she herself will no longer experience. Likewise, Schiller presents the English Queen as isolated and gnawed by her own guilt. The dramatic and aesthetic effect counterbalances the political and religious divide.

CONCLUSION

In this chapter, I have shown how eighteenth-century literature mediated collective memory of the past at the crossroads between high (learned) and low (popular) culture. Literature had long battened upon edifying themes drawn out of the experience of antiquity. By the eighteenth century, however, writers in all genre of literature displayed growing sensitivity to the memorable historical events and personalities of recent centuries and into their own times. In the latter part of the century, this trend was followed by another in which scholars were taking a keen interest in critical interpretation of the ballads, legends, and folklore of popular culture, and set themselves the task of collecting and inventorying them. Considered in its ensemble, therefore, eighteenth-century literature—drama, poetry, and the new genre of the novel—provided a forum in which representation of heroic lives out of high culture came to intermingle with a presentation of the mores of everyday life in popular culture. All of these writers remained faithful to the ancient dictum of Aristotle that literature (poetry) is superior to history in that creative representation of the past should privilege verisimilitude over strict historical accuracy. In other words, literature's highest calling is to revivify the living memory of the past as exemplary of what the moral experience of life is like. This teaching was not far removed from the long-held principle that the task of history itself is to present memorable lives for the edification of its readers. While history as a discipline was being progressively reinvented in the eighteenth century as a science that held the past at a critical distance with a widening eye to its differences from the present, and to the relativity of laws, values and mores, writers and literary critics continued to view history as an art of bringing past into present as living memory based on the permanence of human nature and its passions. In such a view, historical facts might justifiably be adapted to the poetical, and in some cases political, needs of their writings. The common practice of historical parallels helped authors escape censorship and so to use the past as a mirror of their own disturbed times. In this way, history in literature became important as never before, but still as one among the arts of memory.

CHAPTER SEVEN

The Social: Rituals, Faith, Practices, and the Everyday

JENNIFER HILLMAN

INTRODUCTION

At the turn of the eighteenth century, Marguérite de Miramion (1646–1725) paused as she penned the *Life* of her pious mother, to reflect on the legacy of her saintly upbringing: "God grant that the education of such a holy mother will not, one day, be the condemnation of the daughter" (Bibliothèque Mazarine, Ms. 2489: folio 35 (hereafter BM)). The death of her mother, Marie de Miramion, in 1696 had prompted her to write a Life which was, ostensibly at least, a spiritual biography—an account of her mother's untiring devotion to charitable work in Paris during the long Counter-Reformation, as well as an appreciation of her "interior" virtues. Yet the writing of her mother's biography was also an occasion for self-reflection. Marie's exemplary life and commitment to the religious instruction of her daughter triggered a more sobering, soul-searching experience for Marguérite, which was recorded in the text. The boundaries between biography and autobiography became blurred, as the spiritual lives of mother and daughter were recounted.

Beginning with this single, introspective moment helps to capture two broader themes to be explored here. Firstly, in this chapter I illustrate how the study of early modern autobiography necessitates a broadening of scholarly definitions as to what constituted an autobiographical act. It is now generally accepted that early modern actors explored their own identities in a variety of different registers which were sometimes subtler or more creative than a simple diary or memoir (Skura 2008: 2). This shift in the scholarship has already challenged traditional approaches which not only located the origins of autobiography in the late seventeenth and early eighteenth centuries, but also made the genre indistinguishable from narratives of modernity and secularization. Autobiography is thus no longer conceived of as "an almost exclusive hallmark of late modernity," or a genre initiated by Rousseau's *Confessions* (Amelang 1998: 13). Neither is early modern autobiographical writing being lauded as the "forerunner" of modern (read "proper") autobiography as it once was (Skura 2008: 2). Secondly, I note that Marguérite de Miramion's own soul-searching in a biography she wrote of her mother further problematizes the singular conception of subjectivity which has tended to dominate the history of introspection and the self. This is something which has been recently articulated by Adam Smyth in his work on early modern England (Smyth 2010). It is also a point which has long been made by many scholars of female autobiography who have shown that women have, historically, tended to explore their own identities in relation to others (Seelig 2006).

What follows in this chapter is an attempt to explore these two related themes using lay, female-authored spiritual biographies produced in France at the turn of the eighteenth century. Spiritual biographies produced in this context offer an obvious (yet largely unmined) resource for the study of female autobiography because they were usually based on the personal spiritual writings of the subject. Nicholas Paige has revealed, for instance, how female biographers aimed to uncover the "secret recesses of the soul" via the reproduction of the personal writings of their subjects (2001; 2002: 129). This chapter instead aims to show that biographies also functioned as repositories for autobiographical self-expression in a subtler way. It argues that writing the Life of another person could be an opportunity for introspective soul-searching on the part of the *biographer*. As we will see, this appears to have been particularly true of biographers who had a familial or spiritual connection to the subject, or were otherwise connected via friendship or kinship. We know that when biographies were written by "confessor-turned-hagiographers" there was a tendency for these male biographers to insert themselves into the lives of their female subjects—usually as an act of self-promotion (Bilinkoff 2005). However, there has been very little critical attention given to lay female biographers. The premise of this chapter is that since women were becoming more significant contributors to the genre from *c*. 1660 to 1760, there was something of a unique window of opportunity for female self-expression which is highly relevant for the broader study of autobiography in the long eighteenth century.

One might explain the development of autobiography then, as engaging two approaches to memory: the first as public remembrance; the second as personal recollection. At the beginning of the eighteenth century, writers of their own life history recounted their accomplishments as if they were composing a biography, and typically referred to themselves in the third person. By century's end, however, autobiography had become a more intimate exploration of the inner emotional experience of their lives. Third person gave way to first-person narrative. Such a transformation of the meaning of memory for life history required time and found expression in an intermediary stage that I label (auto)biography. This hybrid genre, notably authored by women over the course of the eighteenth century, enables us to understand how this historical transition proceeded. The works I shall discuss in this chapter were written by women who wished to extol the edifying spiritual lives of much admired kin or mentors by praising their acts of steadfast religious devotion. But such exposition gave these biographers the opportunity to use that Life as a frame of reference for exploring their own inner spiritual progress, a memory of a different nature that we have come to characterize as soul-searching. Put somewhat differently, the biography of the edifying life became a prop for autobiographical examination of conscience.

FEMALE AUTOBIOGRAPHY IN EARLY MODERN EUROPE

The writings to be explored in this chapter challenge traditional conceptions of what constitutes autobiography. These are disorderly texts, lacking any neat chronological narrative or order, and were constructed using the first and third person interchangeably. In dealing with texts which do not conform to dominant, traditional ideas about the nature of autobiography, there is much to be learned from the wealth of literature on female autobiography (and life-writing more generally) that has emerged in the last thirty years. The range of scholarship here—especially in the Anglo-American scholarship—is now vast (Seelig 2006; Benstock 1988; Jelinek 1980; Smith and Watson 2001; Dowd and

Eckerle 2007). Female autobiographers in France and Spain have received particularly interesting treatment by scholars (Beasley 1990; Howe 2015). One important strand of this scholarship has been to redefine what signifies autobiography and therefore to challenge the work of influential theorists such as Philippe Lejeune, James Olney, and Georges Gusdorf in particular (Olney 1972; Gusdorf 1980; Lejeune 1989)—as recently synthesized by Lloyd Davis (Davis 2006: 19–34). What is important for our purposes is that autobiography is no longer regarded as the construction of a neatly-ordered "self" that evolves over time. Neither do scholars adhere to those narrow traditional definitions of autobiography as a first-person narrative.

Re-thinking what comprised female autobiography at the turn of the eighteenth century does not require us to abandon entirely the theories of autobiography honed by theorists such as Gusdorf and Olney, but it does require us to expand and lend nuance to their definitions. In turning to spiritual biography to recover female autobiographical experiences, I engage a body of scholarship on female autobiography which has, in various ways, sought to take down the "canonical walls" of the genre (Howe 2015: 2). To the modifications scholars have already made to these definitions, we may add another. A principle of autobiography appears to be that the author considers their life as worthy of recording, or retelling. This is not the case in the writings considered in this chapter. Instead, for our female writers here, their autobiography is buried beneath the narration of the Life of another, more significant woman whose story, the biographer feels, deserves to be told.

If the expansion of what autobiography *is* might be the first significant departure in the scholarship, then the reconfiguring of what autobiography *does* is the second. In his seminal essay of 1956, Gusdorf illuminated the importance of writing in the construction of a "self," an interpretation which scholars generally still accept. Yet many of them now agree that it served to exclude many other kinds of autobiographical writing from the canon. As Susan Stanford Friedman puts it:

First, the emphasis on individualism does not take into account the importance of a culturally-imposed group identity for women and minorities. Second, the emphasis on separateness ignores the difference in socialization in the construction of male and female gender identity.

—Friedman 1988: 34–5

Put succinctly, female lives were often bound-up with those of others and they perceived their own identities in relation to them. Scholars such as Gusdorf saw autobiography beginning with Augustine—the *Confessions* were often cited as the definitive prototype for the genre. Yet as Elizabeth Howe notes, "Rather than solitary weavers busy at the looms of autobiography, women are more appropriately engaged in quilting a patchwork of memories and events from their past" (Howe 2015: 15).

The recognition that women did not always write about their own lives in the same ways as men does not mean that we should universalize their experiences. It does, however, necessitate a more critical interrogation of the ways in which autobiographical writing permitted women to explore their own "selves." This seems particularly relevant for the study of early modern spiritual autobiographical writings which, after all, were supposed to permit deeper, introspective practices in order for the soul to be searched and the conscience to be examined. Just as more "secular" forms of autobiography have been premised on a very narrow, individualistic conception of subjectivity, so too has the scholarship on spiritual autobiography. This is in part a result of the association between

Protestantism and the rise of the individualist self. The spiritual writings associated with the Reformed traditions have arguably received greater critical attention by scholars of autobiography than those produced in the Catholic tradition. In some circumstances, it may also have been a consequence of the more marginal status of Catholic writers—such as in England (Whitehouse 2006: 112). In what follows, I propose that spiritual (auto) biographical writings by women at the turn of the eighteenth century may have offered a unique medium for female soul searching. This kind of writing certainly allowed women to construct and explore their personal spiritual identities, but in a way that inextricably linked their souls with those of others.

WRITING A *LIFE* AND LIFE-WRITING: FRENCH SPIRITUAL (AUTO)BIOGRAPHIES

Spiritual biography constituted an important genre of Baroque spirituality in Catholic Europe and its colonies. Several years ago, Jodi Bilinkoff mined these texts for what they can tell us about female spirituality, and her work continues to be relevant (Bilinkoff 1993; 2000; 2005). *Vitae* were to be edifying, devotional texts which recounted the lives of exemplary, pious individuals in a way which imitated the hagiography of canonized saints. The written testimony of biographers would sometimes be called upon at subsequent canonization trials, after all, and Lives often celebrated the miraculous and saintly occurrences in a "would-be-saint's" life (Suire 2001). Yet biographies also recorded the everyday rituals and practices that comprised a devotional life and they were often substantially based on spiritual autobiographies, letters, and other first-person religious writings. In France, women were already contributing to the genre in different ways by the middle decades of the seventeenth century, often by researching and writing Lives which either enjoyed circulation in manuscript or were later edited and published by a male biographer (Hillman 2018). Female biographers were more numerous within French convents, such as the order of the Visitation, where there tended to be strong traditions of writing *vitae* in convent obituaries. Jacques Le Brun has done important work on the innumerable biographies produced within the order across France (Le Brun 1986; 2013). By the turn of the eighteenth century, however, women both within and beyond the cloister were increasingly fulfilling the role of "official biographer" (Paige 2002: 129). By the early eighteenth century, published spiritual biographies were more likely to be credited to their original author, rather than attributed to a later male editor (Paige 2002: 130). It is within this context, then, of a growing female contribution to the production (and consumption) of devotional Lives that we can consider how they became a vehicle for biographers to search their own souls, as well as those of their subjects.

Soul-searching whilst writing the *Life* of another person was more likely to occur when the biographer had shared some kind of familiarity or even intimacy with their subject. It is important to note that spiritual biographers did not always *know* their subjects. Many biographies published in France in the seventeenth and eighteenth centuries were published by male clerics who had been supplied with narrative outlines of a life, as well as personal writings and other documents by female researchers or ghost writers. However, female-authored biographies in this period tended to be written by biographers who had personal knowledge of their subject—either through shared membership in a religious order or community, friendship, or familial connections. It is this pattern which may explain why female biographers seem to have used *Lives* to explore their own spiritual selves; the retrospective narration of a life which they knew intimately and had perhaps shared, prompted their own self-exploration. To explore this theme more closely, let us now turn to the production of two *Lives* penned at the turn of the eighteenth century.

A HOLY MOTHER

In writing the life of her mother, Marguérite de Miramion, the biographer with whom this essay began, had to do justice to one of the most respected and eminent Parisian *dévotes* of the French Counter-Reformation. Marie de Bonneau was perhaps most well-known for founding an orphanage (Sainte-Enfance), and a congregation of *dévotes* who taught girls (the Filles de Sainte-Geneviève, an amalgamation of an existing community and her own foundation, the *sainte-famille*) (Diefendorf 2004: 182). She was also a committed member of the pious confraternity established by Louise de Marillac and Vincent de Paul, the *Dames de la charité*. Marie has been of considerable interest to historians of the French Counter-Reformation due to the considerable impact she made on social and medical provision in early modern France. During the famine of 1661, for example, she prevented the closure of the Parisian *Hôpital Général* by securing 100,000 livres in donations (Gude 1999: 238–51).

FIGURE 7.1: *Portrait of Madame Marie de Miramion, c.* 1696, Pierre Mignard. Courtesy of the Bibliothèque Nationale de France.

Most scholars have accessed the details of Marie's *Life* either through the early eighteenth-century biography composed by Timoléon François de Choisy (1644–1724), usually known as the abbé de Choisy (Choisy 1706). Others have leaned on a nineteenth-century version (Bonneau-Avenant 1873). This later biography was, in large part, a reworking of Choisy's text by another family descendant: the Comte de Bonneau-Avenant. The contributions that female biographers made to these accounts of her life, have often been overlooked. As Elizabeth Rapley observed: "There have been *two* biographies of Madame de Miramion both by relatives" (Rapley 1990: 97).

Marie's *Life* was, however, initially at least, an oeuvre taken up by her daughter Marguérite. Marie had been widowed at the age of fifteen whilst pregnant with Marguérite. Her daughter was born in 1646, just a few months after her husband's death and spent most of her youth in the Visitation convent on the rue Saint-Antoine, being educated by the mother superior Mère Louise-Eugénie de Fontaine. Miramion also made regular retreats to the Visitandine house and endowed it with large donations (Gude 1999: 245). Choisy was, of course, a prolific writer who published widely in this period, including his own travel writings, orations, and sermons, as well as spiritual biographies. He was later admitted into the *Académie Française* in 1687. He shared a familial link to Marie de Miramion since she had been married to one of Choisy's cousins, Jean-Jacques de Miramion, before his premature death in 1645. Choisy had written the *Life*, he explained in his preface, ten years previously without much intention to publish it. It was based, he claimed, on Marie's own spiritual writings, which her daughter, Marguérite, had been collecting for some thirty years for her own spiritual edification. In his published version, Choisy was modest about his contribution to the writing of this life and professed that his only role was to assemble the material. In reality, however, Choisy made significant edits and changes to the text, including a whitewashing of many of Marguérite's autobiographical experiences. For example, whilst Choisy acknowledges the pious upbringing Marie gave to her daughter, he did not reproduce Marguérite's haunting prayer about its legacy with which this chapter began.

In returning to the manuscript version of Miramion's *Life*, we can see how the writing process provided an opportunity for Marguérite to relate her own spiritual experiences as a lay woman. Marguérite inserted herself in the narrative at a number of points and referred to herself sometimes in the first person and in others in a more distanced way as her daughter, "Mademoiselle de Miramion," and after her marriage included her title "Madame the Presidente de Nesmond." For Marguérite, the advice that her mother had given to her in preparation for marriage during a five-to-six day retreat was particularly formative for her self-understanding as a *"femme chrétienne."*

> She [Marie] inspired in her [Marguérite—i.e. herself] the resolution to renounce early dangerous amusements, representing the Christian life to her as one which must be distanced from all spectacles and games, giving her sage advice distanced from worldly maxims."
>
> —BM, MS. 2489: folio 36 (Choisy 1706: 64)

Marguérite cites this retreat as having inspired in her modesty and care for the poor as well as contempt for immoral entertainments (BM, MS. 2489: ff. 35–7). She refers to herself in the third person throughout this section of the biography, but the account remains strongly autobiographical—"the self as remembered and explained" (Howe 2015: 11). She thus uses her mother's advice to explore her own attitude and values. We learn that this even determined Marguérite's everyday routines of prayer and devotions, as she noted that her mother went into "such detail" that she gave her a daily routine (*règle de journée*) which ensured she spent her days piously ("*pour la passer chrétiennement*"). This is something which she may have written about in later life in a manuscript now held at the Bibliothèque Nationale de France and attributed to her (Bibliothèque Nationale de France, FR, MS. 15238 (hereafter BnF)). The provenance of the manuscript appears to be unknown, however, and other scholars have interpreted it as the work of the *présidente* de Noinville (Timmermans 1993: 209–10). For Marguérite, this may have also been one way of reflecting on her decision not to take religious vows and to take the more spiritually-imperfect path in the world as a married woman. After all, the spiritual counsel which prompted her to do so had come from one of the "century of saints'" most pious and esteemed lay *Dame de la Charité*. Writing the *Life* of one remarkable lay woman perhaps allowed Marguérite to think through her own decision to forgo the religious life and formal vows. This *Life* was, Marguérite noted, something that her mother felt that "God asked" of her daughter (BM, MS. 2489: folio 36). Interestingly, Choisy condensed this lengthy narration of the advice Marie as Marguérite's *directrice* (a word he never used to describe their relationship) gave to her and reframed the instructions as direct quotations from Marie (Choisy 1706: 64). Marguérite's voice and experiences are consequently lost in the published version of the *Life*.

Marguérite did not just use the writing of her mother's *Life* to reflect on her own life choices and piety. Writing the text also allowed her to remember spiritually-rousing stories her mother had told her. The most significant example among these comes in her description of a transformative moment in her mother's life: her decision not to remarry (and to take a vow of chastity) after her widowhood. Marguérite describes a scene which her mother had later shared with her. In the parish church of Saint Nicholas at Christmas time in 1648, she had heard God's voice speak to her as she was venerating the Holy Sacrament. In January 1649, she had heard the voice again and it confirmed her decision to remain in the world as a widowed *dévote*. Marguérite described how her mother was again venerating the holy sacrament when she was suddenly "moved" by God's voice saying "It is your heart that I want." In remembering and describing a spiritual experience had by her mother, Marguérite then reveals how it too became significant for her own spiritual progress. She wrote:

> She has said to me herself that one feels very strongly when it is God who speaks by the impression it makes on one's heart."
>
> —BM, MS. 2489: 165

Marguérite could have only been three years of age at the time of this spiritual experience, but she also recounted a later conversation they had, when her mother explained to her how hearing God's voice had made her feel. In remembering their conversations, Marguérite thus inserted herself into the account of her mother's vow in the first-person. Her account stressed their spiritual relationship as "co-penitents" in life, as well as revealing how evocative was the recounting of her mother's words after her death.

The sharing of this spiritual experience through its retelling in a biography seems significant for explaining how a historical trend in which the edifying life became a mirror for self-analysis. But it can only be accessed in the manuscript version of Miramion's *Life*. Choisy's later version of this episode is largely copied verbatim from Marguérite's, but with one important omission. In this rendering, Marie shared the experience in church with her confessor. "One feels strongly," she told him, "when it is God who speaks, by the impression he makes on one's heart" (Choisy 1706: 31). Clearly, Choisy in his published biography was more attentive to the need to construct Marie as a woman who subjected herself to the authority of the confessor and asked for his expertise as a discerner of spirits before she acted upon the voice she thought she had heard from God. In his reconfiguring of events, Choisy used exactly the same phrase to describe Marie's affective response to her experience, but placed it at the time of the episode—in 1648–9. Marguérite and her mother's spiritual intimacy is therefore concealed, and Marguérite's own introspective moment in remembering it is lost.

In this case, then, returning to the manuscript *Life* of Marie is vital for what it can reveal about how the writing of another *Life* could provoke an autobiographical act. The manuscript restores agency to the (auto)biographer's voice and also sheds light upon this hybrid genre. The issue of gender is crucial to its understanding. Scholars have long been aware that women writers have historically been subjected to "literary erasure." As Elizabeth Howe has recently noted, this is true of well-known female autobiographers in England, such as Margaret Cavendish, Duchess of Newcastle (1623–73), as well as lesser known authors. As she puts it, "their very lives and their right to tell them are in peril of dismissal or even deletion" (Howe 2015: 3). The later, published version of Marie de Miramion's *Life* by the male abbé de Choisy rested upon at least a partial deletion of that act. It simplified the text, offering a neater narrative of Marie's life and her subservience to the confessor. This obscured both the interdependence of Marie and her daughter in the conduct of their devotional lives and the spiritual importance that writing her mother's biography held for Marguérite. Writing at the turn of the eighteenth century, she penned a much more self-reflexive, introspective text which was as much about searching her own soul, as that of her mother.

A SAINTLY AUNT

The spiritual lives of pious mothers were not the only biographies to inspire such introspection. Writing the biography of a *sainte tante* (holy aunt) could also provide inspiration for autobiographical explorations (Trévisi 2008: 471). Moving from the Parisian robe nobility to the French bourgeoisie, let us now turn our attention to Marie-Catherine Homassel (1686–1764) who wrote the Life of her aunt Michelle Homassel (1655–1702). Marion Trévisi has argued that the *sainte tante* became a *figure mythique* in families and their stories were told sometimes down through the generations (Trévisi 2008: 471). Indeed, Marie-Catherine certainly seems to have sought to record the piety and moral reputation of a beloved family member. Like Marguérite de Miramion, she wrote in celebration of a female matriarch and her inimitable piety in order to commemorate her aunt's dedication to her own pious upbringing and education. However, she did not distance herself from the text in the way that Marguérite did and wrote about her experiences entirely in the first person. Far more than the construction of a *sainte tante* figure for posterity, Marie-Catherine's *Life* of her aunt was to be a deeper exploration of her own formative years, lived in the shadow of her saintly aunt.

Marie-Catherine was the daughter of a textile manufacturer from Abbeville in northern France. She is known to scholars less for writing the biography under consideration here, more for her own notoriety as the author of an account reporting the discovery of a "feral" girl raised in the wild, near Champagne in the mid-eighteenth century (Homassel-Hecquet [1755] 2017; Douthwaite 2002). In her own lifetime, she also received public attention as an outspoken and "militant" Jansenist who was interrogated by the church authorities as such. Thomas M. Carr Jr. has argued convincingly that Marie-Catherine's self-identification as a "Jansenist" was initially serendipitous, but that it later became central to her spiritual identity (Carr 2016: 91–105). As he has shown, Marie-Catherine used "private textual self-portraits" as a medium for articulating her theological understanding. She wrote a number of autobiographical texts (or "professions of faith") which have survived in various locations in manuscript, and in some instances, as copies (Carr 2016: 14, n28), (Bibliothèque de la Société de Port-Royal, Bio 338 bis: folios 100–206 (hereafter BSPR)). Marie-Catherine was, thus, a published author and prolific spiritual autobiographer, as well as being a highly literate and educated woman. Probate documents reveal that she owned over 450 titles in her extensive library, for example (Carr 2016: 2). Yet it is in the biography of her aunt—not her own "professions of faith"—that we first access her memories of her upbringing to the age of twelve and where she retrospectively reinterprets moments she later deems to have been transformative in her own life. Unlike her later autobiographical writings, Marie-Catherine's biography of her aunt was not a religio-political statement of her stance on the Jansenist debate. It detailed her early life with a pious—yet entirely orthodox—woman who raised her and whom she clearly considered to have nurtured her spirituality.

The purpose of the biography is explicit in the opening sentence, wherein Marie-Catherine mused how much "love and gratitude" we owe to those who take "care of our education" (BSPR, Ms. 338 bis: folio 1). For the purposes of this essay, I have consulted the recent published version by Nicholas Lyon-Caen (2008: 101–34) but cite the manuscript version at the Bibliothèque de la Société de Port-Royal (Bio 338 bis: 1–98).

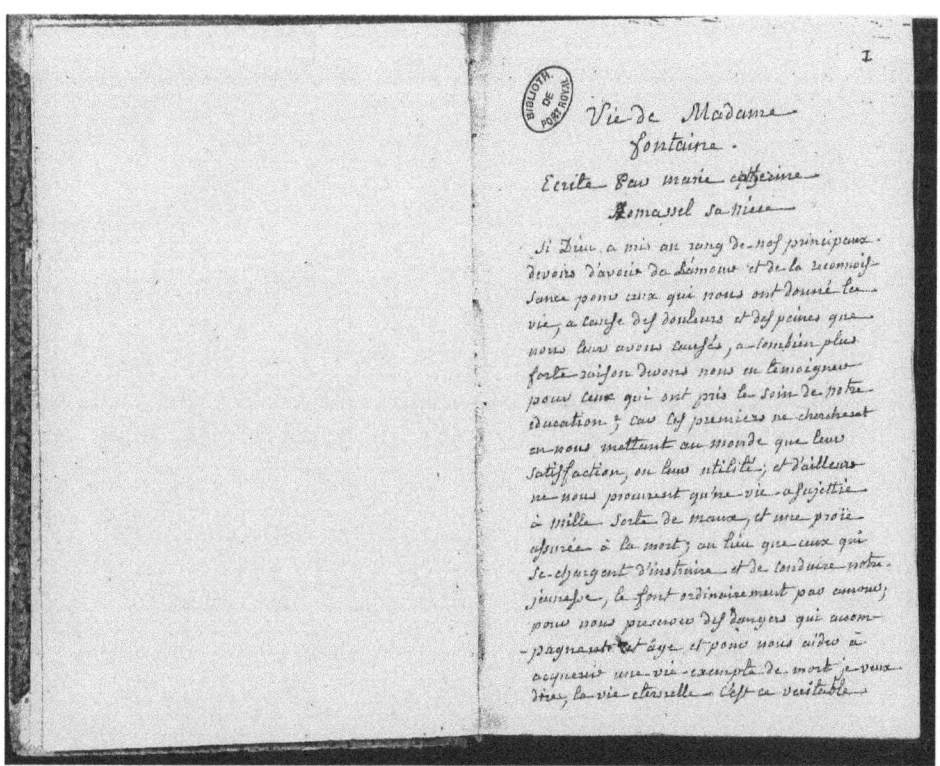

FIGURE 7.2: Title page of Marie-Catherine Homassel's *Life* of her aunt Michelle Homassel. Courtesy of the Bibliothèque de la Société de Port-Royal.

The (auto)biographical texts penned by Marie-Catherine have survived largely because the family considered this portrait of a pious aunt worthy of copying and preserving. Interestingly, as Carr has shown, Marie-Catherine's own professions of faith were also copied by female relatives—her daughter and a granddaughter (Carr 2016: 28).

Marie-Catherine's relationship with her aunt began when she was sent from her family home in Abbeville to live in Paris after the premature death of her mother Marie Hecquet on October 4, 1691. Her biography of her aunt recounts her own arrival there on the evening before the feast of All Saints. Even at this early stage in the account, it becomes clear that Marie-Catherine's memories of her experiences with her aunt prompted her own soul-searching about the legacy of this opportunity. Marie-Catherine noted that she intended to describe her aunt just as she found her, but "prayed to God with all her heart" that he would not ask her to remember rigorously everything she had been taught by her. "Since," she wrote, "the truth obliges me to confess that I have not imitated some, nor profited from others as I should have" (BSPR, Ms. 338 bis: folio 1–2). Just as Marguérite de Miramion felt intimidated by her mother's virtues and daunted by the prospect of fulfilling the expectations she had set for her, Marie-Catherine's own anxieties about having profited from her life with a pious aunt become explicit here.

Early in the text, Marie-Catherine stipulates that her account must rely on events in this eight-year stay (*séjour de huit ans*) with her aunt in Paris, before she returned with her father to Abbeville (BSPR, Ms. 338 bis: folio 2). Although she began with a narration of her aunt's early life in Calais in the mid-seventeenth century, the biography quickly turns

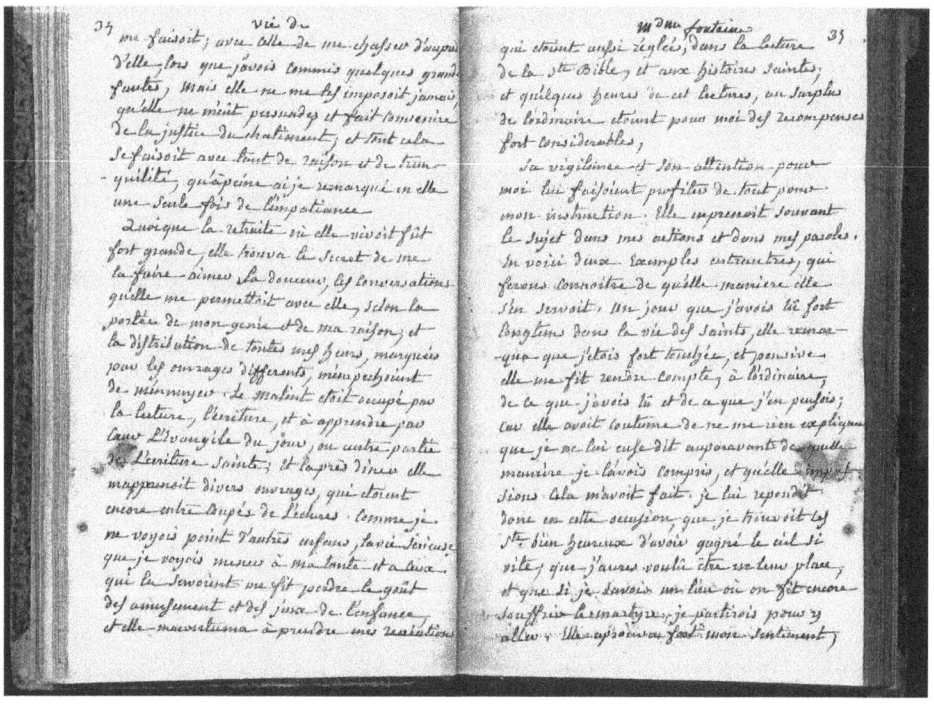

FIGURE 7.3: From the *Life of Michelle Homassel* by Marie-Catherine Homassel. Courtesy of the Bibliothèque de la Société de Port-Royal.

to her own education at the hands of her aunt. Her memories serve to illustrate her aunt's devotion to her religious instruction, and in doing so, allow her to remember and revisit her own devotional routines. We learn that her aunt Michelle taught her to read stories from the Bible and explained their meaning, requiring her to read four times daily before each meal. She discloses how the daily programme kept her amused, despite her aunt's self-imposed solitary life in her house. Her aunt had "found the secret" to ensuring she enjoyed their retreat. Marie-Catherine remembered how her conversations and the punctuation of the day with different works "prevented me from being bored" (BSPR, Ms. 338 bis: folio 33–4). This devotional programme became more stringent as time progressed, and by the late 1690s began at four o'clock in the morning and lasted until ten o'clock in the evening.

As well as offering an opportunity for Marie-Catherine to remember her everyday devotional practices during this upbringing, writing the biography also allowed her to recount specific moments or words which proved to have had a lasting effect on her life. Marie-Catherine's memories of conversations and even rebukes seem to have helped her to strengthen moral lessons and resolutions. On one occasion, for example, she described that her aunt had questioned her response to the reading of some saints' lives. Her aunt had noticed that she had been greatly moved and pensive (*fort touché et pensive*) and asked for her understanding of the lives. Marie-Catherine's response was that her desire to be with the saints in heaven made her pray for martyrdom. Her aunt's sharp reply made her realize that her own desires were the products of pride and presumption and needed to be mortified and punished. There are clear parallels here with Marguérite de Miramion's use of her mother's biography to explore her own life choices outside of the convent. Here, quite possibly because of the connection to the more rigorous practices of self-examination and introspection associated with the Jansenists, the "humiliation" that Marie-Catherine felt as a young child was something she decided to revisit in her relation of her formative experiences with her aunt.

Clearly, the spiritual concerns of the present would shape what stories biographers decided to revisit, and what autobiographical reflections they might make. Just as Marguérite de Miramion used the biography of her mother to reflect on her position as a good, Christian wife and charitable laywoman, Marie-Catherine concentrated on elements of her upbringing which allowed her to explore her spirituality. One strongly autobiographical account in the text, for example, relates another event used by Marie-Catherine's aunt for instilling modesty. The occasion was the procession of the body of Anne-Marie Louise d'Orléans to Saint-Denis in 1693. Marie-Catherine's fondness for modish hairstyles and fashions were punished, she believed, when she accidentally set fire to her own hair with a candle flame as she had dressed-up to watch the spectacle. Marie-Catherine reminisced about how her aunt described the accident as a "punishment for my vanity" (*une punition de ma vanité*) and that "I deserved to be disfigured for the rest of my life" (*je méritais bien d'être défigurée le reste de ma vie*). The next day, Marie-Catherine realized that the fire had only caught the hair on one side of her head; she was not disfigured but the occasion had provided a chilling moral lesson (BSPR, Ms. 338 bis: folios 36–9).

Michelle's words also resonated with Marie-Catherine as she reflected on other occasions when her aunt had tried to challenge her attachment to the world. When she inherited the jewelry of her father's second wife, her exchange with her aunt caused her some anguish. Her aunt had warned her with a "sad and distressed air": "Always remember that Saint Peter forbade Christian women to adorn themselves with pearls, jewels, or precious ornaments, and that he instructed them to adorn themselves only with simplicity and modesty." Marie-Catherine did not heed her aunt's warning and she again rebuked her, alluding to the aunt of Demetriade in the letters of St. Jerome. This time, the warning burdened Marie-Catherine, who noted in the first person that her aunt's words troubled her (BSPR, Ms. 338 bis: folio 60).

Central to Marie-Catherine's introspectiveness in writing this life was her description of the spiritual intimacy she shared with her aunt. At one level, this account may simply have served to lend the biography credibility. If a biographer could claim to know their subjects personally, there was more chance that the biography would be regarded as authentic. More significantly, however, Marie-Catherine appears to have used her position as biographer to remember shared spiritual experiences. Like Marguérite, Marie-Catherine had shared spiritual direction with her aunt. Père Soanen (1647–1740) (later bishop of Senez) jointly directed their devotional lives, and Marie-Catherine describes, for example, detailed preparations for her first communion at the age of nine. She mentions how her aunt had asked her for spiritual writings and reflections on the gospel which she then passed on to Soanen. The communion day itself was recounted by Marie-Catherine who was moved by her aunt's response to the sacrament:

> At last this great day came and I can say that I saw that day in my aunt the greatest joy I ever noticed in her. She received communion with me and I do not doubt that the faith with which I saw her penetrated.
>
> —BSPR, Ms. 338 bis: folios 63–6

As Marie-Catherine reminisced about receiving the sacrament for the first time with her aunt, she considered how her aunt's joy had left an enduring impression on her own faith. What was ostensibly a tribute to her aunt's piety, was also an account of a moving moment in her own life, which she was able to revisit in the text.

It is important to note that Marie-Catherine was not a reluctant writer. We have already observed that she later became a published author, as well as writing several, unpublished though highly controversial professions of faith. Therefore, to suggest that female spiritual biographers used the Lives of others as a pretext for writing their own autobiographies just because they were female would be a misinterpretation of these texts. The fact that Marie-Catherine elected to explore her own spiritual "self" in the first person, in a biography ostensibly about her aunt, is crucial. It highlights how her conception of personal identity was more complex than modern notions of "autobiography" would allow us to understand. Marie-Catherine's self-identity was so closely bound up with her perceptions of her aunt that it was necessary to explore them in relation to one another.

FEMALE BIOGRAPHERS AND AUTOBIOGRAPHY

Despite the differences in social status and age between Marguérite de Miramion and Marie-Catherine de Homassel, as well as their distinct respective spiritual preferences, they both clearly used the writing of a Life to remember and reflect on the religious and moral dimensions of their upbringings. Moments of introspection in both texts allowed them, as biographers, to explore feelings of inadequacy, guilt, and anxiety, and to consider the legacy of their intimacy with such spiritually significant women on their own lives and identities. Common to both of these case studies is, of course, the fact that the texts were not published (at least not contemporaneously). Although many female biographers in this period were writing with publication in mind, in this case we have two biographers writing for small-scale circulation in manuscript or in Marguérite's case, to supply a male cleric with material to write a Life. It is tempting to assume that biographies which were never published contain more of the kind of autobiographical self-reflection explored in this chapter than published accounts; that such biographers disclosed more in texts which might only be shared among their own pious and familial networks. Yet in print, too, female biographers were also interweaving their own spiritual experiences with those of their subject.

Both of the texts explored in this chapter can be contextualized by considering examples, in print, where female biographers inserted themselves into their accounts of other lives. For example, in 1696 Jacqueline-Marie du Plessis published her life of Mère Louise-Eugenie de Fontaine, abbess of the Visitation House on the rue Saint-Antoine (Bonneau du Plessis 1696: 3–4). This was a biography which was written and edited by a community of women: Jacqueline-Marie had been supplied with memoirs by a nun at the convent, Marie-Thérèse Fouquet, before constructing the final narrative herself. Jacqueline-Marie also shared an intimacy with the abbess and noted in the first-person that the biography was premised on their friendship: "I have lost a perfect friend," she remarked (Bonneau du Plessis 1696: 2). The narration of her friend's holy death prompted her reflection on her own death and mortality and throughout the biography she recounts the words that the mother superior had spoken directly to her (Bonneau du Plessis 1696: 283, 400–1). In the final gloss, she noted her own closing reflections: "I can say that in praising this incomparable mother, I praise virtue and in praising virtue I praise her; we have seen in her how the saints live and how they die" (1694: 300–1). There are parallels here with other later eighteenth-century biographies, such as the life that Mademoiselle d'Alès du Corbet wrote of her godfather (d'Alès du Corbet 1760). Here too, the biographer highlights poignant and memorable words spoken to her by him, and uses the biography as a moment to explore their effect on herself. Writing (and even publishing) a biography could be cathartic and offer another mode of self-exploration—just as scholars have noted about other forms of "life-writing" in this period.

CONCLUSIONS

In this essay, I have used female (auto)biographies as a lens through which to view the processes of introspection and soul-searching that women performed via writing at the turn of the eighteenth century in France. In pointing to the blurred boundaries between the genres of spiritual biography and autobiography, I also draw attention to the recent shift in scholarly attention towards *biographers*—exemplified in the work of scholars such as Katherine MacDonald (MacDonald 2007). In doing so, I aim to make a contribution to the reconfiguring of what constituted female autobiographical writing in the long eighteenth century. This period offered women a unique opportunity to write about their lives, as entwined with those of others, and I have argued that (auto-)biographical writings in this context uphold some of the broader theoretical points that scholars have made about female subjectivities in this period. The early eighteenth-century female spiritual (auto)biographers considered in this chapter conceived their own identities as inseparable from those of other women. At one level, biographers such as Marguérite and Marie-Catherine were writing, at least in part, in celebration of the devout families to which they belonged and their work seems to parallel the tradition of convent obituaries—texts which were, by their nature, collective memories (Rapley 2007). As with these conventual lives which were written by and about communities of the female religious, memory was a tool for strengthening the spiritual identities of lay women. Yet, in many ways, then, the "personal-collective" binary is unhelpful for exploring the cultural history of memory in this context. Memory did not function in a way which allowed women like Marguérite and Marie-Catherine to search *only* their own souls, because they could never be divorced from the identities of others—whether they were female relatives whose lives had touched theirs, or other female models and exemplars. Remembering the life of another woman was, at once, a deeply personal, spiritual act for the biographer. Writing a biography could never, therefore, preclude an autobiographical act.

CHAPTER EIGHT

Remembering and Forgetting

VICTORIA E. THOMPSON

MEMORY, HISTORY, COMMEMORATION

When examining the French Revolution, differentiating among the three can be a difficult task. This is due in part simply to the length of the Revolution, commonly dated from 1789 to 1799. Over the span of ten years, events that began as part of living memory were commemorated as foundational to the establishment of a new regime, and also entered into written history. The storming of the Bastille, which occurred on July 14, 1789, is an instructive example. The conquest of the fortress by Parisians ended the standoff between the monarchy and the National Assembly, forcing the former to recognize the legitimacy of the latter. The visit of King Louis XVI to Paris to acknowledge the National Assembly, on July 17, was understood as a moment of reconciliation between the king and the Parisians and the beginning of a new way of configuring the relationship between the monarch and the people. Eyewitnesses, participants, and those who were not present but who understood the political importance of the event immediately produced prints and written accounts that ensured it would enter into the collective memory of Parisians. In July 1790, popular festivities at the site of the Bastille directly commemorated its fall, while the Festival of the Federation indirectly kept this memory alive by including a stone from the fortress on the altar built at the center of the amphitheater on the Champ de Mars. In 1790, the first history of the conquest of the Bastille, based on archival documents and oral accounts, was published (Bailly and Duveyrier 1790). As this example indicates, history, memory and commemoration were all closely intertwined during the period of the Revolution.

The French Revolution effected changes in governmental form (from absolute monarchy to constitutional monarchy to republic) that brought in their wake major legislative changes (such as the abolition of feudalism and titles of nobility), a reconfiguration of institutional life (the royal court shrank and then disappeared while political clubs became significant sites of politicking and sociability), and a shift in how information was communicated (the Church pulpit grew less important while the end of censorship resulted in an increase in pamphlets and newspapers). The changes wrought by the Revolution were far-reaching, of great import, and occurred over a relatively short period of time. Those who lived through the revolutionary decade faced the challenge of making sense of these upheavals. This process entailed explaining, justifying, or denouncing policies, laws and events by placing them within coherent intellectual and affective frameworks. Memory played a key role in this process of meaning-making from the very outset of the Revolution. Memory was important to revolutionary understanding because it linked the political and the emotional as well as the individual and the collective. Through memory—and its corollaries history and commemoration—political events retained or were given an emotional charge that encouraged a feeling of being invested in the course of the Revolution. Memory, history, and commemoration were also powerful tools for demonstrating the ways in which individual experiences could be seen as having collective import.

This chapter examines the role of memory, history, and commemoration during the revolutionary decade 1789 to 1799. It is concerned with collective, rather than individual memory. Collective memory is an aggregate of individual memories that serves to articulate shared values and identity. Collective memory differs from individual memory in several important ways. Individual memory is by its nature idiosyncratic, while collective memory is shared. While individual memory can be fragmented and confused, collective memory is shaped by narrative structures that impart coherence and consistency. A collective memory can be thought of as a shared story about an event that occurred in the past. As with all stories, a collective memory takes on different elements depending upon the storyteller. Some storytellers might emphasize some elements more than others, and over time aspects of the story that once seemed crucial might fade into the background, or disappear altogether, while new dimensions might become more central. Yet to be a collective memory, the story must be recognizable as such. What I mean by this is that despite some expected variation, certain key aspects concerning the event and the manner of relating the event must remain in place for the story to be experienced as collective memory.

French sociologist Maurice Halbwachs argued that collective memory coheres around what he called "localizations": people, places or events that serve as touchstones, giving concrete form to a set of abstract beliefs ([1941] 2008). In establishing a system of localizations, an array of diverse memories held by individuals are pared down into a more concise set of memories that resonate with most members of the group, and contradictions are smoothed over. This set of agreed-upon memories must, to retain their status as memories, be retold on a regular basis. This does not mean that the stories do not change; Halbwachs argues that they do change in response to changing needs and values of the group (1992: 75). Yet even as the content of the stories changes, the act of retelling in itself can serve as a powerful ritual that fosters group cohesion and can be combined with other ritual elements to provide a framework of continuity. Commemorations combine retellings of the event being remembered with practices that have ritual significance to the community, and that therefore aid the community in connecting the event to shared beliefs and values. Similarly, inserting recent events into historical narratives confers meaning to and importance upon the event by associating it with stories a community tells about itself.

This chapter explores the role of memory in the French Revolution by looking first at efforts to establish heroes and martyrs. As Halbwachs noted, individuals often serve as "localizations" for collective memory when values and beliefs important to the group are attributed to them; in the collective memory, they become the incarnation of these values and beliefs. Building upon the eighteenth-century cult of Great Men, revolutionary leaders celebrated intellectuals such as Voltaire and Rousseau as intellectual founders of the Revolution. Those who participated in the revolutionary governments were also memorialized, although with greater difficulty, since shifts in the political landscape made it difficult to celebrate leaders active in one phase of the Revolution during a later period. Less controversial were ordinary men, particularly citizen-soldiers. Revolutionary leaders also had to contend with unwanted martyrs and heroes, the most important of which was the king himself.

Heroes and martyrs were celebrated in many ways, including commemorative rituals. The second section of this chapter focuses on how commemorative ceremonies retold stories of the Revolution as a means to shape collective memory. Commemorative practices created a sense of communal belonging rooted in shared emotion. Commemoration was closely linked to history. Contemporaries drew upon historical allusions in designing and commenting upon commemorative ceremonies. This was part of a larger process of memory-making, by which revolutionary events were placed within the longer narrative of French history. Doing so provided a means of both legitimizing and making sense of the rapid transformations that occurred in so many realms of French life during the Revolution.

These rapid transformations, and the violence that often accompanied them, were painful and difficult for those who lived through them. During the Revolution, people lost family members to sanctioned and unsanctioned political violence and to war. Economic dislocation caused suffering as livelihoods were lost and food became scarce. Fear of reprisals from internal and external enemies (real and imagined) of the Revolution created a climate of intense fear and suspicion. Historians of the Revolution have examined the upheaval of the revolutionary decade through the lens of trauma, and the last section of this chapter turns to this discussion. The use of trauma as a concept to understand the actions of those who lived through the Revolution privileges memory. Individuals suffering from trauma (what we would today call post-traumatic stress disorder) were unable to integrate highly upsetting experience into narratives of their lives. Trauma negatively impacts the ways in which we understand our experiences and thus our sense of who we are. On a collective level, one can speak of trauma when, as Jeffrey Alexander has argued, "patterned meanings of the collectivity are abruptly dislodged" (2004: 10). In other words, and to return to the theme of memory and narrative that I have been developing in this introduction, collective trauma occurs when events cannot be integrated into the stories a group tells about itself, stories that explain events and provide a basis for group identity. In the final section of this chapter, I investigate the ways in which memory as trauma disrupted processes of revolutionary meaning-making.

HEROES AND MARTYRS

Not surprisingly, the French Revolution loomed large in the nineteenth-century imagination, when efforts to define the role it should play in the collective memory preoccupied politicians, participants and observers. With the Restoration of the Bourbon monarchy in 1814 and again in 1815, symbols of the Revolution were destroyed and outlawed, while the memory of Louis XVI and Marie-Antoinette was deployed to legitimize Bourbon rule (Kroen 2000; Fureix 2009; Thompson 2019). Government policies attempted to establish the boundaries of what could be remembered and what should be forgotten, while interest in the Revolution led to the publication of an unprecedented number of memoirs (Petiteau 2012; Luzatto 1991; Rossi 1998; Yalom 1993). The Revolution was also kept alive through what Pascal Dupuy has called "memorial history"—histories of the Revolution that were based on memoirs of those who lived through the event rather than archival evidence (2012: 487; also Orr 1990). And this work of making retrospective sense of the Revolution was not limited to the French. As soon as the Revolution began, foreign travelers such as Arthur Young and Helen Maria Williams penned the first accounts of what the Revolution meant to those outside of France. During the Restoration, travelers returned to France to reflect upon the impact of the Revolution (Thompson 2014). With the defeat of Napoleon in 1815, British historians felt that it was both possible and necessary to write about the Revolution and its impact. As a contributor to the *Quarterly Review* wrote (prematurely) in 1814: "The volcano is now extinguished; and we may approach the crater with perfect security" (quoted in Ben-Israel 1968: 47). In France, the memory of the Revolution continued to influence cultural and political life well into the twentieth century. As Steven Kaplan has shown, preparations for the bicentennial celebration of 1989 elicited widespread debate concerning the legacies of the Revolution in present-day France (1995a and 1995b). Revolutionary efforts to quash the revolt in the Vendée remained a particularly troubling and divisive memory (Martin 1989).

This work of determining what should be remembered as part of the revolutionary legacy began during the Revolution itself. From the outset, revolutionaries attempted to make sense of the Revolution by reference to the past. Revolutionary leaders looked to the past for models of leadership in a continuation of the Enlightenment cult of Great

FIGURE 8.1: *Translation of Voltaire's Remains to the Panthéon français, Paris, 1794*, engraving by Claude Malapeau. Courtesy of the Bibliothèque Nationale de France.

Men (Bonnet 1998; Bell 2001; Clarke 2007). The Pantheon, established in 1791 in the former Church of Saint-Geneviève, was to be the institutional center of this cult. While before 1789 Great Men were to serve as exemplars for individual achievement, during the Revolution, *philosophes* such as Voltaire and Rousseau were celebrated for paving the way, through their writings, for the Revolution (Jourdan 1997: 99). The proposal for creating a Pantheon was prompted by the concern of the marquis de Villette that with the confiscation of clerical property, Voltaire's remains could be sold to whomever purchased the abbey of Scellières, where he was buried. Villette argued that Voltaire's remains "belonged to" the French nation (Bonnet 1998: 266). Although, as discussed below, Mirabeau was the first to be interred in the Pantheon, when Voltaire's remains were placed there shortly afterwards, revolutionary leaders saw this act as linking past, present and future: "In granting the spirit of Voltaire this tribute of admiration . . . we pay the debt of our fathers & we earn the esteem of our nephews" (Charron 1791: 2). By honoring great men of the pre-revolutionary past revolutionaries established a continuity between a past that could be remembered with pride and the Revolution. This was the past of the *philosophes*, not the Bourbon monarchy.

The same logic underlay the translation of the remains of Rousseau to the Pantheon in October 1794. Praising Rousseau as an "apostle of liberty and equality," the President of the Convention stated that this Great Man "was the precursor who called the nation to its path toward glory and happiness." Establishing Rousseau as the author of the "salutatory regeneration" that was the Revolution was a means of establishing a lineage for the Revolution that bypassed the various revolutionary leaders who had fallen in and out of favor (Anon. [1794] 1862: 223). Most importantly, as Andrew Jainchill has argued, the pantheonization of Rousseau was an attempt to break the association between Robespierre and the *philosophe*, thereby rendering Rousseau a "political moderate" (2008: 28).

The propensity to look for heroes in the past encouraged the identification and mythification of revolutionary heroes as well. The citizen-soldier was one of the most influential of these heroes. As Alan Forrest has shown, beginning with the outbreak of war in 1792 and accelerating with the *levée-en-masse* of the Year II (1793), pamphlets, prints, and paintings, commemorative medals, plays, and festivals all attributed to soldiers the values of patriotism and self-sacrifice that would become central to this myth (2009). While during the Directory and Empire military heroes were also celebrated, the citizen-soldier as exemplar demonstrated the ability of ordinary men to contribute in meaningful ways to their country. Even before 1789, the definition of Great Men had been expanding to include ordinary men, such as the father of the family, who were worthy of emulation (Ozouf 1997: 159). Because of the association between fatherhood and monarchy, fatherhood became a site of tension as the Revolution radicalized (Hunt 1992). But ordinariness could still be celebrated by means of remembering the citizen-soldier. In plays from 1792 and 1793, soldiers were portrayed as ordinary men who sacrificed their lives for their country, yet the action was "seldom set on the battlefield," focusing instead on relationships with family members and loved ones (Forrest 2009: 33). Similarly, the Festival of the Supreme Being in the Year II (1793) eschewed the veneration of Great Men in favor of what Mona Ozouf terms an "antiheroic" mood: "There is no hero when all are heroes" (1988: 114). Including children, young men and women, or older men and women was a means of celebrating the ordinary person regenerated by the Revolution.

It was more difficult to identify revolutionary leaders whose memory could withstand the vicissitudes of revolutionary politics. The death of Honoré Gabriel Riqueti, Count of

Mirabeau, on April 2, 1791 inaugurated a public debate over how the Great Men of the Revolution should be remembered. In the hope of creating a revolutionary cult of commemoration that could serve to supplant Catholicism, contemporaries proposed transforming the Church of Saint-Geneviève into a revolutionary necropolis. Opposition to this idea was based on reluctance to dedicate a church to secular heroes, as well as on the conviction that a true cult of revolutionary Great Men required that the public have greater access to the space (Bouwers 2012: 94). Nevertheless, two days after Mirabeau's death, the Assembly decided to rename the church the Pantheon. On its way to the Pantheon, Mirabeau's funeral cortege moved through Paris for five hours, attracting over 300,000 spectators according to one witness (De Baecque 2001: 31). Several plays, including one written by Olympe de Gouges that depicted Great Men from antiquity to the Enlightenment, praised Mirabeau (Goodman 2017: 23). In a print commemorating his consignment to immortality, death unveils his portrait and while one female figure mourns, another rejoices. As the caption suggests, remembering Mirabeau was not only a sign of respect, it was also a source of national regeneration. In contemplating his ashes—whether in the space of the Pantheon or through such prints—the French would "regain all their energy."

However, the decision to place the remains of Mirabeau in the Pantheon was not unanimously approved, and it made the building a site of political contestation. Thus, an

FIGURE 8.2: Commemorative print on the Occasion of the Death of Mirabeau, 1791. Courtesy of the Bibliothèque Nationale de France.

anonymous critic wrote that the Pantheon was a "disgusting charnel house" that posed a danger to both the health and morality of citizens (Anon. n.d.a: 101). Those who had supported Mirabeau's "pantheonization" were shaken by the discovery in 1792 of his secret correspondence with Louis XVI, and following an inquiry it was decided in November 1793 that his body should be removed from the Pantheon. Even Robespierre felt a need to apologize for the decision to place Mirabeau's remains in the Pantheon, vowing to offer "to my country, in expiation of this fault, my entire public life & the eternal persecutions of all the enemies of liberty" (1792: 555). On September 21, 1794, the same day that Mirabeau's once-celebrated memory was to be forgotten by his removal from the Pantheon, the remains of Jean-Paul Marat were to take his place. Great care was taken to ensure that this substitution would be seen as an act of justice. Before Mirabeau's remains were removed, a *huissier* or usher of the National Convention read out the decree; his remains were then turned over the police *commissaire* of the section, as if he were being arrested (Duchosal 1794: 272). Mirabeau's remains were re-buried in a "graveyard set apart for criminals [. . .] without any stone or tablet to mark the spot" (Warwick 1905: 416).

Mirabeau had been seen as a "great man" in the tradition of the Enlightenment, but Jean-Paul Marat was exemplary of the revolutionary cult of martyrs. In the Year II (1793–4), as Annie Jourdan has written, the wounded and mutilated body of the martyr, which was meant to "stimulate emotion and invite sacrifice," became a centerpiece of republican veneration (1997: 113). The martyr served as a "localization" for collective memory in the sense developed by Halbwachs: his body served as a reminder that the Revolution was under assault and thereby elicited a sense of urgency in affirming communal bonds in its defense (De Baecque 1987). Almost immediately following Marat's assassination on July 13, 1793 by Charlotte Corday, the Parisian sections began fighting over the right to bury his remains, while the Society of Republican Revolutionary Women promised to educate their children with his writings (Soboul 1957: 200). The sections of Paris organized over fifty ceremonies in memory of Marat in the fall of 1793 (Bonnet 1986: 102). Souvenirs, such as busts and portraits of Marat, were sold on the streets of Paris, and the Commune built an obelisk in front of the Louvre for the Festival of August 10 that contained Marat's bathtub and inkwell (Clarke 2007: 178). The cult of Marat drew upon both Catholic and revolutionary practice and imagery, and its similarity to Catholicism drew the ire of radicals like Hébert. In the spring of 1794, as revolutionary leaders turned against radicals (Hébert was guillotined on March 24), they also began to turn against Marat (Soboul 1957: 211). His remains entered the Pantheon in September 1794, shortly after the fall of Robespierre. Jean-Claude Bonnet has seen in this a sign of "the incertitude and the contradictions of the beginnings of the Thermidorian Republic," while also noting that Robespierre's opposition to the cult of Marat made the latter's pantheonization an act of revenge against the former (Bonnet 1998: 291). Led by the Gilded Youth, vocal opponents of the Terror, busts of Marat were destroyed in early February 1795, and later that month his body was removed from the Pantheon. As Marat was demonized, Corday became "the only individuated heroine" of the Revolution (Dermenjian et al. 2012: 81; also Mazeau 2009). Remembrance of revolutionary leaders became a means of proclaiming and sustaining adherence to a certain vision of the Revolution. However, the speed with which revolutionary politics evolved made it difficult to establish heroes whose memory should be preserved, as did the lack of consensus over which direction the Revolution should take.

This lack of consensus meant that revolutionary authorities devoted much time and energy to managing collective memory. Several Great Men were nominated for the

Pantheon, but in the midst of revolutionary upheaval, political leaders were "unable to reach consensus over how to define human greatness" (Bouwers 2012: 95). In 1795, the Convention decreed that ten years had to elapse between the death of an individual and the transfer of his remains to the Pantheon, out of fear that facts dishonoring his memory might come to light after his death—a process almost certain to occur as revolutionary tides shifted (Ozouf 1997: 170). Because the determination of who was a martyr for the Revolution changed as the political landscape was transformed, the cult of Great Men returned to favor after Thermidor. The heroes of antiquity were once again in vogue—their reputations having withstood the test of time—and statues of Demosthenes, Cicero, Brutus, Cato, Solon, and Lycurgus graced the meeting room of the Council of Five Hundred (Jourdan 1997: 129). By 1800, some of those dishonored during the Revolution returned to favor; the *Nouveaux Dialogues des Morts*, published in that year included a conversation between Demosthenes and Mirabeau, in which the two debated the relative weight of good and bad actions in shaping the way each should be remembered (De Vixouse 1800).

The search for heroes to remember had its counterpart in efforts to destroy or erase the memory of the king and queen. As many scholars have noted, numerous pamphlets and prints denigrated the king and queen by depicting them as monsters and animals, and by charging the king with impotence and the queen with sexual voraciousness (for example, Thomas 1999; Hunt 1991). Following their executions, concern that they would become martyrs dictated burial practices, not least of all because their deaths (in January and October 1793) occurred at a time when the revolutionary cult of martyrs was spreading. When Louis XVI was executed, precautions were taken to make sure his grave would not become a site of pilgrimage. Helen Maria Williams, who lived in Paris during much of the Revolution, wrote: "The grave was filled with quick lime, and a guard placed over it till the corpse was consumed. The ground was then carefully leveled with the surrounding earth, and no trace or vestige remains of that spot to which, shrouded by the doubtful gloom of twilight, ancient loyalty might have repaired, and poured a tear, or superstition breathed its ritual for the departed spirit" (1796: vol. 4, 39). Similar measures were taken for the burial of Marie-Antoinette and, in 1794, for Louis' sister, Madame Elisabeth. Despite these efforts, attacks upon the royal family in print ensured that the monarchy remained—for better or for worse—important in the collective memory. Following the deaths of the king and queen, royalists produced and circulated images and texts that portrayed Louis and Marie-Antoinette as Christian martyrs (Davenport 1986; Burton 1997; De Baeque 2001).

Authorities were concerned with the bodies of monarchs more distantly deceased as well, and in July 1793 the Convention ordered the exhumation of royal tombs at the Saint-Denis Basilica (Le Gall 2009). Over the course of several days during the following autumn, bodies in varying states of decay were carried outside the building and thrown into trenches dug into the cemetery ground, then covered with quicklime (Anon 1825: vol. 3, 407–17). The destruction of the deceased bodies of kings was extended to likenesses of their living bodies. In 1793 and 1794, statues of monarchs were destroyed and royal insignia of all sorts was removed from public and private buildings. During the summer of 1793 this work included removing the royal coat of arms on the former Pont Royal, a bas-relief of the king over the main entrance of the Ecole de Chirurgie, as well as all "symbols of feudalism" from the Fontaine des Innocents (Barzin 1793; Dorotte/Scellier 1793; Daujon 1793). Through such efforts, authorities sought to erase the memory of the monarchy.

One of those present at Saint-Denis was Alexander Lenoir, founder of the Musée des Monuments français, housed in what today is the Ecole des Beaux-Arts in Paris. Lenoir's

FIGURE 8.3: *Apotheosis of Louis XVI, 1793*, engraving by Francesco Bartolozzi. Courtesy of the Bibliothèque Nationale de France.

efforts to safeguard works of art endangered by revolutionary politics began in 1791, when he was put in charge of a warehouse for artworks in metal and marble from the religious institutions that had been confiscated by the state as *biens nationaux* (Poulot 1997: 1521; also Stara 2013). Lenoir's storehouse was open temporarily to the public in 1793 and was designated as a museum in 1795. According to Christopher Greene, witnessing the destruction of the royal tombs at Saint-Denis gave Lenoir the idea of "creating a museum dedicated solely to an historical and chronological exhibition of French sculpture" (1981: 211). Peopled with statues taken from churches and royal tombs, the museum had a funerary element to it; as Dominique Poulot has argued, it served as an alternative Pantheon, where statues and busts of Great Men from the Old Regime that Lenoir believed were worth remembering could be housed (1997: 1523). As in so many other examples of revolutionary remembering, the museum was not without its critics. Lenoir's conviction that in a Republic, all Great Men, no matter what their birth or achievement, were equals, lent itself to a degree of confusion. "It was the true mirror of our revolution," wrote Louis-Sebastien Mericer, "what contrasts! What games of chance and of caprice, what a unique chaos!" (Mercier 1994: 946). Stripped from their original locations and thus from a complex of associations and experiences, the monuments of Lenoir's museum could not serve as effective localizations of collective memory.

COMMEMORATING THE REVOLUTION

Commemoration is one means of establishing a story about a past event. Particularly when sponsored by state authorities, commemorative efforts can influence which elements of the event are remembered and which are not. Old Regime France was a society rich with religious holidays, celebrations of the monarchy, and festivities surrounding momentous events such as peace treaties. These traditions shaped commemorative festivals during the Revolution. The processional through town or city, the recourse to altars and fountains, and the publication of descriptions of revolutionary festivals were all drawn from a pre-revolutionary repertoire of celebration and commemoration. Thus, although revolutionary festivals sought, as Mona Ozouf has noted, to demonstrate that "the era of the Republic was no longer the era of kings, and to mark this absolute beginning" (Ozouf 1988a: 159), festivals throughout the revolutionary period were shaped by a dialectic between past and present.

As with the celebration of individuals, commemoration of revolutionary events was a troublesome proposition, not least because efforts to establish a commemorative calendar were always undermined by the course of events themselves. The Constitution of 1791 called for national festivals that would "preserve the memory of the French Revolution" (Ozouf 1988a: 61). In spring 1792, the Committee of Public Instruction was tasked with establishing a list of such festivals; this task was revisited in the spring of 1794, and again following the fall of Robespierre (Ozouf 1988a: 61, 106, 119–20). The choice of which dates to celebrate changed over time. Robespierre decided in the spring of 1794 that the October days should no longer be commemorated, but that the insurrection that led to the arrest of the Girondins, on May 31, 1793, should be remembered (Ozouf 1988a: 110). The Directory no longer celebrated May 31; it maintained the celebrations for July 14, August 10, and January 21, and added to that calendar a celebration of 9 Thermidor. Some events, such as the September Massacres, were never celebrated. Yet while certain dates remained part of the revolutionary commemorative calendar, the tenor of the celebrations altered their meaning. Hans Lüsebrink and Rolf Reichardt analyzed speeches given at commemorations of the fall of the Bastille to show how references to popular sovereignty gave way over time to an emphasis on military conquest and expansion outside of France (1997: 156–64). This shift corresponds to the transition noted above in regard to the commemoration of Great Men, who increasingly during the Directory were military heroes. These trends would be continued under Napoleon's rule.

The conquest of the Bastille on July 14, 1789 and the visit of the king to Paris on July 17 were the first events of the Revolution to be commemorated officially, on July 14, 1790. The storming of the Bastille would remain an important commemorative event throughout the Revolution; it was included in the list of civic festivals prepared by Robespierre and adopted by the Convention in the Year II (1793–94) as well as in the list of festivals instituted by the Directory with the Law of 23 Nivôse Year IV (1796). Even before the official commemoration, "spontaneous" popular commemorations began as early as August 1789, while prints and published accounts ensured that it would become part of the revolutionary collective memory (Lüsebrink and Reichardt 1997: 149).

The storming of the Bastille was immediately recognized as a foundational event in the Revolution, for it ended the stand-off between monarchy and the newly created National Assembly in favor of the latter, thereby initiating a transition from absolutist to constitutional monarchy and opening the door to a wide array of legislative reforms. However, it was also marked by mob violence. The military commander of the Bastille, de Launay, was killed by the Parisian crowd as he was taken to the city hall to be judged, as was the prévôt des marchands, Jacques de Flesselles. Commemoration of this event was important, but also difficult, not least because members of the National Assembly saw little differentiation between the crowd that attacked the Bastille and the crowd that killed de Launay. The first official commemoration in 1790 was thus called the Festival of the Federation, a name that reveals how, as Pascal Dupuy has argued, authorities wished to emphasize with this celebration the unity of the nation, the king and the constitution, and in so doing, "artificially concealed the insurrection of an angry crowd" (2012: 491).

In fact, the official celebration of the Festival of the Federation barely evoked the conquest of the Bastille or evoked it only obliquely: national guard troops were prominent in the ceremony and the altar upon which the oath to the nation was taken was built from stones taken from the fortress. The king's throne was set on the same level as that of the President of the National Assembly, a visual reminder of the great transformation in France's government that occurred as a result of the conquest of the Bastille (Etlin 1975: 28). The oath-taking occurred in an amphitheater built for this purpose at the Champ de Mars. The amphitheater evoked antiquity, while the Champ de Mars connected the celebration to French history, in particular to Charlemagne gathering his nobles before setting off for war (Etlin 1975: 26). Historical precedents for the events of July 1789 were established by the decision that the procession, on its way to the Champ de Mars, should stop in the rue de la Ferronnerie, where Henri IV was assassinated, to pay their respects to this "good" king. Yet any direct reference to the conquest of the Bastille—such as a mock battle or the destruction of a model of the prison—was rejected (Etlin 1975: 35).

Yet this example also demonstrates how difficult it is to establish a single narrative remembering an event. In an unofficial celebration on July 14, 1790 men and women danced on the ruins of the fortress, in the middle of which was placed a column "the same height as the Bastille, on the top of which a tri-colored flag floated in the wind, bearing the single work *Liberté*" (Anon. n.d.b: 18). Dancing was a tradition carried over from the Old Regime, when orchestras played in the royal squares of Paris. Dancing on the site of the Bastille both continued this tradition and transformed its meaning. It was no longer simply a celebration or an occasion to let off steam; it now became a means of signifying the occupation of a space associated with monarchical "despotism" and the transformation of a people from "slaves" to free citizens. As the president of the 11th arrondissement of Paris proclaimed on the occasion of the commemoration of July 14 in the Year VII (1799): "We suffered in its awful dungeons, we dance on its remains" (Gauthier n.d.: 3). The power of this unofficial celebration can be seen in the way it remained part of the collective memory, as in numerous prints that depicted the dancing. Including dancing at the Bastille in official commemorations (as in the festival of 30 Vendémiaire, Year II (1793), which ended with music and dancing at the Bastille, the Pantheon, and the Tuileries garden) became a means of keeping the memory of the storming of the Bastille continuously present for Parisians in a way that encouraged ordinary Parisians to participate, and yet replaced violence with celebration (*Journal des théâtres* Year III: 510).

As we see with the first Festival of the Federation, which celebrated both the fall of the Bastille and the king's visit to Paris, multiple events were often included within a single

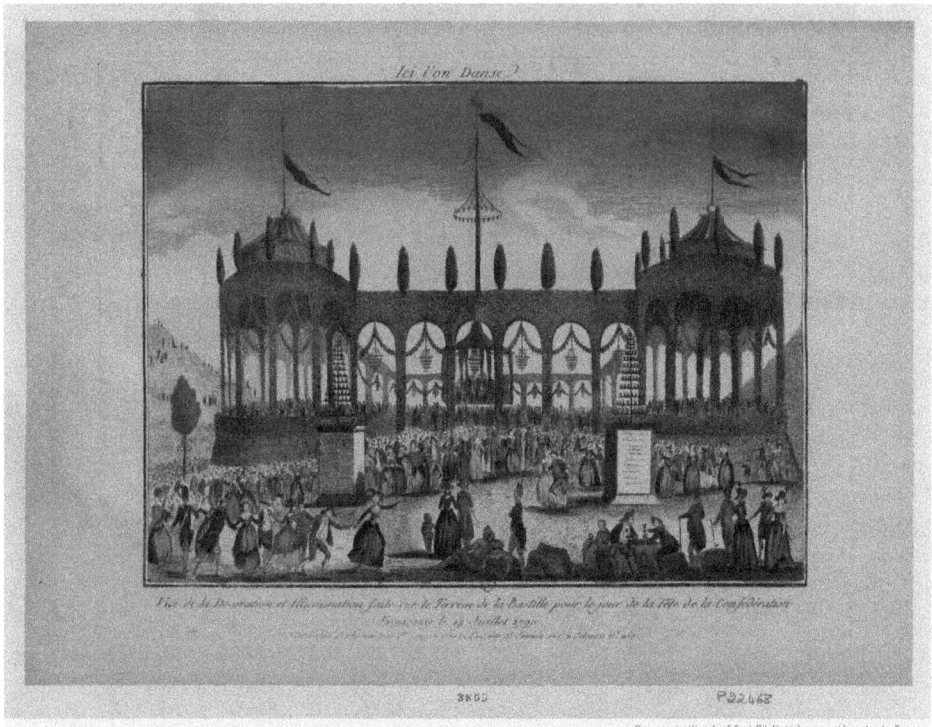

FIGURE 8.4: *"Ici l'on danse"* (Here we dance): *a view of the decorations and lighting constructed on the former site of the Bastille for the festival of the French Confederation, July 14, 1790.* Courtesy of the Bibliothèque Nationale de France.

festival. Similarly, the Festival of the Reunion on August 10, 1793 commemorated the attack on the Bastille and march on Versailles in 1789, the 1790 Festival of the Federation, and the execution of the king in 1793 (Ozouf 1988a: 84, 155–6). These events were not celebrated chronologically—while the festival began at the Place de la Bastille it ended at the Champ de Mars (site of the Festival of the Federation) after stopping at the Place de la Revolution, where the king was executed. The narrative was thus not meant to be historically accurate, but was rather meant to provide a framework for the events of the Revolution that proceeded from the initial actions demonstrating a realization of popular sovereignty (the Bastille and the October Days) to the destruction of the monarchy to the realization of national unity.

Commemorative festivals were themselves the object of commemoration. Prints and published accounts followed upon each festival. In 1794, the 1793 Festival of the Réunion that commemorated the August 10, 1792 insurrection leading to the suspension of the monarchy, was re-enacted on stage. It was performed in the meeting hall of the Convention, as well as at the National Opera (*Journal des théâtres* Year III: 320). More permanent means of commemorating memorial festivals were also imagined. Following the Festival of the Federation, numerous projects for monuments commemorating the event were proposed, some of which were envisioned as being built at the Place de la Bastille. As with so many other major commemorative monuments, the financial and political vicissitudes

FIGURE 8.5: *A Temple dedicated to liberty, proposed for the site of the ruins of the Bastille*, engraving by Jean-Louis Prieur, c. 1789–91. Courtesy of the Bibliothèque Nationale de France.

of the revolutionary decade meant that these monuments would never be built (Leith 1991). The dream of "immortalizing" the Revolution in stone would remain just that: a dream.

REVOLUTIONARY TRAUMA

Because many of the events of the Revolution were unprecedented, because they had a direct impact on people's lives, and because they often involved literal or figurative violence, memories of revolutionary events tended to be emotionally charged. The city of Paris was itself a profound reminder of the losses many experienced during the Revolution. To take the most obvious example, no one who crossed the current Place de la Concorde could help but remember that this was the site of the executions of Louis XVI, Marie Antoinette, and Robespierre. When the émigré Pauline de Noinville returned to Paris after a ten-year absence, she described how, in walking with her aunt across this plaza, their "hearts were oppressed" at the thought of the French blood spilled there (1893: 290). As the anonymous author of an 1824 work noted, the Parisian landscape was dotted with sites that evoked the turmoil of the Revolution: "the memory of the Temple [prison], of the murder of the royal victims, of the horrible and deceased Bastille, of the awful prison of Sainte-Pélagie, and of the frenzy of the revolutionary mob, strikes fear into the soul of he who has traversed history, and who, in seeing these places, cannot escape from his painful memories" (Anon 1824: 15).

As Ronen Steinberg has written, it is tempting to view the experience of those who survived the Revolution through the lens of trauma. During the Revolution "many in France had good reason to experience the intense feelings of fear and helplessness associated with [modern concepts of] trauma" (Steinberg 2015b: 29). Trauma, as we understand it today, has at its core the inability of an individual to integrate a difficult experience into the narrative of her life story. Dominick LaCapra has written that a memory site (*lieux de mémoire*) can also function as a site of trauma if "memory has not been effective in coming to terms with it, notably through modes of mourning" (1998: 10). As the above examples indicate, these sites of trauma could include places, such as the Place de la Concorde, or people. Barry Shapiro has argued that Louis XVI served as such a site of trauma for deputies to the National Assembly. The events leading up to and following the conquest of the Bastille in July 1789 created a great deal of fear among Parisians and among members of the Third Estate, who were convinced that their defiance of the king would lead to their arrest and/or slaughter. Afterwards, deputies were unable to reconcile their feelings of betrayal and fear of the king with their traditional respect for him. As a result, they were torn by the need to both remember and forget his actions. Shapiro argues that the political vacillations of the deputies in the early years of the Revolution were shaped by this experience of trauma (2009). Silence can also be a response to trauma. Sylvie Mouysset has noted the ways in which authors of memoires censored themselves, out of a "fear of being heard, read and betrayed," but also because of a perceived "impossibility to give full rein to one's emotions, so frightening, even a long time after the events" (2013: 18). Refusing to write about certain aspects of the Revolution was an impediment to mourning; the pain caused by the memories of these events made it impossible to integrate experiences into an account of the Revolution.

Using trauma to understand those who lived through the Revolution allows us to feel empathy for their sufferings, while also providing us with analytical tools that help us analyze the relationship between emotions and politics. However, Steinberg cautions us that trauma was not a concept available to revolutionaries and that applying this concept retroactively must be done with care. As he argues, experiences that we might assume would be traumatic were sometimes understood in more complicated ways. The Terror "was seen, by some at least, as a rejuvenating, constructive, even therapeutic experience" (Steinberg 2015b: 30). What we assume to be negative emotions, such as fear, could also serve positive ends, and thus were remembered. The happy resolution of the crisis of July 1789 was greeted with intense relief. In remembering these events, those who wrote about it evoked both this relief and the fear that preceded it. As a critic wrote of the 1791 play commemorating the storming of the Bastille, "each scene retraces for inhabitants of Paris the troubles that agitated them, & the dangers they faced" (quoted in Darlow 2010: 396). Without remembering the fear surrounding the events, Parisians could not remember the relief, and the joyous moments of fraternal unity, that followed the crisis (Thompson 2016: 47). Contemporaries made sense of their fear and of the violence of the July crisis by placing it within a larger story about the Revolution.

Commemorative ceremonies could also mitigate trauma. These ceremonies offered those who were emotionally distressed by events an opportunity to come together with others who may have been similarly affected. They also provided a framework for making sense of events that could help participants process their emotions. The funeral ceremonies for those who were killed in the storming of the Bastille served both of these functions.

Large crowds of mourners attended ceremonies held in each parish of the French capital, where "patriot priests ... explained the Revolution as God's will and embraced the turmoil as a miraculous transformation heralding the nation's re-birth" (Clarke 2007: 54). The Catholic liturgy as well as the presence of friends and neighbors probably comforted mourners whose lost loved ones were also recast as heroes who sacrificed for the nation. As with the citizen-soldier, the appellation "vainqueur de la Bastille" allowed people to make sense of a loved one's death by placing it within a larger narrative of national regeneration.

Narratives of martyrdom were equally comforting to those whose loved ones had been designated enemies of the Revolution, and religion was a powerful consolatory force throughout the Revolution. Religion was not only important to those who opposed the Revolution; as we have seen, Catholic imagery and practice remained alive within revolutionary politics, through incorporation into the cult of martyrs and in the use of the processionals during festival days. Following the death of Robespierre, Catholic practices became visible once again. In 1795, many priests who had previously sworn oaths to the Constitution retracted those oaths and participated in efforts to revive Catholic ceremony and devotion (Desan 1990: 86). In the fall of 1797, tolerance for the public practice of Catholicism came to an end with a second effort at dechristianization. Yet as Suzanne Desan has shown, French men and women did not abandon Catholicism, and efforts to decrease, or even eliminate, the authority of the Catholic Church and its role in people's lives led to lay ministers preforming the functions of priests. In 1795 and 1800—following the two periods of dechristianization—Catholics in the department of the Yonne cleaned their churches from top to bottom in order to "purify" and reclaim them (1990: 97). Such efforts brought members of the community together and served as a symbolic means of putting the past behind them. By literally scrubbing away the memory of dechristianization, purification attempted to relegate the more radical and troubling aspects of the Revolution to a past that had no place in the present.

Jeffrey Alexander has argued that events that are perceived as collective traumas prompt concerns over the establishment and maintenance of boundaries (2004: 22). Cleaning the Church as a means to reclaim it for the community was one way of marking a boundary between past and present. The intense efforts of revolutionary authorities to erase all reminders of a past that was no longer sanctioned could also be seen as a means of policing the boundaries of collective memory. In June 1794, members of the Arsenal section (an administrative district of Paris) seized a watch with hands that ended in *fleurs-de-lys* and members of the *Indivisibilité* section (another such district) confiscated a purse embroidered with *fleurs-de-lys* from a sixty-six-year-old woman (Anon. Year II (1793–94)). Yet as these examples indicate, official efforts to define the limits of collective memory could never be fully successful as long as individuals and groups established their own "localizations" for memory—localizations that in the context of government efforts to police memory, tended to take the form of personal items such as watches and purses, or more ephemeral stories and songs.

The impossibility of containing or controlling memory created anxiety that was expressed through fear of inexistent or insufficient boundaries. Marie Hélène Huet has argued that the burial practices that were meant to prevent those executed during the Revolution from becoming martyrs—indiscriminately burying victims of different rank and political outlook in the same location, burials in mass graves, and secret burials—created a sense of anxiety that contemporaries expressed as a fear of disease spread through close proximity with improperly buried corpses (1997: 138–43). This concern with an absence of boundaries between the living and the dead was also expressed as a fear of ghosts. In March 1794, a Parisian told a group who had gathered around the guillotine that a friend would not join them, for he was convinced "that several of those executed returned to haunt the spot" (Arasse 1989: 111). In 1798, the phantasmagoria, a Parisian attraction staged in the abandoned Capucin convent, claimed to bring forth the specters of Voltaire, Mirabeau, and Marat (Steinberg 2015a: 258). Fear of miasmas and ghosts prevented the dead from becoming memories; instead their presence intruded into the lives of the living in ways that were painful and unsettling.

For an individual, trauma is experienced as an inability to integrate damaging experiences into a coherent life story, with the result that some aspects of an experience are forgotten (repressed) while others come unbidden to consciousness in damaging ways.

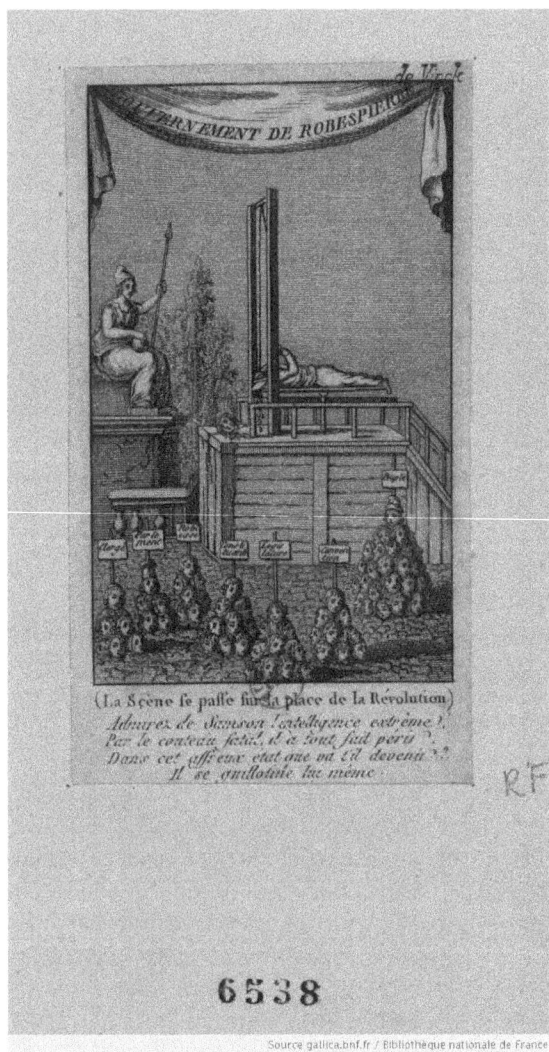

FIGURE 8.6: *Government by Robespierre*, 1794. Courtesy of the Bibliothèque Nationale de France.

By contrast, collective trauma may encourage memorial practices. Jeffrey Alexander has argued that if an experience is defined by a group as having harmed the identity of the group, this identity will need to be "revised" by means of "a searching re-remembering of the collective past" (2004: 22). Because communication within the group is only possible through creating narratives that others can understand, collective trauma may prompt the construction of multiple narratives about the past as a means to rewrite the history of the group. This is suggested not only by the examples I've discussed in this chapter, but also by the proliferation of memoires concerning the Revolution in the early nineteenth century as well as the numerous histories of the Revolution that continue to be written and read today. Yet, as Maurice Halbwachs indicated in his study of collective memory, as stories concerning the past are rewritten, they are shaped to fit the evolving concerns of the group. Those who wrote and read memoirs of the Revolution in the early nineteenth century were trying to come to terms with the ways in which the Revolution had impacted their lives, their families and their careers.

CONCLUSION

Acknowledging the close connections between history, commemoration and memory during the Revolution is important, because the Revolution has so often been interpreted as an event that encouraged forgetting. This interpretation of the Revolution is rooted in part in the view of contemporaries, that—for better or for worse—the Revolution ushered in a new era and gave birth to a "new man". The Revolution was thus seen as severing the present from the past. This was the basis of Edmund Burke's critique of revolutionary leaders: that they were so enamored of what was new that they jettisoned all ties to tradition. The rhetoric of regeneration was, as Mona Ozouf has argued, central to revolutionary ideology (1988b).

Yet as we have seen, the past was crucial in the construction of a revolutionary present, and in efforts to establish a collective memory. In 1789, the French state had a tradition of drawing upon the past to legitimize the present. From royal ceremonial to the Cult of Great Men, the past legitimized the present—as it was and as it might be. The Revolution, by accelerating the pace of political change, encouraged more self-conscious uses of the past as a means to establish a collective memory that could unite the population and stabilize politics. If one unified collective memory of the Revolution did not emerge triumphant, it was not for lack of trying. Memorial practices proliferated during the Revolution, not least because rapid and successive changes in the political landscape produced and exacerbated conflict over who and what should be remembered. As a result, it was almost impossible to "forget" the Revolution, despite efforts of political leaders to encourage French men and women to forget the damage inflicted by those with different political beliefs. It was this type of forgetting that Louis XVI recommended in his last testament: "I advise my son, if he has the misfortune of becoming King . . . that he should forget all hatred and all resentment" (Louis XVI [n.d.]: 3). State policies also encouraged such forgetting as a means to stabilize politics in the years between the fall of Robespierre and the fall of the Restoration. As Sheryl Kroen has argued, the politics of *oubli* (forgetting) was an attempt to avert civil discord. Yet the power of the Revolution was such that even those who encouraged forgetting also implemented a selective remembering as a means to construct political legitimacy.

This process of promoting some elements of the past while attempting to silence others is one that we have become accustomed to associate with modern states. Memory—and the past in general—have always been used for political purposes. However, with the Revolution, a new relationship between the past and the present emerged, as history and memory were called on to legitimize progress and change. As Paul Connerton has written, a "radical beginning" is not "even thinkable without its element of recollection—of recollection both explicit and implicit. The attempt to establish a beginning refers back inexorably to a pattern of social memories" (1989: 13). The Revolution drew upon—and produced—multiple pasts and multiple memories. These memories have been used by successive generations to fight for and oppose change, and to legitimate and undermine the status quo. This multiplicity of memories is one of the enduring legacies of the French Revolution.

BIBLIOGRAPHY

Alexander, Jeffrey C. (2004), "Toward a Theory of Cultural Trauma," in Jeffrey C. Alexander et. eds *Cultural Trauma and Collective Identity*, 1–30, Berkeley: University of California Press.

Amelang, James (1998), *The Flight of Icarus: Artisan Autobiography in Early Modern Europe*, Stanford: Stanford University Press.

Anderson, Benedict (2006), *Imagined Communities: Reflections on the Origin and Spread of Nationalism*, rev. ed., London: Verso.

Andress, David (2005), *The Terror: The Merciless War for Freedom in Revolutionary France*, New York: Farrar, Straus and Giroux.

Anon. (n.d.a), *Les finances, ou le pot-au-feu national du grand Mirabeau: Avis au peuple français*, Paris: Chez Senneville.

Anon. (n.d.b), *Antiquités nationales. I. La Bastille*, N.p.: n.p.

Anon. ([1794] 1862), "Fête célébrée en l'honeur de Jean-Jacques Rousseau, le 20 vendémiaire, l'an 3 de la république française," *Réimpression de l'ancien Moniteur*, vol. 22: 223–4, Paris, Henri Plon.

Anon. (Year II (1793–94)), Bureau de la surveillance administrative de la police générale. Rapport du 11 Messidor, an II; Rapport du 28 Messidor, an II, Archives nationales de France F/7/3821.

Anon. (1824), *L'Hermite rôdeur, ou observations sur les moeurs et usages des anglais et des français au commencement du XIXe siècle*, Paris: Malepeyre.

Anon. (1825), *A History of Paris, from the Earliest Period to the Present Day*, 3 vols., Paris: A. and W. Galignani.

Arasse, Daniel (1989), *The Guillotine and the Terror*, London: Penguin.

Ariès, Philippe ([1954] 1986), *Le Temps de l'histoire*, Paris: Seuil.

Ariès, Philippe ([1960] 1973), *L'Enfant et la vie familiale sous l'Ancien Régime*, Paris: Editions du Seuil.

Ariès, Philippe (1988), "L'Histoire des mentalités," in Jacques Le Goff, ed., *La Nouvelle Histoire*, 167–90, Paris: Editions Complexe.

Assmann, Aleida (2011), *Cultural Memory and Western Civilization*, Cambridge: Cambridge University Press.

Assmann, Jan (1992), *Das kulturelle Gedächtnis: Schrift, Erinnerung und politische Identität in frühen Hochkulturen*, Munich: Beck.

Assmann, Jan (2011), *Cultural Memory and Early Civilization*, Cambridge: Cambridge University Press.

Aulard, Alphonse (1904), *Le Culte de la raison et le culte de l'être suprême*, Paris: Alcan.

Bailly, Jean-Sylvain and Honoré Duveyrier (1790), *Procès-verbal des séances et délibérations de l'Assemblée générale des électeurs de Paris, Réunis à l'Hôtel-de-Ville le 14 Juillet 1789. Rédigé depuis le 26 Avril jusqu'au 21 Mai 1789 par M. Bailly [. . .] Et depuis le 22 Mai jusqu'au 30 Juillet 1789*, Paris: Baudoin.

Baecque, Antoine de (1987), "Le corps meurtri de la Révolution: Le discours politique et les blessures des martyrs (1792–1794)," *Annales historiques de la Révolution française* 267: 17–41.

Baecque, Antoine de (2001), *Glory and Terror: Seven Deaths Under the French Revolution*, trans. Charlotte Mandell, New York: Routledge.
Baker, Keith (1990), *Inventing the French Revolution: Essays on French Political Culture in the Eighteenth Century*, New York: Cambridge University Press.
Barzin (1793), *Mémoire du Citoyen Barzin, entrepreneur des bâtiments*, août, Archives nationales de France, F/13/212.
Beasley, Jerry C. (1976), "Romance and the 'New' Novels of Richardson, Fielding, and Smollett," *Studies in English Literature, 1500–1900*, 16 (3): 437–50.
Beasley, Faith E. (1990), *Revising Memory: Women's Fiction and Memoirs in Seventeenth-Century France*, New Brunswick, NJ: Rutgers University Press.
Beaune, Colette (1991), *The Birth of an Ideology: Myths and Symbols of Nation in Late-Medieval France*, ed. Fredric L. Cheyette, trans. Susan Ross Huston, Berkeley: University of California Press.
Becker, Carl (1932), *The Heavenly City of the Eighteenth-Century Philosophers*, New Haven: Yale University Press.
Becq, Annie ([1984], 1994), *Genèse de l'esthétique française moderne 1680–1814*, Paris: Albin Michel.
Beecher, Jonathan (1986), *Charles Fourier: The Visionary and His World*, Berkeley: University of California Press.
Behrens, C.B.A. (1967), *The Ancien Regime*, New York: Harcourt, Brace, and World.
Bell, David A. (2001), *The Cult of the Nation in France: Inventing Nationalism, 1680–1800*, Cambridge, MA: Harvard University Press.
Bellaigue, Christopher de (2017), *The Islamic Enlightenment: The Struggle between Faith and Reason, 1798 to Modern Times*, New York: Liveright.
Ben-Israel, Hedva (1968), *English Historians on the French Revolution*, Cambridge: Cambridge University Press.
Bending, Stephen (2016), "Writing in Ruins: immediacy and emotion in the English landscape garden," *Studies in the History of Gardens & Designed Landscapes* 36: 272–81.
Benstock, Shari, ed. (1988), *The Private Self: Theory and Practice of Women's Autobiographical Writings*, London: University of North Carolina Press.
Berger, Stefan, Heiko Feldner, and Kevin Passmore, eds (2020), *Writing History: Theory and Practice*, London: Bloomsbury Publishing.
Berlin, Isaiah (1976), *Vico and Herder: Two Studies in the History of Ideas*, New York: Random House.
Berlin, Isaiah ([1980] 2013), *Against the Current*, ed. Henry Hardy, Princeton, NJ: Princeton University Press.
Bevis, Richard R. (1995), *English Drama: Restoration and Eighteenth Century (1660–1789)*, London and New York: Longman.
Bibliothèque Mazarine, Paris, France, Ms. 2489.
Bibliothèque Nationale de France, FR, MS. 15238.
Bibliothèque de la Société de Port-Royal, Bio 338 bis.
Blair, Hugh (1853), *Lectures on Rhetoric and Belles Lettres*, Philadelphia: Troutman & Hayes.
Bilinkoff, Jodi (1993), "Confessors, Penitents and the Construction of Identities in Early Modern Avila," in Barbara Diefendorf and Carla Hesse, eds., *Culture and Identity in Early Modern Europe 1500–1800: Essays in Honor of Natalie Zemon Davis*, 83–102, Ann Arbor: University of Michigan Press.

Bilinkoff, Jodi (2000), "Confession, Gender, Life-Writing: Some Cases (Mainly from Spain)," in Katharine J. Lualdi and Anne. T. Thayer, eds, *Penitence in the Age of Reformations*, 169–83, London: Ashgate.

Bilinkoff, Jodi (2005), *Related Lives: Confessors and their Female Penitents 1450–1750*, Ithaca, NY: Cornell University Press.

Blix, Göran (2009), *From Paris to Pompeii: French Romanticism and the Cultural Politics of Archaeology*, Philadelphia: University of Pennsylvania Press.

Bloom, Rori (2009), *The Abbé Prévost between Novel and Newspaper*, Lewisburg: Bucknell University Press.

Bonneau du Plessis, Jacqueline-Marie, (1696), *La Vie de la vénérable mère Louise-Eugénie de Fontaine Religieuse du Monastère de la Visitation de Sainte-Marie de Paris, Rue Saint-Antoine, morte le 29 Septembre de l'année 1694*, Paris: François Muguet.

Bonneau-Avenant, Alfred (1873), *Madame de Miramion: sa vie et ses oeuvres charitables, 1629–1696*, Paris: Didier.

Bonnet, Jean-Claude (1986), "Les formes de célébration," in Jean-Claude Bonnet, ed., *La mort de Marat*, 101–27, Paris: Flammarion.

Bonnet, Jean-Claude (1998), *Naissance du Panthéon: Essai sur le Culte des Grands Hommes*, Paris: Fayard.

Bossuet, Jacques-Bénigne ([1681] 1976), *Discourse on Universal History*, ed. Orest Ranum, Chicago: University of Chicago Press.

Bouwers, Eveline G. (2012), *Public Pantheons in Revolutionary Europe: Comparing Cultures of Remembrance, c. 1790–1840*, Houndmills, UK: Palgrave Macmillan.

Boyer, Ferdinand (1961), "Les Collections et les ventes de Jean-Joseph de Laborde", *Bulletin de la société de l'histoire de l'art français*: 137–52.

Boym, Svetlana (2002), *The Future of Nostalgia*, New York: Basic Books.

Briant, Pierre (2012), *Alexandre des Lumières, fragments d'histoire européenne*, Paris: Gallimard.

Brown, Homer Obed (1979), "Tom Jones: The 'Bastard' of History," *Boundary*, 7 (2): 201–45.

Browning, Reed (1993), *The War of the Austrian Succession*, New York: St. Martin's Press.

Burke, Peter (2017), "Shaping Memories," in Mihaela Irimia, Drago Manea, Andreea Paris eds., *Literature and Cultural Memory*, 19–30, Leiden: Brill.

Burgdorf, Wolfgang (1998), *Reichskonstitution und Nation: Verfassungsreformprojekte für das Heilige Römische Reich Deutscher Nation im politischen Schrifttum von 1648 bis 1806*, Mainz: von Zabern.

Burton, Richard D.E. (1997), "From Scapegoat to Martyr: The Image of Marie-Antoinette in Nineteenth-Century Catholic-Monarchist Thought," *Australian Journal of French Studies* 34 (2): 196–201.

Burwick, Frederick (2011), *Playing the Crowd: London Popular Theater, 1780–1830*, Basingstoke, New York: Palgrave Macmillan.

Carr, Thomas, M, Jr. (2016), "Jansenist Women Negotiate the Pauline Interdiction," *Arts et Savoirs*, 2016.

Casid, Jill H. (2005), *Sowing Empire: Landscape and Colonization*, Minneapolis: University of Minnesota Press.

Catala, Sarah and Gabriel Wick, eds., *Hubert Robert et la fabrique des jardins*, Paris: Réunion Des Musees Nationaux.

Cayeux, Jean de (1987), *Hubert Robert et les jardins*, Paris: Herscher.

Cayeux, Jean de (1968), "Hubert Robert et sa collaboration à Méréville," *Bulletin de la société de l'histoire de l'art français*: 127–33.

Ceserani, Giovanna (2013), "Antiquarian transformations in eighteenth-century Europe," in Alain Schnapp, ed., *World Antiquarianism: comparative perspectives*, Los Angeles: Getty Research Institute.

Cerutti, Joseph-Antoine-Joachim (1792), *Les Jardins de Betz, Poème, Accompagné de Notes instructives sur les travaux champêtres, sur les arts, les lois, les révolitions, la noblesse, le clergé, etc.*, Paris: Chez Desenne.

Charron, Joseph (1791), *Translation de Voltaire à Paris, et détails de la cérémonie qui aura lieu le 4 juillet*, Paris: Lottin l'aîné et J-R Lottin.

Chartier, Roger (1982), "Intellectual History or Socio-Cultural History?" in Dominick LaCapra and Steven L. Kaplan, eds, *Modern European Intellectual History: Reappraisals and New Perspectives*, 30, Ithaca, NY: Cornell University Press.

Chartier, Roger (1989), "The Practical Impact of Writing," in Roger Chartier, ed., *A History of Private Life: Passions of the Renaissance*, 3: 111–59, Cambridge, MA: Harvard University Press.

Chartier, Roger (1991), *The Cultural Origins of the French Revolution*, Durham: Duke University Press.

Chartier, Roger (1998), "Introduction," in Roger Chartier, ed., *Cultural History. Between Practice and Representations*, 4, Cambridge: Cambridge University Press.

Choisy, François-Timoléon de (1706), *La Vie de Mme de Miramion par François-Timoléon de Choisy*, Paris: A. Dezallier.

Choppin de Janvry, Olivier (1969), "Méréville," *L'Oeil*, no. 180 (December): 30–40, 83, 96.

Clark, Andy (2008), *Supersizing the Mind: Embodiment, Action, and Cognitive Extension*, Oxford: Oxford University Press.

Clark, John O.E., ed. (2016), *Maps that Changed the World*, London: Pavilion Books.

Clarke, Joseph (2007), *Commemorating the Dead in Revolutionary France: Revolution and Remembrance, 1789–1799*, Cambridge: Cambridge University Press.

Coffin, David R. (1994), *The English Garden: Meditation and Memorial*, Princeton, NJ: Princeton University Press.

Collé, Charles ([1768], 1974), "La Partie de Chasse de Henry IV, Théâtre de société," in Jacques Truchet, ed., *Théâtre du XVIIIe siècle*, vol. 2, Paris: Gallimard, La Pléiade.

Colley, Linda (2012), *Britons: Forging the Nation, 1707–1837*, rev. ed., London: Yale University Press.

Condorcet, Nicholas Caritat, marquis de ([1793] 2012), "The Sketch," in Steven Lukes and Nadia Urbinati, eds., *Political Writings*, 1–147, Cambridge: Cambridge University Press.

Confino, Alon (2008), "Memory and the History of Mentalities," in Astrid Erll and Nünning Asgar, eds., *Cultural Memory Studies*, 77–84, Berlin: Walter de Gruyter.

Connerton, Paul (1989), *How Societies Remember*, Cambridge: Cambridge University Press.

Conroy, Jane (1999), *Terres tragiques: l'Angleterre et l'Ecosse dans la tragédie française du XVIIe siècle*, Tübingen: Gunter Narr Verlag.

Cooper, Kirsten L. (2019), "Honest Germans and Perfidious French: National Ideas in Pamphelt Propaganda During the Wars of Louis XIV," PhD Diss., University of North Carolina at Chapel Hill.

Cooper, Kirsten L. (2020), "Political Fear during the Wars of Louis XIV: The Danger of Becoming French," in Michael Pickering and Thomas Kehoe, eds., *Representations of Fear in the German-Speaking World 1600–2000*, 15–39, London: Bloomsbury Publishing.

Corneille, Pierre ([1660] 1987), *Les Trois Discours sur le poème dramatique*, in Georges Couton ed., *Œuvres Complètes*, 3: 117–90, Paris: Gallimard.

Coy, Jason, Benjamin Marschke and David Warren Sabean, eds (2010), *The Holy Roman Empire, Reconsidered*, New York: Berghahn Books.

Cramer, Kevin (2007), *The Thirty Years War and German Memory in the Nineteenth Century*, Lincoln: University of Nebraska Press.

D'Alès du Corbet (1760), *Abrégé de la Vie de M. Le Pelletier, mort à Orléans, en odeur de sainteté, par Mlle d'Alès du Corbet*, Orléans: Chez Couret de Villeneuve.

Darlow, Mark (2010), "History and (Meta-) Theatricality: The French Revolution's Paranoid Aesthetics," *The Modern Language Review* 105 (2): 385–400.

Darnton, Robert (1979), *The Business of Enlightenment; A Publishing History of the Encyclopédie, 1775–1800*, Cambridge, MA: Harvard University Press.

Darnton, Robert (1982), *The Literary Underground of the Old Regime*, Cambridge, MA: Harvard University Press.

Darnton, Robert (1984), *The Great Cat Massacre and Other Episodes in French Cultural History*, New York: Basic Books.

Darnton, Robert (1995), *Forbidden Best-Sellers of Pre-Revolutionary France*, New York: W.W. Norton & Co.

Darnton, Robert (2009), *The Case for Books, Past, Present, and Future*, New York: Basic Books.

Daujon (1793), *Mémoire de Citoyen Daujon, juin 1793*, Archives nationales de France, F/13/212.

Davenport, Nancy (1986), "Maenad, Mother, Martyr: Marie-Antoinette Transformed," *Proceedings of the Consortium on Revolutionary Europe, 1750–1850*: 66–84.

Davis, Lloyd (2006), "Critical Debates and Early Modern Autobiography," in Lloyd Davis, Ronald Bedford, and Philippa Kelly, eds., *Early Modern Autobiography: Theories, Genres, Practices*, 19–34, Ann Arbor: University of Michigan Press.

Deelman, Christian (1964), *The Great Shakespeare Jubilee*, New York: Viking Press.

Defoe, Daniel ([1722] 2003), *A Journal of the Plague Year*, London: Penguin.

Dehaene, Stanislaus (2010), *Reading in the Brain: The New Science of How We Read*, New York: Penguin.

Dermenjian, Geneviève, Jacques Guihaumou, Karine Lambert, and Martine Lapied (2012), "L'autre Panthéon: femmes et héroïsation sous la Révolution française," in Serge Bianchi with Bernard Gainot and Pierre Serna, eds., *Héros et héroïnes de la Révolution française*, 81–95, Paris: Editions du Comité des travaux historiques et scientifiques.

Desan, Suzanne (1990), *Reclaiming the Sacred: Lay Religion and Popular Politics in Revolutionary France*, Ithaca, NY: Cornell University Press.

Diefendorf, Barbara (2004), *From Penitence to Charity: Pious Women and the Catholic Reformation in Paris*, Oxford: Oxford University Press.

Delille, Jacques (1825), *L'Imagination*, 2 vols., Paris: L.G. Michaud.

Delumeau, Jean (1971), *Le Catholicisme entre Luther et Voltaire*, Paris: Presses Universitaires de France.

Denton, Margaret Fields (2003), "Death in French Arcady: Nicolas Poussin's 'The Arcadian Shepherds and Burial Reform in France c. 1800," *Eighteenth-Century Studies*, 36 (2): 202–3.

Derrida, Jacques (1984), *Otobiographies*, Paris: Editions Galilée.

Des Essarts, Nicolas-Toussaint (1773), *Causes célèbres, curieuses et intéressantes, de toutes les cours souveraines du royaume, avec les jugements qui les ont décidées*, Paris: Lacombe.

Desfontaines, Pierre-François Gugot (1724), *Histoire de Juan de Portugal fils de D. Pedre et d'Ines de Castro*, Paris: Prissot.

Diderot, Denis, and Jean le Rond d'Alembert, eds. ([1751–72] 2017), *Encyclopédie*, Chicago: University of Chicago ARTFL *Encyclopédie* Project.

Dobson, Michael (1992), *The Making of the National Poet: Shakespeare, Adaptation, and Authorship, 1660–1769*, Oxford: Clarendon Press.

Dodd, William (1752), *Beauties of Shakespeare*, London: Waller.

Dorotte/Scellier (1793), *Mémoire des ouvrages de maçonnerie, 29 juillet*, Archives nationales de France, F/13/212.

Douthwaite, Julia V. (2002), *The Wild Girl, Natural Man, and the Monster*, Chicago: University of Chicago Press.

Dowd, Michelle. M, and Julie A. Eckerle, eds. (2007), *Genre and Women's Life Writing in Early Modern England*, London: Ashgate.

Draper, James David and Guilhem Scherf, eds. (1998), *Augustin Pajou: Royal Sculptor, 1730–1809*, New York: Metropolitan Museum of Art.

Dryden, John (1668), *An Essay of Dramatic Poesy*, ed. Jack Lynch. Available on line: https://andromeda.rutgers.edu/~jlynch/Texts/drampoet.html

Duchosal, Marie-Emile-Guillaume (1794), *Journal des théâtres et des fêtes nationales* no. 34, 4E sans-culotide.

Dugas, Don-John (2006), *Marketing the Bard: Shakespeare in Performance and Print, 1660–1740*, Columbia: University of Missouri Press.

Dupuy, Pascal (2012), "The Revolution in History, Commemoration, and Memory," in Peter McPhee, ed., *A Companion to the French Revolution*, 468–501, Chichester: John Wiley & Sons.

Dziembowski, Edmond (1998), *Un Nouveau Patriotisme Français, 1750–1770: La France face à la puissance anglaise à l'époque de La Guerre de Sept Ans*, Oxford: Voltaire Foundation.

Eisenstein, Elizabeth L. (2005), *The Printing Revolution in Early Modern Europe*, 2nd ed., Cambridge: Cambridge University Press.

Elias, Norbert ([1939] 1978), *The Civilizing Process: The History of Manners*, New York: Urizen.

Erll, Astrid, ed. (2008), *Cultural Memory Studies: An International and Interdisciplinary Handbook*, Berlin: de Gruyter.

Etlin, Richard A. (1975), "Architecture and the Festival of Federation, Paris, 1790," *Architectural History* 18: 23–42.

Febvre, Lucien ([1952] 1992), *Combats pour l'Histoire*, Paris: Armand Colin.

Ferrone, Vincenzo (2015), *The Enlightenment: History of an Idea*, Princeton, NJ: Princeton University Press.

Field, G.W. (1960), "Schiller's Maria Stuart," *University of Toronto Quarterly*, 29 (3): 326–40.

Fink, Gonthier-Louis (2002), "Du discours de Rousseau aux contes des frères Grimm. Le mythe du peuple et le miroir de la bourgeoisie," *Etudes germaniques*, 57 (2): 233–66.

Fink, Gonthier-Louis (2003), "Goethes Mythus des Janusköpfigen Volkes in der Zeit des Sturm und Drang," in Werner Frick, Susanne Komfort-Hein, eds., *Aufklärungen: Zur Literaturgeschichte der Moderne: Festschrift für Klaus-Detlef Müller zum 65 Geburtstag*, 73–94, Tübingen: Walter de Gruyter.

Foer, Joshua (2011), *Moonwalking with Einstein*, New York: Penguin.

Forrest, Alan (2009), *The Legacy of the French Revolutionary Wars: The Nation-in-Arms in French Republican Memory*, Cambridge: Cambridge University Press.

Foucault, Michel (1977), "What is an Author?" in Donald F. Bouchard, ed., *Language, Counter-Memory, Practice; Selected Essays and Interviews by Michel Foucault*, 113–38, Ithaca, NY: Cornell University Press.

Foucault, Michel (1978), *A History of Sexuality, An Introduction*, vol. 1, New York: Pantheon.

Foucault, Michel (1980), *Power/Knowledge*, ed. Colin Gordon, New York: Pantheon.

Friedman, Susan, Stanford (1988), "Women's Autobiographical Selves: Theory and Practice," in Shari Benstock, ed., *The Private Self: Theory and Practice of Women's Autobiographical Writings*, 34–62, London: University of North Carolina Press.

Fritzsche, Peter (2004), *Stranded in the Present: Modern Time and the Melancholy of History*, Cambridge, MA: Harvard University Press.

Funk, Robert and Roy Hoover, eds. (1993), *The Five Gospels*, New York: HarperCollins.

Fureix, Emmanuel (2009), *La France des larmes: Deuils politiques à l'âge romantique (1814–1840)*, Paris: Editions Champs Vallon.

Furet, François (1981), *Interpreting the French Revolution*, Cambridge: Cambridge University Press.

Gadamer, Hans-Georg ([1960] 1992), *Truth and Method*, 2nd ed., New York: Crossroad.

Gagliardo, John (1980), *Reich and Nation: The Holy Roman Empire as Idea and Reality, 1763–1806*, Bloomington: Indiana University Press.

Garrick, David, *An Ode upon Dedicating a Building and erecting a Statue to Shakespeare at Stratford upon Avon* ed. D.G., London: T. Beckett and P.A. de Hondt.

Gauthier, Laurent-Marie (n.d.), *Discours pour la fête de l'anniversaire du 14 juillet, prononcé dans le temple de la Victoire, le 26 messidor an VII, par le président de la municipalité du 11e arrondissement*, Paris: Guilhemat.

Gay, Peter (1958), "Carl Becker's Heavenly City," in Raymond O. Rockwood, ed., *Carl Becker's Heavenly City Revisited*, 27–51, Ithaca, NY: Cornell University Press.

Gazier, G. (1906), "La mort de J.-J. Rousseau récit fait par Thérèse Levasseur à l'architecte Pâris, à Ermenonville," *Revue d'histoire littéraire de la France*: 101–9.

Gélis, Jacques (1989), "The Child: From Anonymity to Individuality," in Roger Chartier, ed., *A History of Private Life*, 3: 309–25, Cambridge, MA: Harvard University Press.

Gellner, Ernest (1997), *Nations and Nationalism*, London: Weidenfeld & Nicolson.

Germa, Antoine (2002), "Les Promenades du château de La Roche-Guyon: étude de l'aménagement d'un parc," MA diss., Université de Paris XIII.

Gifford, William (1802), *The Satires of Decimus Junius Juvenalis*, London: Bulmer & Co.

Girardin, René-Louis, marquis de (1777), *De la composition des paysages ou des moyens d'embellir la Nature autour des Habitations, en joignant l'agréable à l'utile*, Geneva: P.M. Delaguette.

Girardin, Stanislas de (1788), *Promenade ou itinéraire des jardins d'Ermenonville auquel on a joint vingt-cinq de leurs principales vues*, Paris: Mérigot père.

Goldmann, Lucien (1964), *The Hidden God*, London: Routledge & Kegan Paul.

Goldmann, Lucien (1967), *The Hidden God. A Study of Tragic Vision in the Pensées of Pascal and the Tragedies of Racine*, 17, London: Routledge.

Goodman, Dena (1994), *The Republic of Letters: A Cultural History of the French Enlightenment*, Ithaca, NY: Cornell University Press.

Goodman, Dena (2009), *Becoming a Woman in the Age of Letters*, Ithaca, NY: Cornell University Press.

Goodman, Jessica, ed. (2017), *Commemorating Mirabeau: Mirabeau aux Champs-Elysées and Other Texts*, Cambridge: Modern Humanities Research Association.

Gorski, Philip S. (2006), "Pre-modern Nationalism: An Oxymoron? The Evidence from England," in Gerard Delanty and Krishan Kumar, eds., *The SAGE Handbook of Nations and Nationalism*, 143–56, London: SAGE Publications.

Gouiric, Nicole (2017) "Hubert Robert et Méréville," in Sarah Catala and Gabriel Wick, eds., *Hubert Robert et la fabrique des jardins*, Paris: Réunion des musées nationaux.

Goulemot, Jean Marie (1996), Le Règne de l'histoire, discours historique et révolutions, XVIIE–XVIIIE siècles, Paris: Albin Michel.

Grabes, Herbert (2008), "Cultural Memory and the Literary Canon," in Astrid Erll and Ansgar Nünning, eds., *Cultural Memory Studies*, 311–19, Berlin: Walter de Gruyter.

Grafton, Anthony (1997), *The Footnote: A Curious History*, Cambridge, MA: Harvard University Press.

Grazia, Margareta de (1991), *Shakespeare Verbatum: The Reproduction of Authenticity and the 1790 Apparatus*, Oxford: Clarendon Press.
Greenblatt, Stephen (1991), *Marvelous Possessions: The Wonder of the New World*, Chicago: University of Chicago Press.
Greene, Christopher M. (1981), "Alexandre Lenoir and the Musée des monuments français during the French Revolution," *French Historical Studies* 12 (2): 200–22.
Greenfeld, Liah (1992), *Nationalism: Five Roads to Modernity*, Cambridge, MA: Harvard University Press.
Grell, Chantal (1982), *Herculanum et Pompéi dans les récits des voyageurs français du XVIIIe siècle; Mémoires et documents sur Rome et l'Italie méridionale*, Naples: Centre Jean Bérard.
Gribbin, William (1972), "Rollin's Histories and American Republicanism," *The William and Mary Quarterly*, 29 (4): 611–22.
Grimm, Jacob and Wilhelm ([1819, 1857] 1980), *Kinder- und Hausmärchen*, Heinz Rölleke, ed., Stuttgart: Philip Reclam.
Grimsley, Ronald (1969), *Jean-Jacques Rousseau: A Study in Self-Awareness*, Cardiff: University of Wales Press.
Groom, Nick (1996), "Introduction," in Thomas Percy, *Reliques of Ancient English Poetry*, London: Routledge/Thoemmes Press.
Gude, Mary, L. (1999), "Madame de Miramion and the Friends of Vincent de Paul," *Vincentian Heritage Journal* 20 (2): 238–51.
Gusdorf, Georges (1980), "Conditions and Limits of Autobiography," in James Olney, ed., *Autobiography: Essays Theoretical and Critical*, 28–48, Princeton, NJ: Princeton University Press.
Habermas, Jurgen ([1962] 1989), *The Structural Transformation of the Public Sphere*, Cambridge, MA: MIT Press.
Haddock, Bruce (1986), *Vico's Political Thought*, Swansea: Mortlake Press.
Halbwachs, Maurice ([1941] 2008), *La Topographie légendaire des évangiles en Terre Sainte*, Paris: Presses Universitaires de France.
Halbwachs, Maurice (1992), *On Collective Memory*, trans. Lewis A. Coser, Chicago: University of Chicago Press.
Hartog, François (2015), *Regimes of Historicity*, New York: Columbia University Press.
Harvey, David Allen (2012), *The French Enlightenment and Its Others*, New York: Palgrave Macmillan.
Hastings, Adrian (1997), *The Construction of Nationhood: Ethnicity, Religion and Nationalism*, Cambridge: Cambridge University Press.
Havelock, Eric (1963), *Preface to Plato*, Cambridge, MA: Harvard University Press.
Hecht, Jennifer (2003), *Doubt: A History*, New York: HarperCollins.
Herzog, Günter (1989), *Hubert Robert und das Bild im Garten*, Worms: Wernersche Verlagsgesellschaft.
Hesse, Carla, and Thomas Laqueur (1994), "Introduction," *Representations*, 47: 1–12 (Special Issue: National Cultures before Nationalism).
Hillman, Jennifer (2018), "Writing a Spiritual Biography in Early Modern France: The 'Many Lives' of Madeleine de Lamoignon," *French Historical Studies*, 42 (1): 1–34.
Hirschi, Caspar (2012), *The Origins of Nationalism: An Alternative History from Ancient Rome to Early Modern Germany*, Cambridge: Cambridge University Press.
Hobsbawm, Eric (1992), *Nations and Nationalism since 1780: Programme, Myth, Reality*, 2nd ed., New York: Cambridge University Press.

Hobsbawm, Eric and Terence Ranger, eds. (1983), *The Invention of Tradition*. Cambridge: Cambridge University Press.

Hommasel-Hecquet, Marie-Catherine ([1755] 2017), *Histoire d'une jeune fille sauvage, trouvée dans les bois à l'âge de dix ans*, Paris: Gallimard.

Howe, Elizabeth Teresa (2015), *Autobiographical Writing by Early Modern Hispanic Women*, London: Ashgate.

Huet, Marie-Hélène (1997), *Mourning Glory: The Will of the French Revolution*, Philadelphia: University of Pennsylvania Press.

Hume, David ([1775] 1965), "Of the Poems of Ossian," in David Norton and Richard Popkin, eds., *David Hume: Philosophical Historian*, 390–400, Indianapolis: Bobbs-Merrill Company.

Hume, David (2008), *Dialogues* [1779] and *Natural History of Religion* [1757], ed. J.C.A. Gaskin, Oxford: Oxford University Press.

Hunt, John Dixon (1992), *Gardens and the Picturesque: Studies in the History of Landscape Architecture*, Cambridge, MA: MIT Press.

Hunt, Lynn (1984), *Politics, Culture, and Class in the French Revolution*, Berkeley: University of California Press.

Hunt, Lynn (1989), "Introduction: History, Culture, Text," in Lynn Hunt, ed., *The New Cultural History*, 19, Berkeley: University of California Press.

Hunt, Lynn (1991), "The Many Bodies of Marie-Antoinette: Political Pornography and the Problem of the Feminine in the French Revolution," in Lynn Hunt, ed., *Eroticism and the Body Politic*, 108–30, Baltimore: The Johns Hopkins University Press.

Hunt, Lynn (1992), *The Family Romance of the French Revolution*, Berkeley: University of California Press.

Hunt, Lynn (1993), "Obscenity and the Origins of Modernity," in Lynn Hunt, ed., *The Invention of Pornography*, 10–35, New York: Zone.

Hutton, Patrick (1981), *The Cult of the Revolutionary Tradition*, Berkeley: University of California Press.

Hutton, Patrick H. (1988), "The Print Revolution of the Eighteenth Century and the Drafting of Written Constitutions," *Vermont History* 56: 154–65.

Hutton, Patrick H. (1992), "Inventing Constitutions: The Vermont Constitution and the Print Revolution of the Eighteenth Century," in Michael Sherman and Jennie Versteeg, eds., *We Vermonters: Perspectives on the Past*, 277–89, Burlington: Center for Research on Vermont.

Hutton, Patrick H. (1993), *History as an Art of Memory*, Hanover, NH: University Press of New England.

Hutton, Patrick H. (2016), *The Memory Phenomenon in Contemporary Historical Writing: How the Interest in Memory Has Influenced Our Understanding of History*, New York: Palgrave Macmillan.

Israel, Jonathan (2001), *Radical Enlightenment*, Oxford: Oxford University Press.

Jacob, Margaret C. (1991), *Living the Enlightenment*, Oxford: Oxford University Press.

Jacob, Margaret C. (2006), *The Origins of Freemasonry*, Philadelphia: University of Pennsylvania Press.

Jainchill, Andrew (2008), *Reimagining Politics after the Terror: The Republican Origins of French Liberalism*, Ithaca, NY: Cornell University Press.

Jelinek, Estelle, ed. (1980), *Women's Autobiography: Essays in Criticism*, Bloomington: Indiana University Press.

Jourdan, Annie (1997), *Les Monuments de la Révolution, 1770–1804: Une histoire de représentation*, Paris: Honoré Champion.

Journal des théâtres et des fêtes nationales (Year III [1793–94]).

Kaiser, Thomas E. (1996), "Madame de Pompadour and the Theaters of Power," *French Historical Studies* 19 (4): 1025–44.

Kammen, Michael (1986), *A Machine That Would Go of Itself; The Constitution in American Culture*, New York: Knopf.

Kaplan, Steven Laurence (1995a), *Farewell Revolution: Disputed Legacies, France 1789/1799*, Ithaca, NY: Cornell University Press.

Kaplan, Steven Laurence (1995b), *Farewell Revolution: The Historians' Feud, France 1789/1989*, Ithaca, NY: Cornell University Press.

Kelley, Donald (1998), *Faces of History: Historical Inquiry from Herodotus to Herder*, New Haven: Yale University Press.

Kim, Dae Kweon, (2002), *Sprachtheorie im 18. Jahrhundert: Herder, Condillac und Süssmilch*, Saarbrücken: Röhrig Universitätsverlag.

Koselleck, Reinhart (1985), *Futures Past: On the Semantics of Historical Time*, Cambridge, MA: MIT Press.

Krobb, Florian (2005), "Friedrich Schiller: 'The First Historiographer in Germany'? An Appreciation to Mark the 200th Anniversary of His Death," *Archivium Hibernicum*, 59: 277–89.

Kroen, Sheryl (2000), *Politics and Theater: The Crisis of Legitimacy in Restoration France, 1815–1830*, Berkeley: University of California Press.

Kuhn, Thomas (1970), *The Structure of Scientific Revolutions*, 2nd edn, Chicago: University of Chicago Press.

La Chapelle, Jean de (1704), *Lettres d'un Suisse à un François ou l'on voit les véritables intérêts des princes et des nations de l'Europe qui sont en guerre*, 8 vols., Basel.

La Rochefoucauld, Alexandrine-Charlotte-Sophie de (2001), *Lettres de la duchesse de La Rochefoucauld à William Short*, ed. Doina Pasca Harsanyi, Paris: Mercure de France.

Laborde, Alexandre de (1808), *Description des nouveaux jardins de la France et de ses anciens châteaux mêlée d'observations sur la vie de la campagne et la composition des jardins par Alexandre de Laborde*, Paris: impr. de Delance.

LaCapra, Dominick (1998), *History and Memory after Auschwitz*, Ithaca, NY: Cornell University.

Lassus, Simone de (1976), "Quelques détails inédits sur Méréville," *Bulletin de la société de l'histoire de l'art français*: 273–87.

Le Brun, Jacques (1986), "À corps perdu: Les biographies féminines du XVIIe siècle," in Charles Malamoud and Jean-Pierre Vernant, eds., *Corps des dieux; Le Temps de la réflexion*, 389–408, Paris: Gallimard.

Le Brun, Jacques (2013), *Soeur et amante: les biographies spirituelles féminines du XVIIe siècle*, Geneva: Droz.

Le Gall, Jean-Marie (2009), "Violence et révolution: Exhumation et profanation des tombes royales à Saint-Denis," in Annie Duprat, ed., *Révolutions et mythes identitaires: Mots, violences, mémoire*, 157–71, Paris: Nouveau Monde éditions.

Le Roy Ladurie, Emmanuel (1981), *The Mind and Method of the Historian*, Chicago; University of Chicago Press.

Leerssen, Joep (2010), *National Thought in Europe: A Cultural History*, Amsterdam: Amsterdam University Press.

Lefebvre, Georges ([1939] 1947), *The Coming of the French Revolution*, Princeton, NJ: Princeton University Press.

Leith, James A. (1991), *Space and Revolution: Projects for Monuments, Squares, and Public Buildings in France, 1789–1799*, Montreal: McGill-Queen's University Press.

Lejeune, Phillippe (1989), *On Autobiography*, ed. Paul John Eakin, Minneapolis: University of Minnesota Press.

Lemierre, Antoine-Marin (2005), *Théatre*, France Marchal Ninosque, ed., Paris: Honoré Champion.

Lenglet Du Fresnoy, Nicolas (1734), *De l'usage des romans, où l'on fait voir leur utilité & leurs différens caractères*, Amsterdam, Veuve de Poilras.

Lepore, Jill (2010), *The Whites of Their Eyes: The Tea Party's Revolution and the Battle over American History*, Princeton, NJ: Princeton University Press.

Lessing, Gotthold Ephraim ([1767–9] 1981), *Hamburgische Dramaturgie*, Stuttgart: Philip Reclam jun.

Levine, Joseph (1999), *The Autonomy of History; Truth and Method from Erasmus to Gibbon*, Chicago: University of Chicago Press.

Lichtheim, George (1967), *The Concept of Ideology*, New York: Random House.

Lilla, Mark (1993), *G.B. Vico: The Making of an Anti-Modern*, Cambridge, MA: Harvard University Press.

Lilti, Antoine (2015), *The World of the Salons: Sociability and Worldliness in Eighteenth-Century Paris*, Oxford: Oxford University Press.

Lilti, Antoine (2017), *The Invention of Celebrity*, Cambridge: Polity.

Lindfield, Peter and Christie Margrave, eds. (2015), *Rule Britannia? Britain and Britishness 1707–1901*, Newcastle upon Tyne: Cambridge Scholars Publishing.

Louis XVI (n.d.), *Testament de notre bon roi Louis XVI*, Paris: Imprimerie de Mame frères.

Löwith, Karl (1949), *Meaning in History*, Chicago: University of Chicago Press.

Lüsebrink, Hans-Jürgen and Rolf Reichardt (1997), *The Bastille: A History of a Symbol of Despotism and Freedom*, trans. Norbert Shürer, Durham: Duke University Press.

Luzatto, Sergio (1991), *Mémoire de la Terreur: Vieux montagnards et jeunes républicains au XIXe siècle*, trans. Simone Carpentari-Messina, Lyon: Presses Universitaires de Lyon.

Lynn, John A. (1999), *The Wars of Louis XIV, 1667–1714*, New York: Longman.

Lyon-Caen, Nicholas (2008), *Un roman bourgeois sous Louis XIV: Récits de vies marchandes et mobilité sociale: les itinéraires des Homassel*, Limoges: Pulim.

MacDonald, Katherine (2007), *Biography in Early Modern France 1540–1630*, Oxford: Modern Humanities Research Association and Routledge.

Mackrell, J.Q.C. (1973), *The Attack on 'Feudalism' in Eighteenth-Century France*, Toronto: University of Toronto Press.

Macpherson, James ([1765] 1996), *A Dissertation concerning the Antiquity, of the Poems of Ossian the son of Fingal*, in Howard Gaskill, ed., *The Poems of Ossian and related works*, Edinburgh: Edinburgh University Press.

Maës, Antoine (2016), "Hubert Robert et Rambouillet," in Guillaume Faroult and Catherine Voiriot, eds., *Hubert Robert 1733–1808, Un peintre visionnaire*, Paris: Musée du Louvre éditions/Somogy éditions d'art.

Mah, Harold (1994), "The Epistemology of the Sentence: Language, Civility, and Identity in France and Germany, Diderot to Nietzsche," *Representations*, 47: 64–84 (Special Issue: National Cultures before Nationalism).

Mah, Harold (2003), *Enlightenment Phantasies: Cultural Identity in France and Germany, 1750–1914*, Ithaca, NY: Cornell University Press.

Maignien, Edmond (1890), *Bibliographie des écrits relatifs à Mandrin*, Grenoble: E. Baratier.

Manuel, Frank (1962), *Prophets of Paris*, Cambridge, MA: Harvard University Press.

Marmontel, Jean-François ([1787] 2005), *Eléments de littérature*, ed. Sophie Le Ménahèze, Paris: Desjonquères.

Marshall, Louise (2008), *National Myth and Imperial Fantasy, Representations of Britishness on the Early Eighteenth-Century Stage*, Basingstoke: Palgrave Macmillan.

Martin, Jean-Clément (1989), *La Vendée de la mémoire 1800–1980*, Paris: Editions du Seuil.

Martin, John Rupert (1977), *Baroque*, New York: Harper & Row.

Martin, Meredith (2011), *Dairy Queens: The politics of pastoral architecture from Catherine de Medici to Marie-Antoinette*, Cambridge, MA: Harvard University Press.

Martin-Decaen, André (1912), *Le Dernier ami de J.-J. Rousseau: le marquis René de Girardin (1735–1808) d'après des documents inédits*, Paris: Perrin.

Maskill, David (2006), "Death in a French Garden: The Laborde and Cook Monuments at Méréville and the Landscape of Loss," in Martin Calder, ed., *Experiencing the Garden in the Eighteenth Century*, 145–60, Bern: Peter Lang.

Matsuda, Matt K. (2012), *Pacific Worlds*, Cambridge: Cambridge University Press.

Mazeau, Guillaume (2009), *Le bain de l'histoire: Charlotte Corday et l'attentat contre Marat (1793–2009)*, Paris: Editions Champ-Vallon.

McIntosh, Fiona (2002), *La Vraisemblance narrative en question*, Paris: Presses de la Sorbonne Nouvelle.

McLuhan, Marshall ([1962] 2011), *The Gutenberg Galaxy: The Making of Typographic Man*, Toronto: University of Toronto Press.

McNeil, Kenneth (2012), "Ballads and Borders," in Fiona Robertson, ed., *The Edinburgh Companion to Sir Walter Scott*, 22–34, Edinburgh: Edinburgh University Press.

Melton, James van Horn (2001), *The Rise of the Public in Enlightenment Europe*, Cambridge: Cambridge University Press.

Mercier, Louis-Sébastien (1772), *L'An deux mille quatre cent quarante : rêve s'il en fût jamais*, Lausanne: François Grasset.

Mercier, Louis-Sébastien (1994), *Journal de Paris* 11 vendémiaire an VI, reprinted in Louis-Sébastien Mercier, *Le Nouveau Paris*, ed. Jean-Claude Bonnet, Paris: Mercure de France.

Merrick, Jeffrey (1990), *The Desacralization of the French Monarchy in the Eighteenth Century*, Baton Rouge: Louisiana State University Press.

Merrill, Michael (1976), "Interview with E.P. Thompson," in H. Abelove, et al. eds, *Visions of History*, 20f, Manchester: Manchester University Press.

Mettler, Heinrich, and Heinz Lippuner (1989), *Wilhelm Tell: das Drama der Freiheit*, Paderborn: Schöningh.

Moatti, Claude (1993), *The Search for Ancient Rome*, New York: Harry Abrams.

Mondon, Christine (2007), "Le mythe du peuple: de Herder aux romantiques de Heidelberg," in Jean-Marie Paul, ed., *Le peuple, mythe et réalité*, Rennes: Presses universitaires de Rennes.

Montagu, Elizabeth (1769), *The Essay on the writings and genius of Shakespear, compared with the Greek and French dramatic poets : with some remarks upon the misrepresentations of Mons. de Voltaire*, ed. Jack Lynch, London: Doddsley.

Montesquieu, Charles-Louis de Secondat, baron de ([1748] 1989), *The Spirit of the Laws*, trans. Anne M. Cohler, Basia C. Miller, Harold S. Stone, Cambridge: Cambridge University Press.

Moreland, Caroll C. (1935), "Ritson's life of Robin Hood," *PMLA*, 50 (2): 522–36.

Mornet, Daniel (1933), *Les Origines intellectuelles de la Révolution française*, Paris: Armand Colin.

Mortier, Roland (1974), *La poétique des ruines en France: ses origines, ses variations de la Renaissance à Victor Hugo*, Geneva: Droz.
Moser, Friedrich Carl von (1765), *Von dem deutschen National-Geist*.
Moser-Verrey, Monique (2015), "La 'nouvelle-anecdote' en circulation entre la France, la Suisse et l'Autriche: une contribution singulière de M. et Mme d'Ussieux," in Geneviève Haroche-Bouzinac, Camille Esmein-Sarrazin, Gaël Rideau, Gabriele Vickermann-Ribémont, eds, *L'Anecdote entre littérature et histoire*, 299–311, Rennes: Presses Universitaires de Rennes.
Mosse, George (1961), *The Culture of Western Europe*, New York: Rand McNally & Company.
Mosse, George (1975), *The Nationalization of the Masses*, New York: New American Library.
Mosser, Monique (1983), "Le rocher et la colonne: un thème architectural au XVIIIème siècle," *Revue de l'Art* 58–9: 53–74.
Mosser, Monique and Hervé Brunon (2014), *L'Imaginaire des Grottes dans les Jardins Européens*, Paris: Hazan.
Mouysset, Sylvie (2013), "'Silence de mort et craintes extrêmes': La peur et son for privé à l'époque révolutionnaire," *Annales historiques de la Révolution française*, 373 (July–Sept): 11–34.
Münkler, Herfried, Hans Grünberger, and Kathrin Mayer (1998), *Nationenbildung: die Nationalisierung Europas im Diskurs humanistischer Intellektueller: Italien und Deutschland*, Berlin: Akademie Verlag.
Noinville, Pauline de (1893), *Souvenirs d'une octégenaire*, quoted in Hervé, vicomte de Broc, ed., *Dix ans de la vie d'une femme pendant l'émigration. Adélaïde de Kerjean Marquise de Falaiseau*, Paris: Plon.
Nora, Pierre, ed. (1984–92), *Les Lieux de mémoire*, 3 vols., Paris: Gallimard.
Nora, Pierre (1986), "La Nation-mémoire," in Pierre Nora, ed., *Les Lieux de mémoire*, 2: 647–58, Paris: Gallimard.
Olick, Jeffrey K., Vered Vinitzky-Seroussi, and Daniel Levy (2011), eds. *The Collective Memory Reader*, Oxford: Oxford University Press.
Olney, James (1972), *Metaphors of the Self: The Meaning of Autobiography*, Princeton: Princeton University Press.
Olney, James, ed. (1980), *Autobiography: Essays Theoretical and Critical*, Princeton: Princeton University Press.
Ong, Walter (1982), *Orality and Literacy: The Technologizing of the Word*, London: Methuen.
Orr, Linda (1990), *Headless History: Nineteenth-Century French Historiography of the Revolution*, Ithaca, NY: Cornell University Press.
Ozouf, Mona (1988a), *Festivals and the French Revolution*, trans. Alan Sheridan, Cambridge, MA: Harvard University Press.
Ozouf, Mona (1988b), "La Révolution française et l'idée de l'homme nouveau," in Colin Lucas, ed., *The French Revolution and the Creation of Modern Political Culture. Vol. 2: The Political Culture of the French Revolution*, 213–32, Oxford: Pergamon Press.
Ozouf, Mona (1997), "Le Panthéon: L'école normale des morts," in Pierre Nora, ed., *Les Lieux de mémoire*, 1:155–178, Paris: Gallimard.
Paige, Nicholas (2001), *Being Interior: Autobiography and the Contradictions of Modernity in Seventeenth-Century France*, Philadelphia: University of Pennsylvania Press.
Paige, Nicholas (2002), "Enlightened (Il)literates: Problems of Gender and Authority in Early Modern Devotional Writing," in David Lee Rubin and Julia V. Douthwaite, eds., *Rethinking Cultural Studies 2: Exemplary Essays*, 115–40, Charlottesville: Rookwood Press.

Palmer, Robert Roswell (1960), *The Age of the Democratic Revolution*, 2 vols., Princeton: Princeton University Press.
Pascal, Roy ([1937] 1971), *Shakespeare in Germany, 1740–1815*, New York: Octagon.
Paulin, Roger (2003), *The Critical Reception of Shakespeare in Germany, 1682–1914: Native Literature and Foreign Genius*, New York: Georg Ohms Verlag.
Paulin, Roger, ed. (2015), *Voltaire, Goethe, Schlegel, Coleridge: Great Shakespeareans, Vol. 3*, London: Bloomsbury.
Pemble, John (2005), *Shakespeare Goes to Paris: How the Bard Conquered France*, London: Hambledon and London.
Peraldo, Emmanuelle (2010), *Daniel Defoe et l'écriture de l'histoire*, Paris: Honoré Champion.
Percy, Thomas ([1765] 1996], *Reliques of Ancient English Poetry*, introduction Nick Groom, London: Routledge, Thoemmes Press.
Petiteau, Natalie (2012), *Ecrire la mémoire: Les mémorialistes de la Révolution et de l'Empire*, Paris: Les Indes Savantes.
Phillips, Mark Salber (2013), *On Historical Distance*, New Haven: Yale University Press.
Pincus, Steven (1995), "From Butterboxes to Wooden Shoes: The Shift in English Popular Sentiment from Anti-Dutch to Anti-French in the 1670s," *The Historical Journal* 38 (2): 333–61.
Pincus, Steven (2009), *1688: The First Modern Revolution*, New Haven: Yale University Press.
Pinto, John A. (2012), *Speaking Ruins: Piranesi, Architects, and Antiquity in Eighteenth-Century Rome*, Ann Arbor: University of Michigan Press.
Plessner, Helmuth (1959), *Die verspätete Nation: über die politische Verführbarkeit bürgerlichen Geistes*, Stuttgart: W. Kohlhammer.
Pocock, J.G.A. (1972), *Politics, Language, and Time: Essays on Political Thought and History*, London: Methuen.
Pomian, Krzysztof (1992), "Les Archives," in Pierre Nora, ed., *Les Lieux de mémoire*, 3: 163–233, Paris: Gallimard.
Postert, Kirsten (2010), *Tragédie historique ou Histoire en Tragédie? Les sujets d'histoire moderne dans la tragédie française (1550–1715)*, Tübingen: Narr Verlag.
Poulot, Dominque (1997), "Alexandre Lenoir et les musées des monuments français," in Pierre Nora, ed., *Les Lieux de mémoire*, I: 1515–43, Paris: Gallimard.
Radisich, Paula Rea (1995), "'La chose publique,' Hubert Robert's decorations for the 'petit salon' at Méréville," in Ann Bermingham and John Brewer, eds., *The Consumption of Culture, 1600–1800: Image, Object, Text*, London: Routledge.
Ranum, Orest (1976), "Introduction," in *Discourse on Universal History by Jacques-Bénigne Bossuet*, xiii–xliv, Chicago: University of Chicago Press.
Rapley, Elizabeth (1990), *The Dévotes: Women and the Church in Seventeenth-Century France*, Montreal: McGill-Queen's University Press.
Rapley, Elizabeth (2007), "'Un tresor enfoui, une lampe sous un boisseau:' Seventeenth-Century Visitandines Describe Their Vocation," in Thomas M. Carr, ed., *The Cloister and the World: Early Modern Convent Voices*, 155–66, Charlottesville: Rockwood Press.
Reddy, William M. (2001), *The Navigation of Feeling: A Framework for the History of Emotions*, Cambridge: Cambridge University Press.
Redfield, Marc (1996), "The Dissection of the State: *Wilhelm Meisters Wanderjahre* and the Politics of Aesthetics," *The German Quarterly*, 69: 15–31.
Ritson, Joseph ([1795]1883), *Robin Hood, a collection of all the ancient poems, songs, and ballads, now extant, relative to that celebrated English outlaw. To which are prefixed historical anecdotes of his life*, London: John C. Nimmo.

Roberts, Peter (1998), "Tudor Wales, National Identity and the British Inheritance," in Brendan Bradshaw and Peter Roberts, eds., *British Consciousness and Identity: The Making of Britain, 1533–1707*, 8–42, Cambridge: Cambridge University Press.
Robespierre, Maximillien (1792), "Maximillien Robespierre, à Prudhomme," *Révolutions de Paris, dédiées à la nation*, 8–15 décembre 1792: 554–6.
Rollin, Charles (1740), *Histoire ancienne des Égyptiens, des Carthaginois, des Assyriens, des Babyloniens, des Mèdes et des Perses, des Macédoniens, des Grecs*, Paris: Veuve Estienne.
Rollin, Charles ([1738] 1823), *Histoire romaine*, in Jean-Antoine Letronne, ed., *Œuvres complètes*, vol. 1, Paris: Firmin Didot.
Rose, Mary Beth (1986), "Gender, Genre and History: Seventeenth-Century English Women and the Art of Autobiography," in Mary Beth Rose, ed., *Women in the Middle Ages and the Renaissance: Literary and Historical Perspectives*, 245–78, Syracuse: Syracuse University Press.
Rosenberg, Daniel and Anthony Grafton (2010), *Chronologies of Time*, New York: Princeton Architectural Press.
Rossi, Henri (1998), *Mémoires aristocratiques féminins 1789–1848*, Paris: Honoré Champion.
Rossi, Paolo (1984), *The Dark Abyss of Time*, Chicago: University of Chicago Press.
Rossi, Paolo (2000a), *The Birth of Modern Science*, Oxford: Blackwell Publishers.
Rossi, Paolo ([1983] 2000b), *Logic and the Art of Memory*, Chicago: University of Chicago Press.
Rousseau, Jean-Jacques ([1782] 1979), *Reveries of the Solitary Walker*, ed. Peter France, London: Penguin.
Rousseau, Jean-Jacques (1966), *Emile ou de l'éducation*, ed. Michel Launay, Paris: Flammarion.
Rousso, Henry (2016), *The Latest Catastrophe*, Chicago: University of Chicago Press.
Rudé, George (1964), *The Crowd in History, 1730–1848*, New York: John Wiley & Sons.
Rymer, Thomas ([1693] 1970), *Short View of Tragedy*, New York: AMS Press.
Sahlins, Peter (1989), *Boundaries: The Making of France and Spain in the Pyrenees*, Berkeley: University of California Press.
Sahut, Marie-Catherine and Nicole Garnier (1979), *Le Louvre d'Hubert Robert*, Les dossiers du département des peintures, Paris: Editions de la Réunion des Musée Nationaux.
Scales, Len (2012), *The Shaping of German Identity: Authority and Crisis, 1245–1414*, Cambridge: Cambridge University Press.
Schiller, Friedrich (1792), *Vorrede*, in François Gayot de Pitaval, ed., *Merkwürdige Rechtsfälle als ein Beitrag zur Geschichte der Menschheit*, Iena: Christ. Heinz Cuno.
Schillinger, Jean (1999), *Les pamphlétaires allemands et la France de Louis XIV*, Bern: P. Lang.
Schmidt, Peer (2001), *Spanische Universalmonarchie oder teutsche Libertet: das spanische Imperium in der Propaganda des Dreissigjährigen Krieges*, Stuttgart: Steiner.
Schoenbaum, Samuel (1993), *Shakespeare's Lives*, Oxford: Oxford University Press.
Schumann, Jutta (2011), *Die andere Sonne: Kaiserbild und Medienstrategien im Zeitalter Leopolds I*, München: Oldenbourg Akademieverlag.
Scott, Walter ([1814] 1986), *Waverley; or, "Tis Sixty Years Since,"* Oxford: Oxford University Press.
Seelig, Sharon Cadman (2006), *Autobiography and Gender in Early Modern Literature: Reading Women's Lives 1600–1680*, Cambridge: Cambridge University Press.
Shapiro, Barry M. (2009), *Traumatic Politics: The Deputies and the King in the Early French Revolution*, University Park: Pennsylvania State University Press.
Sheehan, James J. (1981), "What Is German History? Reflections on the Role of the Nation in German History and Historiography," *The Journal of Modern History* 53 (1): 1–23.

Simeone, William E. (1953), "The Historic Robin Hood," *The Journal of American Folklore*, 66 (262): 303–8.
Skura, Meredith, Anne (2008), *Tudor Autobiography: Listening for Inwardness*, Chicago: University of Chicago Press.
Smith, Jay M. (2005), *Nobility Reimagined: The Patriotic Nation in Eighteenth-Century France*, Ithaca, NY: Cornell University Press.
Smith, Sidonie and Julie Watson, eds. (2001), *Reading Autobiography: A Guide for Interpreting Life Narratives*, Minneapolis: University of Minnesota Press.
Smyth, Adam (2010), *Autobiography in Early Modern England*, Cambridge: Cambridge University Press.
Soboul, Albert (1957), "Sentiment religieux et Cultes populaires pendant la Révolution: Saintes patriotes et martyrs de la liberté," *Annales historiques de la Révolution française* 29: 193–213.
Stafford, Fiona (1996), "Introduction," in Howard Gaskill, ed., *The Poems of Ossian and Related Works*, v–xxi, Edinburgh: Edinburgh University Press.
Stanton, Domna C. (2014), *The Dynamics of Gender in Early Modern France: Women Writ, Women Writing*, London: Routledge.
Stanzel, Franz K., ed. (1999), *Europäischer Völkerspiegel: imagologisch-ethnographische Studien zu den Völkertafeln des frühen 18. Jahrhunderts*, Heidelberg: Winter.
Stara, Alexandra (2013), *The Museum of French Monuments 1795–1816: "Killing art to make history,"* Farnham: Ashgate.
Stedman Jones, Gareth (1983), *Languages of Class: Studies in English Working-Class History 1832–1986*, 22, Cambridge: Cambridge University Press.
Steinberg, Ronen (2015a), "Between Silence and Speech: Spectres and Images in the Aftermath of the Reign of Terror," *Acta Academica* 47 (1): 247–65.
Steinberg, Ronen (2015b), "Trauma and the Effects of Mass Violence in Revolutionary France: A Critical Inquiry," *Historical Reflections/Réflexions historiques* 41 (3): 28–46.
Steinberg, Ronen (2019), *The Afterlives of the Terror*, Ithaca, NY: Cornell University Press.
Stochholm Johanne M. (1964), *Garrick's Folly; The Shakespeare Jubilee of 1769 at Stratford and Drury Lane*, New York: Barnes and Noble.
Stone, Lawrence (1977), *The Family, Sex, and Marriage in England, 1500–1800*, New York: Harper & Row.
Stoye, John (2006), *The Siege of Vienna*, new ed., Edinburgh: Birlinn.
Suire, Éric (2001), *La Sainteté française de la réforme catholique (XVI–XVIII siècles d'après les textes hagiographiques et les procès de canonisation)*, Pessac: Presses Universitaires de Bordeaux.
Tagliacozzo, Giorgio (1993), *The "Arbor Scientiae" Reconceived and the History of Vico's Resurrection*, Atlantic Highlands, NJ: Humanities Press International.
Tantillo, Astrida Orle (1999), "Herder and National Culture: A Case Study of Latvia," in David Bell, Stéphane Pujol and Ludmila Pimenova, eds., *Raison universelle et culture nationale au siècle des Lumières*, 31–46, Paris: Champion.
Taylor, Charles (1989), *Sources of the Self*, Cambridge, MA: Harvard University Press.
Taylor, Owen Reece (1970), "Introduction," in *The Complete Works of Voltaire, La Henriade*, Geneva: Institut et Musée Voltaire.
Taylor, Susan B. (1990), "Ut pictura horti: Hubert Robert and the Bains d'Apollon at Versailles", PhD Diss., Philadelphia: University of Pennsylvania.
Thomas, Chantal (1999), *The Wicked Queen: The Origins of the Myth of Marie-Antoinette*, trans. Julie Rose, Cambridge, MA: The MIT Press.
Thompson, E.P. (1963), *The Making of the English Working Class*, New York: Random House.

Thompson, Victoria E. (2014), "An Alarming Lack of Feeling: Urban Travel, Emotions, and British National Character in Post-Revolutionary Paris," *Urban History Review/Revue d'histoire urbaine* 42 (2): 8–17.

Thompson, Victoria E. (2016), "Memories of Fear in the Early French Revolution," *Journal of the Western Society for French History* 44: 35–48.

Thompson, Victoria E. (2019), "Restoring the Royal Family: 'Les adieux de Louis XVI' and the Family of Louis XVIII," in Nimisha Barton and Richard Hopkins, eds., *Practiced Citizenship: Women, Gender and the State in Modern France*, 51–74, Lincoln: University of Nebraska Press.

Tilly, Charles (1964), *The Vendée: A Sociological Analysis of the Counter-Revolution of 1793*, Cambridge, MA: Harvard University Press.

Timmermans, Linda, (1993), *L'accès des femmes à la culture (1598–1715): un débat d'idées de Saint François de Sales à la Marquise de Lambert*, Paris: H. Champion.

Toews, John E. (1987), "Intellectual History after the Linguistic Turn: The Autonomy of Meaning and the Irreducibility of Experience." *American Historical Review* 92, 4 (Oct.): 879–907.

Trévisi, Marion, (2008), *Au coeur de la parenté: oncles et tantes dans la France des Lumières*, Paris: Presses de l'Université Paris-Sorbonne.

Van Kley, Dale K. (1996), *The Religious Origins of the French Revolution: From Calvin to the Civil Constitution, 1560–1791*, New Haven: Yale University Press.

Vazsonyi, Nicholas (1999), "Montesquieu, Friedrich Carl von Moser, and the 'National Spirit Debate' in Germany, 1765–1767," *German Studies Review* 22 (2): 225–46.

Vick, Brian E. (2014), *The Congress of Vienna: Power and Politics after Napoleon*, Cambridge, MA: Harvard University Press.

Vico, Giambattista ([1744] 1968), *The New Science*, 3d ed., ed. Thomas Goddard Bergin and Max Harold Fisch, Ithaca, NY: Cornell University Press.

Vico, Giambattista ([1709] 1990), *On The Study Methods of Our Times*, Ithaca, NY: Cornell University Press.

Vixouse, François-Xavier Pagès de (1800), *Nouveaux dialogues des morts entre les plus fameux personnages de la Révolution française et plusieurs hommes célèbres, anciens et modernes, morts avant la Révolution*. Paris: Laurens jeune.

Voltaire ([1728] 1816), "Essai sur la poésie épique," in *La Henriade, poème*, avec les notes et variantes, 290–402, Paris: A. Égron.

Voltaire ([1732] 1974), "Zaïre, épître dédicatoire," in Jacques Truchet, ed., *Le Théâtre du XVIIIe siècle*, 684–91, Paris: Gallimard, La Pléiade

Voltaire [1756] (1963), *Essai sur les moeurs et l'esprit des nations et sur les principaux faits de l'histoire depuis Charlemagne jusqu'à Louis XIII*, ed. René Pomeau, Paris: Garnier frères.

Vovelle, Michel (1974), *Mourir autrefois: Attitudes collectives devant la mort aux XVIIe et XVIIIe siècles*, Paris: Gallimard.

Vovelle, Michel (1983), *La Mort et l'Occident de 1300 à nos jours*, Paris: Gallimard.

Walsh, Marcus (1997), *Shakespeare, Milton, and Eighteenth-Century Literary Editing: The Beginnings of Interpretive Scholarship*, Cambridge: Cambridge University Press.

Warner, Michael (1990), *The Letters of the Republic: Publication and the Public Sphere in Eighteenth-Century America*, Cambridge, MA: Harvard University Press.

Warwick, Charles F. (1905), *Mirabeau and the French Revolution*, Philadelphia: George W. Jacobs & Company.

Watt, Ian ([1957] 2001), *The Rise of the Novel*, Berkeley: University of California Press.

Watteville, Alexandre-Louis ([1754] 1757), *Histoire de la Confédération helvétique*, Gottschall & Co.

Weber, Eugen (1976), *Peasants into Frenchmen: The Modernization of Rural France, 1870–1914*, Stanford, CA: Stanford University Press.

Welch, Ellen R. (2013), "Dancing the Nation: Performing France in Seventeenth-Century Ballets des Nations," *Journal for Early Modern Cultural Studies* 13 (2): 3–23.

West, Shearer (2012), "Shakespeare and the Visual Arts" in Fiona Ritchie and Peter Sabor, eds., *Shakespeare in the Eighteenth Century*, 227–53, Cambridge: Cambridge University Press.

Whaley, Joachim (2012), *Germany and the Holy Roman Empire*, vols. 1 & 2, New York: Oxford University Press.

Whately, Thomas (1770), *Observations on Modern Gardening illustrated by descriptions*, London: T. Payne.

Whitehouse, Tessa (2006), "Structures and Processes of English Spiritual Autobiography from Bunyan to Cowper," in Adam Smyth, ed., *A History of English Autobiography*, 103–18, Cambridge: Cambridge University Press.

Wick, Gabriel (2014), *Un paysage des Lumières: le jardin anglais du château de la Roche-Guyon*, Paris: Artlys.

Wick, Gabriel (2017), "The Princesse de Monaco, Hubert Robert and the invention of the 'Vieux château' of Betz," *Studies in the History of Gardens & Designed Landscapes*, published online, February 2017.

Wiebenson, Dora (1978) *The Picturesque Garden in France*, Princeton, NJ: Princeton University Press.

Williams, Helen Maria (1796), *Letters from France: Containing a Great Variety of Interesting and Original Information concerning the most Important Events that have lately occurred in that Country and particularly respecting the Campaign of 1792*, 2nd ed., 4 vols., London: G.G. and J. Robinson.

Withers, Charles W. J. (2007), *Placing the Enlightenment*, Chicago: University of Chicago Press.

Wrede, Martin (2004), *Das Reich und seine Feinde: Politische Feindbilder in der reichspatriotischen Publizistik zwischen Westfälischem Frieden und Siebenjährigem Krieg*, Mainz: P. von Zabern.

Wulf, Andrea, (2015), *The Invention of Nature; Alexander von Humboldt's New World*, London: John Murray.

Yalom, Marilyn (1993), *Blood Sisters: The French Revolution in Women's Memory*, New York: Basic Books.

Yates, Francis (1966), *The Art of Memory*, Chicago: University of Chicago Press.

Zahra, Tara (2008), *Kidnapped Souls: National Indifference and the Battle for Children in the Bohemian Lands, 1900–1948*, Ithaca, NY: Cornell University Press.

Zaretsky, Robert (2015), *Boswell's Enlightenment*, Cambridge, MA: Harvard University Press.

Zerubavel, Eviatar (2003), *Time Maps: Collective Memory and the Social Shape of the Past*, Chicago: University of Chicago Press.

CONTRIBUTORS

Kirsten L. Cooper completed her PhD from the University of North Carolina at Chapel Hill in 2019. Her dissertation analyzed the use of national rhetoric in French and German-language political pamphlets during the Wars of Louis XIV (1667–1714). More broadly she is interested in alternative understandings of nation and uses of national ideas in the early modern and modern periods, as well as the development of new forms of nationalism in the world today. Her work has been featured in journals such as the *Journal of World History* and the *Journal of the Western Society for French History*, as well as several edited collections. She is the recipient of numerous grants and fellowships for research and study in Austria, Germany, France, and most recently South Korea.

Jennifer Hillman is Visiting Research Fellow and tutor in History in the Department of History and Archaeology at the University of Chester, UK. She is a historian of early modern France and her first monograph was published as *Female Piety and the Catholic Reformation in France* (London: Routledge, 2014).

Patrick H. Hutton is Professor of History Emeritus at the University of Vermont, USA. He has published a number of books, scholarly articles, and review essays germane to scholarship on memory and history and the historiography of memory studies, notably *The Cult of the Revolutionary Tradition* (1981), *History as an Art of Memory* (1993), *Philippe Ariès and the Politics of French Cultural History* (2004), and *The Memory Phenomenon in Contemporary Historical Writing* (2016).

Fiona McIntosh-Varjabédian is Professor for the Faculty of Humanities at the University of Lille, France. She teaches comparative literature and her research interests are centered on British, French and German eighteenth- and nineteenth-century literature. She is the author of *La Vraisemblance narrative, Walter Scott, Barbey d'Aurevilly*, (Paris: Presses de la Sorbonne Nouvelle, 2002); *Ecriture de l'histoire et regard rétrospectif, Clio et Epiméthée*, (Geneva: Champion, 2010) and of many collective books. Her last one co-directed with Pr Eléonore Le Jallé, *Libéral, libéralité, libéralisme: histoire et enjeux philosophiques, culturels et littéraires*, was published in 2018.

Tom Simone is Professor of English at the University of Vermont, USA. He is an award-winning teacher and was a founding member of its Integrated Humanities Program. He has written a book and numerous articles on Shakespeare and has recently translated with commentary Dante's *Divine Comedy* (Hackett Publishing 2007).

Victoria E. Thompson is Associate Professor of History at Arizona State University, USA. Her research focuses on politics, culture and identity in Paris in the eighteenth and early nineteenth centuries. She is currently completing a monograph entitled *Inventing Public Space in Paris, 1748–1790*.

Gabriel Wick is Lecturer in the History of Design and the Built Environment at the Paris campuses of NYU and Parsons. He received his doctorate in history from Queen Mary University of London, UK, and also holds masters degrees in landscape architecture from UC Berkeley, USA, and landscape conservation from the École Nationale Supérieure d'Architecture Versailles, France. He has edited and authored a number of books on eighteenth-century landscape gardens in France and curated an exhibition on the built landscapes of Hubert Robert at the château of La Roche-Guyon.

INDEX

Addison, Joseph 74
Alembert, Jean le Rond d' 7, 9, 63, 94, 99, 114
Alexandre, Jeffrey 145, 157, 159
Alighieri, Dante 8
American War of Independence 29, 124
Andersen, Hans-Christian 60
Anderson, Benedict 19, 36
antiquarianism, transformed in the eighteenth
    century 38
antiquity, Greco-Roman
    archaeological excavations and the
        evocation of memories of antiquity
        38–40, 42, 55, 101
    memorable figures of antiquity in
        eighteenth-century literature 114
    and models for modern government 3, 13
    modern aesthetic uses of its culture 37, 113
    scholarly interest in 101, 118
    see also history of preliterate societies
archives, as memory banks 59
Aristotle, verisimilitude in his theory of poetics
    113, 128
Arne, Thomas 86
Assmann, Aleida, memory as *ars* and as *vis* 58
Augustine of Hippo 98, 109, 131
autobiography 11, 58, 109–12, 129–42
    (auto)biography, concept of 129–30
    female authored spiritual biography/
        autobiography as a hybrid genre
        130, 132–3, 136, 140–2
    gender issues in 131–2, 141

Banks, John 115, 126
baroque 97
    art and architecture 7, 9
    and the concept of the decay of nature 10
Barré, Jean-Benoît 49, 52, 56
Bayle, Pierre 119
Beaumont, Francis 73
Beaune, Collette 22
Becker, Carl, his interpretation of the
    Enlightenment 3, 96
Belanger, François-Joseph 49, 52

Bell, David 22, 27–8
Berlichingen, Götz von, the legendary 92, 122
Berlin, Isaiah, and the concept of Counter-
    Enlightenment 4
Betterton, Thomas 74, 84
Bilinkoff, Jodi 132
biography
    as literary genre 11, 61–2
    as religious genre 129–42
Blackwell, Thomas 119
Bonnet, Jean-Claude 149
Bordes, Jean de 126
Bossuet, Jacques Bénigne 93
    compared with Augustine of Hippo 98
    compared with Condorcet 96–7, 100–1
    his theist philosophy of history 96–9
Boswell, James 61, 81, 87
Bougainville, Louis-Antoine 16
Boursault, Edmé 126
Boydell, John 89–90
Boym, Svetlana, and the concept of reflective
    nostalgia 5
Brooke, Henry 115
Buchanan, George 126
Burke, Edmund 13, 159

Cammaert, Frans 115
Capell, Edward 79, 80–1
Carr, Thomas M. 136, 138
Casid, Jill 49
Castelvetro, Ludivico 114
Cavendish, Margaret 136
celebrity
    and the birth of the "fan" 69
    changing conceptions of 69
    and the concept of the memorable
        personality 3
    and the cult of Great Men 146–7
Cerutti, Joseph 37
Charles II (England) 74
Charles VII (Wittelsbach Holy Roman
    Emperor), and the War of the
    Austrian Succession 25, 31

Chartier, Roger, on techniques of reading and writing 60–1
Choiseul, Etienne de 41, 49
Choisy, Timoléon François de 134–6
Cibber, Colley 114
Collé, Charles 116
Colley, Linda 25, 29
commemoration, practices 8, 144
    and the French Revolution 17, 69–70, 144–5, 152–9
    and heroes and martyrs 145–52
    and history 145
    and memory-making 145
    and pantheons 17, 69–70, 147–53
    and the politics of forgetting 159–60
    and the quest for continuity between past and present 147
    and Shakespeare 81–90
    and writers and statesmen 69–70
communication, modes of 58
    autobiography 58, 109–11
    corresponding societies 66
    letters 64
    memoirs 58, 117, 145–6
    novels 12, 58, 64, 109, 117
    orality vs. literacy 58–9
    personal letters 58
Condorcet, Nicholas, marquis de 93, 94
    compared with Bossuet 96–7, 100–1
    his humanist philosophy of history 100
    role in the French Revolution 99–100
Connerton, Paul 160
Cook, Captain James, 16
    cenotaph of 51
Corday, Charlotte 149
Cordel, Henry 76
Corneille, Pierre 114, 124
Corneille, Thomas 115
Crevier, Jean-Louis 118
Cromwell, Oliver 73, 116

D'Alès du Corbet 141
Darnton, Robert 64
    and the *Encyclopédie* 63
Davenant, William 74
Defoe, Daniel 7, 116
Delille, the Abbé 41
Desan, Suzanne 157
Des Essarts, Nicholas-Toussaint 117–18
Desfontaines, Pierre-François 116
Desprez, Louis Jean 55
Deverell, Mary 126

Diderot, Denis 7, 9, 42, 63, 114
Digges, Leonard 82
Dreyden, John 73–4
Dupuy, Pascal 153
    and the concept of memorial history 145

encyclopedias
    Cyclopedia (Ephraim Chambers) 63
    Encyclopédie, the 6, 7, 9, 38, 63–4, 114
Enlightenment, the 1, 27
    and the cult of Great Men 146–50, 159
    as an epoch in cultural history 94
    interpretations of 96
    and liberal vs. radical ideas 7
    scope 7
    and women of the salon 7
Eusebius of Caesarea 98

family, as a unit of intimacy 12
Ferrone, Vincenzo 94
Fletcher, John 73
Foucault, Michel, and discourse about asylums 5–6
Fourier, Charles 4, 96
Francis I (Holy Roman Emperor) 26
Franklin, Benjamin, as celebrity 69
freemasons 57, 67–9
    and mnemonic symbols 9, 67
French Revolution 3, 12–13, 63, 64, 94, 95, 99, 100, 117, 118, 122, 124, 143–60
    and the Old Regime 3, 8, 152
    and the revolutionary tradition 14, 146
    and trauma 8, 145, 155–9
    and the Terror 17, 149, 156
French Revolution, commemoration of 17, 152–5
    festivals 143, 147, 149, 152–5
    and iconoclasm concerning the heritage of monarchy 150
    martyrs and heroes 144–5, 145–52, 157
    museum for the heritage of the monarchy 150–2
    and the Pantheon 17, 147–53
Friedman, Susan Stanford 131
Fuseli, Henry 89

Gay, Peter 3
Garrick, David
    his *Ode* to Shakespeare 86–8
    merges Shakespeare's persona with his own 75, 85

as Shakespearean actor 75, 84–6
and his "Shakespeare Jubilee" of 1769 at Stratford-upon-Avon 85–90
Gellner, Ernest 19, 36
George I (Great Britain) 25
George II (Great Britain) 25
George III (Great Britain) 29, 30, 31
Gibbon, Edward 119
Girardin, René-Louis, marquis de, and the gardens and tomb of Rousseau at Ermenonville 42–6, 55
Goodman, Dena 64
Goethe, Johann von 12, 34, 64, 91–2, 109, 117, 122
Gottsched, Johann Christoph 114
Greene, Christopher 151
Gusdorf, Georges 131
Gouiric, Nicole 49, 54
Grancourt, Pierre Bergeret de 38
Grazia, Margareta de 81, 82
Grell, Chantal 38
Grimm, Wilhelm and Jacob 60, 103, 120–1
Groom, Nick 119

Habermas, Jürgen, and the concept of the public sphere 7, 65
Halbwachs, Maurice
  and the concept of localization 144, 149, 157
  his theory of collective memory 144, 159
Hegel, Georg 95
Hemminges, John 76
Herder, Johann 2, 4, 8, 13, 34, 91, 94, 95, 103, 119, 121
Hesse, Carla 20, 36
Hill, Aaron 115
historicism 18, 93
  the "new historicism" 16
historiography
  Annales scholarship 5
  of autobiography 130–2
  and the concept of "post-modern" 6
  and the concept of progress 1, 3, 18, 94, 100
  and the elaboration of historical chronologies 102
  and the Enlightenment 1–2, 18
  and the grand narrative of nation-building 5, 94
  and the heritage of Greco-Roman antiquity 1
  history and memory, relationship between 93, 112
  and history as the story of exemplary lives 8, 94
  and the philosophy of history 8, 94–101
  and scholarship on collective memory 3–8
  see also philosophy of history
history
  of the ancient world 117–18
  as an autonomous scholarly discipline 101
  and chronicles 117
  and the concept of a primordial social contract 102
  and the critique of myth and legend 108, 119
  and historical fiction 116–17
  and national literary traditions 114–18
  of preliterate societies 101–9
Hobbes, Thomas 12
Hobsbawm, Eric 19, 36
Holy Roman Empire 23, 24, 25
Homassel, Marie-Catherine 136–41
  biographer of her aunt, Michelle 136–40
  parallels with the biography by Miramion 139, 140–2
Homassel, Michelle 136–40
Hood, Robin, the legendary 121–2
Howe, Elizabeth 131, 136
Huet, Marie Hélène 157
Humbolt, Alexandre von 16
Hume, David 110, 126
  compared with Vico 104, 108–9
  as historian 108, 118
  his ideas about memory 108
  on the origins of the civilizing process in preliterate societies 104
  on the origins of religion 106–8
  his theory of knowledge 104
Hume, Patrick 76, 79
Hunt, Lynn 17, 64
Hutton, James 101

identity, issues concerning 8
  civic props and rituals 17
  and shared heritage 13
ideology, concept of 16
introspection 58, 64
  and autobiography 109–11, 129–36
  as an art of memory 12, 61
  and portrait painting 11
  techniques of 8, 11

Jainchill, Andrew 147
Janvry, Olivier Choppin de 52

Johnson, Ben 73, 76, 82
Johnson, Samuel 61–2, 74, 78, 81
Joseph II (Austria) 10, 26

Kant, Immanuel 94, 95
Kaplan, Steven 146
Kent, William 82
Kroen, Sheryl 159

Laborde, Alexandre de 56
Laborde, Jean-Joseph de 49, 51, 52
Laborde, Natalie de, her Laiterie at Méréville 52–5
LaCapra, Dominick 156
La Chapelle, Jean de 23–4
Lapeyrère, Isaac de 102
Laqueur, Thomas 20, 36
law, ideas about 58, 70–1
    the American Constitution 71
    the concept of founding fathers 71
    from constitutional traditions to written constitutions 58, 70–1
    the French Constitution 71
    the Vermont Constitution 71
Le Brun, Jacques 132
Lejeune, Philippe 131
Lenoir, Alexandre 150–2
Le Sueur, Philippe 44
Le Tourneur, Pierre 90–1
Lefebvre, Georges 3
Lemierre, Antoine-Marin 123–4
Leopold I, (Hapsburg Holy Roman Emperor) 24, 25, 30, 31
Lessing, Gothold Ephraim 91, 115, 116
literature, see Memory, cultural
Lilti, Antoine 67, 69
Louis, chevalier de Jaucourt 38
Louis-Alexandre, duc de La Rochefoucauld 48
Louis XIV (France) 22, 29
    wars of 20, 23, 24
Louis XVI (France) 49, 143, 159
    execution of 17, 24, 29, 30, 155
    remembrance of 145, 150, 151, 156
Löwith, Karl 106
Lüsebrink, Hans 152
Lyon-Caen, Nicholas 137

MacDonald, Katherine 141
McLuhan, Marshall, and the "Gutenberg Galaxy" 58
Macpherson, James 60, 103, 119–20
Mah, Harold 20, 35

Malone, Edmond 79, 80, 81
manners, the cult of 14, 67
Mandrin, Louis, in life and legend 121–2
manuscript culture 58–9, 71
    and the classical art of memory 59
    and resistance to innovation 59–60
    and the uses of rhetoric 59
Marat, Jean-Paul 158
    commemoration of 149
    interment in the Pantheon 149
Maria Theresa (Holy Roman Empress) 9, 26
Marie-Antoinette (France)
    execution, of 17, 155
    memory of 145 150
Marmontel, Jean-François 113, 114
Mary Stuart (Queen of Scots) 115, 123
    dramas and writings about 126–7
    in life and legend 126–7
Maupeou, René de 24–5
    Maupeou Coup 24, 26, 27
media 8
    and the decline of the ancient art of memory 10, 57
    and the democratization of print culture 7, 10–11, 57–8, 71–2, 123
    print and manuscript culture compared 57
    print media and the power of publicity 58
    see also print culture
Melchtal, Arnold von, the legendary 124
Melton, James, on rates of literacy 60
memory, collective
    and antiquity 38, 42
    and collective mentalities 4–5, 59
    as a concept 144
    and the concept of habit 2, 5, 59, 71, 108
    and the concept of the sublime 52
    and the construction of meaning 144, 145
    and cosmology 8–10
    and folklore and mythology 105, 119–23
    and the idea of historical origins of modern institutions 40
    and the idea of a universal memory 40
    institutional foundations of 5, 7
    and an imagined future 3, 5
    and legendary heroes and martyrs 121–3, 145–52
    mediated by literature 113–28
    nature as an archetypal source of 15
    relationship to history 8, 18, 93, 128
    scholarship concerning 3–7

INDEX

and the traditions of ordinary people 4–5
and trauma 7–8, 145, 155–9
and the world map 15–16
memory, cultural
   Ancients vs. Moderns 1, 13
   and history in the literature of high culture 114–15
   literature and high culture 114–18
   literature and popular culture 113, 118–23
   literature and the interplay of high and popular culture 123–7
   literature as *lieu de mémoire* 113
   some prominent themes in uses of 8–18
   verisimilitude vs. historical accuracy in literature 114
   William Shakespeare as icon of cultural memory 73–92
memory, personal
   and autobiography 58, 61, 109–12, 129–42
   and emotional sensibility 14
   and introspection 8, 11–12, 58, 61, 111, 129–35
   and memoirs 58
   and rituals of mourning 45–6
   and the widening divide between public and private memory 11, 72
mentalities, collective 59
Mercier, Louis Sébastien 39–40
Michelet, Jules 95
mimesis, concept of 2 105
Mirabeau, comte de (*pseud* for Honoré Gabriel Riqueti) 69–70, 147–8, 158
   interment in the Pantheon 147, 148–9
Miramion, Marguérite de 129, 133–6, 139
   biographer of her mother Marie 129, 133
   parallels with the biography by Homassel 139, 140–2
Miramion, Marie de 129, 133–4
mnemonics 3
   and the classical art of memory 10, 59, 111
   and historical timelines 18, 94
   the idea of nation as metonym 20, 24, 34
   as method of framing and modelling 8
   and rituals of mourning 11–12, 45–6
   and rituals of religion 9
   and schemes of the cosmos 8–10
   schemes in the philosophy of history 94–101
   of time 3, 18, 94
Montagu, Elizabeth 91
Montchrestien, Antoine de 126

Montesquieu, Charles-Louis de Secondat, baron de 16, 27
Mornet, Daniel 69
Mortier, Roland 42
Moser, Friedrich Carl von, and his theory of the nation 32–3
Mosser, Monique 48, 53
Mouysset, Sylvie 156
Müller, Johannes 124

Napoleon, military campaigns of 69
nation, ideas about 19–36
   and changing conceptions of sovereignty 25, 28
   comparisons among nations 20, 23, 26–7, 35
   debated and reconceived 25, 27–35, 36
   and dynastic politics 19, 21–7, 35
   early uses of 20
   in France 24–5, 27–9
      during the French Revolution 34–5
   in Germany 25–6, 30–4
   in Great Britain 25, 29–30
   vs. ideas about nationalism 19, 34–5
   as an imagined community 12
   and the making of the nation-state 16, 18, 25
   in myths of heritage 19, 22, 23
   in political rhetoric and propaganda 22, 23
   and social identity 20
   uses in political opposition 27, 29
Noinville, Pauline de 155
nostalgia 5, 13, 60
   its aesthetics for an emerging aristocracy 14–15
   for the Old Regime 15
   and Rococo art 14
Novalis (*pseud.* for Friedrich von Hardenberg), and the cultural foundations of German identity 2

Old Regime (France) 1, 3, 8, 15, 69, 152
Olney, James 131
oral traditions 59
Ozouf, Mona 147, 152, 159

Paige, Nicholas 130
Pajou, Augustin 43
Pantheons 69–70
   French 17, 147–53
Percy, Thomas 60, 103, 119–20, 121
Perrault, Charles 60

philosophy of history, the
    common characteristics 18, 94–6
    and the concept of Providence 95, 96, 104, 106–7
    as grand narrative 94
    as a hybrid scholarly discipline 94
    mnemonic schemes in 94–5
    theist vs. humanist conceptions of 96–101
Pincus, Steven 22
Piranesi, Giovanni Battista 38, 45, 48, 54
Pitaval, François Gayot de 117
Plessis, Jacqueline-Marie du 141
Plutarch 93
Pope, Alexander 78, 79, 80, 82
Prévost, Antoine François, the abbé 116
print culture
    its democratization 57–8, 71
    fostering introspection 64
    and the historicizing of storytelling 60
    and practices of learning and communication 58, 100
    print media as mobile cultural archive 57–8
    and the rising power of public opinion 58, 65, 66
    and the trend toward independence of mind 58
Ptolemy, Claudius, and the ancient conception of the cosmos 8
public sphere
    its celebrities 66, 69
    the idea of 65–6
    its institutions 66–9
    and writing as a profession 66–7
Purcell, Henry 74

Racine, Jean 114, 115, 124
Radisich, Paula Rea 49
Rapley, Elizabeth 134
reading, arts and techniques of
    the appeal of new kinds of reading matter 58
    the concept of the canon reconceived 63
    and the concept of taste 63
    the diversification of reading matter 62–5, 123
    and difficulties of learning 60
    habits of reading 63, 72
    from intensive to extensive reading 58
    literacy rates in the eighteenth century 59–60
    the novel and the cultivation of sentiment 64
    pornography as a secret literature 64–5
    from religious to secular literature 58
    silent reading and its cultural effects 61–2
    vis-à-vis orality 59, 60
    women readers 61
Regnault, Charles 126
Reichardt, Rolf 152
Republic of Letters 4, 14, 58, 72
    its burgeoning influence 66, 69, 72
    and coffee houses 57, 67
    and corresponding societies 66
    and educated women 67
    as an imagined community 3, 66
    and Masonic societies 67
    and reading clubs and lending libraries 69
    and salons 67
    and the subversion of the Old Regime 69
Richardson, Samuel 64
Ritson, Joseph 121
Robert, Hubert
    and the cenotaph of James Cook 51
    as designer of the Baths of Apollo at the gardens of Versailles 37, 40, 47, 48
    as designer of the gardens at Méréville 37, 49–56
    at Mauperthius 48, 56
    as designer of gardens with ornamental ruins (fabriques) 37–8, 55–6
    as designer of the Laiterie at Méréville 52–5
    at Rambouillet 53
    as designer of the Tower of Guy at the château of La Roche-Guyon 46–8
    his education 41–2
    his evocation of the heritage of classical antiquity 37–8, 40–1, 47–8, 51–2
    his landscape project for the tomb of Rousseau at Ermenonville 37, 42, 44, 52
    as painter of architecture and of ruins 41–2, 46–8, 52
    his painting of the demolition of the Bastille 17
        of the Grand Gallery of the Louvre 37
    as pioneer of the concept of the public museum 37
    his reputation as the "poet of time" 37
Robertson, William 126
Robespierre, Maximilien 158
    execution of 155
    and the politics of commemoration 147, 149

Robin Hood, the legendary 121–2, 123
Rob Roy, the legendary 121, 123
Rohan-Chabot, Louis-Antoine and Louise-Elizabeth 46–8
Rollin, Charles 118, 124
Rousseau, Jean-Jacques
  and autobiography 10, 11, 109–12, 129
  as celebrity 69
  commemoration during the French Revolution 144, 147
  on the government of Poland 13
  interment in the Pantheon 70
  and landscapes as sources for moral edification 40
  mnemonic scheme in his *Reveries of a Solitary Walker* 111
  and the modern novel 12, 64, 109
  and the social contract 27
  his tomb at Ermenonville 42–6
  on walking and the recovery of dormant memory 40
Rowe, Nicholas 77–8, 79–80, 81, 82
Rymer, Thomas 75

Sade, Donatien, marquis de 64
St. John, John 126
Saint-Non, the abbé 55
Saint-Simon, Henri de 4, 95–6
Sahlins, Peter 22
salon, the 7, 14, 57, 67
  role of women in 14, 67
Scaliger, Joseph Just 114
Schiller, Friedrich 91, 114, 117, 124–5, 126–7
Schlegel, Friedrich 91
Scott, Walter 116, 117, 122–3
Seven Years War 26, 29, 31
Shakespeare, William
  the eighteenth-century editions 77–81
  famous Shakespearean actor 84
    see also Garrick, David
  growing sophisticated readership and the commercial book trade 76, 79, 82
  his influence abroad 90–2
  as literary icon in eighteenth-century cultural memory 73–92
  popular dramatic performances and adaptations of his plays 74–5, 79, 84
  printed texts and the historicizing of Shakespeare 75, 80
  the seventeenth-century folios 76, 77, 79, 80, 82
  textual editing and scholarly treatment of his plays 75–81
Shakespeare, William, commemorations 81–90
  engraved portraits 81–2
  funeral monument at Stratford-upon-Avon 82, 84
  David Garrick's contribution to Shakespeare's fame 85–91
  memorial statue in the Poets Corner of Westminster Abbey 82, 83–4
  and the Shakespeare Ladies Club 75, 83
  Stratford-upon-Avon as a memorial town for Shakespeare 85
  the Shakespeare Gallery of John Boydell 89–90
  in the Temple of Worthies at Stowe 82
Shapiro, Barry 156
Shawcross, John 76
Sheemakers, Peter 82
Smith, Charlotte 117
Smith, Jay 27–8
Smyth, Adam 129
Staël, Germaine de 35, 117
Steevens, George 79
Steinberg, Ronen 156

Tate, Nathan 74
Taylor, Susan 40, 48
Tell, William
  dramas and writings about 123–5
  the legendary 121, 123–5
Temple, Richard 82
Theobald, Lewis 79, 80
Thévenin, Jacques-Jean 53
Thierry, Augustin 122
Thirty Years War, memory of 8
Tieck, Ludwig 91
Tonson, John and Jacob 76–7, 79, 81
traditions
  and folklore and storytelling 60, 103–4, 119–23
  the French revolutionary tradition 14, 71
  immemorial 2, 5, 6, 19, 40, 48, 58, 60, 70
  vs. invented 13, 19, 36
  nature of tradition reconceived 13–14
  oral traditions 102–4
    their waning authority 58–60
  and power 6

trauma, effects of
    and the French Revolution 8, 18, 143, 155–9
    and persistent anxiety 8
    and the will to forget 7
Trévisi, Marion 136

Ussieux, Louis d' 117

Vazsonyi, Nicholas 33
verisimilitude, concept of 113, 114
Vick, Brian 35
Vico, Giambattista 4, 18, 60, 93, 94, 103
    compared with Hume 104, 108–9
    and the debasement of learning in print culture 60
    ideas about memory 104–6
    his method: philology and philosophy 105–6
    on the origins of the civilizing process among preliterate people 104–6
Voltaire (*pseud* for François-Marie Arouet) 1, 8, 16, 27, 70, 90, 94, 95, 114, 115, 158
    as celebrity 69
    commemorated during the French Revolution 144, 147

Wallace, William the legendary 121
Walpole, Robert 82
Walsh, Marcus 76, 81
War of the Austrian Succession 25, 26, 31
Washington, George, as celebrity 69
Watt, Ian 116
Watteville, Alexandre-Louis 124
Welch, Ellen 22
Wellek, René 76
Wesley, John 14
Whately, Thomas 43
Wilkes, John 14, 29
Williams, Helen Maria 146
Winckelmann, Johann Joachim 38, 101
Wordsworth, William
    and nature as a resource for memory 15
    and screen memories 64
writing
    as a profession 66–7
    as a skill separate from reading 61
Wrede, Martin 31

Young, Arthur 146

Zerubavel, Eviatar, and the concept of the mnemonics of progress 3